# ARSÈNE WHO?

# ARSÈNE WHO?

## THE STORY OF THE WENGER REVOLUTION

# RYAN BALDI

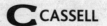

First published in Great Britain in 2024 by Cassell, an imprint of
Octopus Publishing Group Ltd
Carmelite House
50 Victoria Embankment
London EC4Y 0DZ
www.octopusbooks.co.uk

An Hachette UK Company
www.hachette.co.uk

The authorized representative in the EEA is Hachette Ireland,
8 Castlecourt Centre, Dublin 15, D15 XTP3, Ireland (email: info@hbgi.ie)

Distributed in the US by
Hachette Book Group
1290 Avenue of the Americas
4th and 5th Floors
New York, NY 10104

Distributed in Canada by
Canadian Manda Group
664 Annette St.
Toronto, Ontario, Canada M6S 2C8

A

ISBN 978-1-78840-455-6

CIP catalogue record for this book is available from the British Library.

Printed and bound in Great Britain

Typeset in 12/18pt FreightText Pro by Jouve (UK), Milton Keynes

5 7 9 10 8 6

MIX
Paper | Supporting
responsible forestry
FSC® C104740

Publisher: Trevor Davies
Senior Editor: Alex Stetter
Picture Research Manager: Giulia Hetherington
Assistant Production Manager: Lisa Pinnell

For Sophie, Dylan and Finlay, my world.

# Contents

# CONTENTS

# Calmness and Swagger

## A foreword by Lee Dixon

I'll have an argument as long as anyone wants over the quality of the sides from Arsenal's most successful period under Arsène Wenger. If you take the 1998 Double winners, the 2002 Double team and the 'Invincibles' of 2004, the '98 side was the best.

I say that because we still had the back four at its peak – Tony Adams alongside either Martin Keown or Steve Bould at centre back, Nigel Winterburn and myself at full back. We were hugely experienced and still very, very fit. And then Wenger just sprinkled this amazing talent in front of us. Nicolas Anelka was unplayable. The two midfield players, Patrick Vieira and Emmanuel Petit, were the best in the league as a duo. We had pace from Marc Overmars, industry from Ray Parlour and invention from Dennis Bergkamp. Ian Wright was still deadly and, in David Seaman, we had the best goalkeeper in my book.

The 2002 team was brilliant and the Invincibles were amazing, but if we all had to play each other in a round robin, I think the '98 side would come out on top.

If you wrote a script – or a book! – about how Arsenal's 1997–98 season was going to end, you wouldn't be far off writing it the way it played out. It culminated in an incredible run of victories as we were chasing down Manchester United, playing some brilliant football in front of the crowd at Highbury.

Then, when we hosted Everton on that perfect Sunday afternoon in May, the icing on the cake: Mr Messi himself – aka Bouldy – chipped the ball over to Tony Adams, our captain who'd been through so much. The way Tony lashed it into the net with his left foot, it was fantasy stuff.

I'm sure we all dreamed it would end like that. The way we played that year and the way Tony scored such an uncharacteristically beautiful goal to cap it off – plus his iconic celebration that's been immortalized as a statue outside the Emirates Stadium – it summed up everything that was good about that era under Arsène Wenger. He brought a calmness and a swagger to what had been a military brand of football before he arrived, a very regimented style of play.

Arsène gave us all freedom, and Tony epitomized that with a left-footed volley in the sunshine. I feel quite emotional thinking about it now.

# Arsène for Arsenal

It started with a spark. The snap of a lighter. Arsène Wenger leaned forward and ignited his cigarette. It was 2 January 1989. The AS Monaco manager had spent part of the French football season's winter break in Istanbul, watching Galatasaray in preparation for an upcoming European Cup quarter-final meeting with the Turkish champions. Having decided to stop over in London for a few days before returning to the principality, he'd called the agent of Glenn Hoddle, Monaco's English midfielder and former Tottenham Hotspur icon, to ask for help arranging to see a match during his short stay in England's capital. That's how the Frenchman – distinctive for his lanky, six-foot-three frame, thick-rimmed spectacles and beige trench coat – found himself in the exclusive cocktail room within the bowels of Arsenal's Highbury stadium.

Arsenal beat local rivals Tottenham 2-0 that afternoon, with goals from Paul Merson and Michael Thomas. It was a result that would prove crucial in what was to be one of the tightest and most dramatic title races in First Division history, with the Gunners beating Liverpool 2-0 at Anfield on the final day of the campaign to pip the Merseysiders to the championship by virtue of having scored eight more goals across the course of the season, with total points and goal difference dead even between the two clubs.

The 45,129 spectators crammed into Arsenal's quaint home ground for that New Year derby showdown with Spurs had no idea that serendipity would shine on the Gunners that day to reward them with more than simply three points for their victory and bragging rights over their North London nemesis. The spark of a distant bright future was about to be lit.

At the time, women were not permitted to enter Highbury's directors' box within 45 minutes of kick-off on match days. As such, the female companions of the club's executives congregated in the cocktail lounge, where VIP guests were also stationed. When Wenger sought a light for his cigarette, it was a friend of the vice-chairman David Dein's wife, Barbara, who obliged.

After the trio exchanged small talk, Barbara Dein alerted her husband to the presence of this intriguing French football manager. David Dein introduced himself to Wenger at half time. 'I went through and met Arsène and had a chat,' Dein says. 'I remember him standing there, in this long raincoat, with what looked like National Health glasses. He didn't look like a football manager at all; he looked like a professor. I said to him, "What are you doing here?" He said, "I've been to Istanbul, Turkey. I'm just staying overnight. I'm going back to Monaco tomorrow." I said to him, "What are you doing tonight? My wife and I are going out for dinner at a friend's house. Would you like to join us?" The next answer changed all our lives. He said, "Yes, I would be delighted to." So I hijacked him. He came out for dinner with us. My friend happened to be in showbiz, and at the end of the evening we found ourselves playing charades. I said to him, because he didn't speak great English at the time, "Do you want to play?" And he said, "OK." Five minutes later, he's acting out *A Midsummer Night's Dream*. I looked at him and I thought, "This guy's a bit special." He speaks multiple languages and is highly intelligent.'

Dein had purchased a 16 per cent stake in Arsenal in 1983, investing in his beloved club with the wealth earned through his rise from manning an exotic fruit stall on Shepherd's Bush market to running an international sugar exports company with offices in Pall Mall. His initial investment in the flagging Gunners, who'd gone 12 years without a league championship and 4 without a trophy of any kind, was at the time described as 'dead money' by chairman Peter Hill-Wood. But by 1991, Dein would increase his shareholding to 42 per cent while Arsenal claimed their second league title in three years. He would also be one of the architects of the Premier League's formation in 1992, as one of five directors from top English clubs who pushed through a breakaway from the Football League. With a knack for wielding gentle influence, he was once described by *The Guardian*, not entirely flatteringly, as an 'instinctive politician'. But there can be little doubt that Dein's weathervane for football – both the game itself and its surrounding business – was as accurate as any. And in Wenger, he saw the future. Arsenal's future.

'I'm not spiritual,' he says, 'but I sort of saw it in the sky: Arsène for Arsenal. It's destiny. It's going to happen one day.'

# Arsène Who?

Peter Hill-Wood couldn't help but be impressed by Arsène Wenger. The Arsenal chairman had agreed to meet with the French coach at David Dein's insistence. They sat across from each other at a white-clothed table in Ziani, an Italian restaurant in the heart of Chelsea, around a mile east of Stamford Bridge and a stone's throw from the banks of the Thames. Over some of London's finest Venetian cuisine, Wenger charmed as he laid out his footballing philosophies.

Arsenal needed a manager. George Graham's trophy-laden eight seasons at the Highbury helm had ended in disgrace months earlier, in February 1995. A Premier League inquiry found he had accepted an illicit payment of £425,000 from Norwegian agent Rune Hauge relating to the 1992 signings of John Jensen and Pål Lydersen, two of Hauge's clients. The Arsenal board had no alternative but to sack Graham. The FA levied him with a one-year ban and the term 'bung' entered the football vernacular.

Dein had stayed in regular contact with Wenger ever since their first meeting in 1989. The Gunners' vice-chairman had a yacht docked at Antibes, on the French Riviera, and would visit Wenger at Monaco. He also sent tapes of Arsenal games for the Frenchman to peruse.

'He didn't realize, but he was auditioning,' Dein says. 'I could see how he interacted with the Monaco players, with the board, with the fans, with the press. I would send videos weekly, after every game.

He was interested in the team and the players. I kept him up to speed. I thought, "This guy's one for the future."'

When Graham's sacking unexpectedly created a vacancy in the Highbury dugout, Dein lobbied for Wenger. Although Hill-Wood enjoyed Wenger's company and was engaged by his ideas on the game, he did not wish to appoint the Frenchman – or any Frenchman, indeed any foreigner. There had only been two non-British or Irish managers in the history of top-flight English football at the time – the Slovak Dr Jozef Vengloš at Aston Villa and the Argentinian World Cup winner Ossie Ardiles at Tottenham in the 1990s. Ardiles was a Spurs legend as a player, but he lasted just 56 games in charge at White Hart Lane, losing more than he won. In Vengloš's ill-fated single season in the First Division, Villa finished seventeenth in the league after being runners-up the year before. Neither was seen as a ringing endorsement of foreign coaches' suitability for the English game. Scepticism pervaded. Hill-Wood, an old Etonian and merchant banker, was the third generation of his family to serve as Arsenal chairman, after his grandfather Samuel and his father, Denis. In 1995, he was not ready to usher in the club's first ever foreign manager. The board – with the exception of Dein – agreed.

'I got comprehensively outvoted,' Dein says, 'because the board thought we needed to have an English person. George came up from the lower divisions. It's got to be something like that.'

They didn't plump for an Englishman but rather another Scot. Bruce Rioch had just overseen Bolton Wanderers' promotion to the Premier League via the First Division play-offs. He was seen as similar enough to Graham in tone but also someone who could implement a more progressive style of play than his predecessor.

Graham's success had been built on the foundation of a rigid defence. In six of his eight full seasons as Arsenal manager, the Gunners boasted one of the three best defensive records in the top flight. When they won the title in 1990–91, they conceded just 18 goals in 38 matches and were beaten only once. Graham's style was effective yet hardly entertaining. Arsenal's form had already begun to deteriorate before Graham's sacking. At the point of his departure, they were twelfth in the Premier League table with 28 games played and had conceded more goals than they'd scored. Assistant manager Stewart Houston stepped in as caretaker boss for the remainder of the campaign, but he couldn't improve Arsenal's league position. They lost seven of their last fourteen matches and finished with their worst defensive record since before Graham's tenure. Their defence of the UEFA Cup Winners' Cup, which they'd won the prior season, brought hope as they once again reached the final, but it ultimately ended in despair: former Tottenham midfielder Nayim scored with an outrageous lob over David Seaman from near the halfway line in the last minute of extra time to claim the cup for Real Zaragoza.

Rioch was a coach on the rise. He'd taken Bolton from the third tier to the Premier League, with his last match in charge being a 4-3 victory over Reading in the 1995 First Division play-off final at Wembley. That was Bolton's second trip to the national stadium that season, having reached the League Cup final in February, losing 2-1 to Liverpool. The previous season, Rioch's Wanderers had eliminated Arsenal, the holders, from the FA Cup in the fourth round. After Bolton dispatched the Gunners with a 3-1 after-extra-time victory in a replay at Highbury, the England manager Terry Venables approached Rioch. 'That was some of the best football I've seen from a visiting team,' he said.

To help Rioch institute a similarly entertaining style of play from Highbury's home dugout, Arsenal signed England captain David Platt from Sampdoria and the gifted Dutch striker Dennis Bergkamp, who arrived from Internazionale for a club-record £7.5 million. Rioch attempted to stamp his mark in North London by reshuffling what had been the Gunners' most established unit – the back four. He switched to a back three, with Tony Adams, Steve Bould and Martin Keown as the bedrock and full backs Lee Dixon and Nigel Winterburn reimagined as flying wing backs.

The results were . . . fine. There was embarrassment in the FA Cup when Arsenal were knocked out in the third round by second-tier Sheffield United, but they finished fifth in the Premier League, enough to secure a place in the following season's UEFA Cup. Their goals-per-game average had risen slightly (from 1.24 the previous season to 1.29). It was by no means a disastrous campaign for the Gunners, yet it would be Rioch's first and last.

'I didn't particularly enjoy playing under Bruce Rioch,' Dixon says. 'It was a very difficult season, coming after George leaving. George leaving was probably not the right circumstances, but the team was starting to not be as successful. There was a breakdown in the relationships between the players and him. You can only be told and shouted at so many times. It was coming to its end, whether it was him getting rid of us lot and rebuilding, like Alex Ferguson used to do at Manchester United, or indeed him moving on. The fact that it happened how it did was unfortunate.

'Then Bruce came in. That season was difficult for me. Although I played virtually every game, I was playing as a wing back. It's a very physical position to play and I hadn't played it much, so a whole season playing as a wing back – ask Nigel Winterburn – it was brutal. And because I never really got injured and rotation wasn't a thing back then, you play every game, so it was tough. I didn't particularly like the way we were playing. Bruce was fine; I got on well enough with him. But I was open to getting a new manager.'

'Although we'd had a reasonably successful season, there was a little bit of . . . I wouldn't say unrest, but there was a very strong dressing room that had its own views,' says Platt. 'It was a difficult job for Bruce because he was trying to change things around. But it was a difficult dressing room to change around. Did it come as a surprise when he was sacked? To a certain extent. But, really, if you thought about it, it didn't.'

It was the breakdown of two key relationships that sealed Rioch's Arsenal downfall. The first was with the club's star striker, Ian Wright.

Rioch came from a military family – his father had been a sergeant major in the Scots Guards – and he took a militaristic hardline approach to football management. He had once, while Middlesbrough manager, fined his entire team £100 each on the spot after a defeat. When it was pointed out that one of the team's youngsters was still an apprentice and earned less than £50 a week, Rioch is said to have responded, 'Fair point. He can pay in instalments.' After Arsenal's preseason friendly against St Albans on 15 August 1995, five days before the new Premier League season was to begin, he singled out Wright for a post-match reprimand. Arsenal had won 5-0, with Wright among the goal scorers, yet Rioch let rip on the England forward in front of the team. Wright bristled. And when Rioch stopped one training session to insist that Wright could learn a thing or two about the art of a striker's movement by studying John McGinlay, the centre forward Rioch worked with at Bolton, Wright told the manager to 'Fuck off' and headed for the showers. In March of that season, Wright walked into Rioch's office and slapped a written transfer request on the desk. 'You've made my life a misery from practically the moment you arrived,' he said.

Wright also sent a copy of his letter to David Dein. His transfer request was rejected, but it alerted the vice-chairman to the disharmony within the team. And then Dein's own relationship with Rioch reached breaking point over the subject of transfers. Since Graham's bung scandal, Dein had taken a lead role in negotiating the club's signings. In a modern-day context, it is not unusual for the processes of player identification and transfer dealings to fall under the remit of a club executive – such as a director of football – with the manager's involvement secondary. In English football in the mid-1990s, this kind of Continental approach to the transfer market was rare. To the managers of the time, it was anathema. Rioch and Dein butted heads over how much control the manager should have over the club's incomings and outgoings. Rioch clashed with the board over failed attempts to sign Andrei Kanchelskis, Roberto Carlos and Alan Shearer. Despite this discord, Rioch signed a new, three-year contract with the club in July. However, when he went to Highbury expecting to witness the countersigning on 12 August, just eight days before the start of the 1996–97 season, he was told his services were no longer required.

Rioch's reign lasted just 431 days, the shortest spell any Arsenal manager had overseen in almost a century. The Gunners were on the hunt for a new coach again, and this time Dein was determined to get his man.

'When Bruce didn't work out, I decided to really go big time to the board,' he says. 'I said, "Luckily, I'm still in touch with Arsène. I don't know if he'll come, but we missed out first time. We've really got to get him now."'

\*

Dein, Hill-Wood and majority shareholder Danny Fiszman flew to Nagoya, Japan, to meet with Wenger at his apartment in the city. His seven years in charge of Monaco had ended in September 1994. He won a league championship at the Stade Louis II in 1987–88 and a Coupe de France in 1991. His team were also twice runners-up to a Marseille side later convicted of match fixing. He'd made stars of Youri Djorkaeff, Lilian Thuram and George Weah and Bayern Munich tried to appoint him, only for Monaco to refuse to allow him to leave. The cachet he'd accumulated in the principality apparently counted for little after a poor start to the 1993–94 season, though. Monaco sacked him two months into the campaign.

In October 1994, FIFA, world football's governing body, invited Wenger to speak at a convention in the United Arab Emirates for developing football nations. He delivered a technical report on the past summer's World Cup and the attendant Japanese delegation was particularly impressed. The J.League, Japan's national championship, had been founded the previous year and, with clubs owned by major Japanese companies, significant resources were being pumped into the nascent competition. A representative from Toyota, owners of Nagoya Grampus Eight, approached Wenger with an offer to take charge of their club. After ten years of working in Ligue 1, the French first division, Wenger welcomed the chance of a change of pace.

The name Grampus Eight was somewhat familiar to English football fans because former England and Tottenham striker Gary Lineker had spent the final two seasons of his career with the club. But Wenger took over a struggling side – they'd finished bottom of the league the previous season and a toe injury had forced Lineker to retire.

'You always monitor and follow your former clubs, even though it was a difficult period at the end of my career because I didn't play many games due to my toe injury,' Lineker says. 'I was looking to see how they were doing and I was genuinely surprised at the success they'd had, because they were near the bottom of the league when I was there – maybe it was my fault! Wenger clearly made a difference.'

That difference: an Emperor's Cup, runners-up in the league format and a J.League Manager of the Year Award. The 1996 Japanese season was approaching its final stretch when Arsenal made their move for the Frenchman and he was ready to bring his eastern excursion to a close. Negotiations with the Highbury executives were smooth and swift.

'I had decided to return to Europe only on the condition that I went to a big club, and that it was a real challenge,' Wenger wrote in *My Life in Red and White*, his 2020 autobiography. 'Arsenal was a sizeable one. Within an hour we came to an agreement. I would join the London club as soon as possible, but I would not abandon Nagoya mid-season without a manager.'

The finer details of the agreement were hashed out over a series of faxes, and the correspondence wired from Nagoya carried the name of a figure much more familiar in North London than Wenger, albeit thanks to a history with the Gunner's hated neighbours.

'Our times in Japan didn't overlap at all,' Lineker explains, 'but Arsène moved into the apartment that I had stayed in for two years. I left a fax machine there. That was how we communicated back then. There were no mobile phones. The deal that was done with Arsenal was over fax and my name was at the top of the paper that Arsène was sending to David Dein.'

More than seven years after their chance meeting in the Highbury cocktail lounge – and a year later than he'd hoped – Dein had got his man.

It was Arsène for Arsenal. Destiny fulfilled.

Arsenal were struggling when Wenger walked into the away dressing room at the Müngersdorfer Stadion in Cologne, Germany. It was 25 September 1996 and, although he'd been unveiled as the Gunners' new manager at a press conference a few days earlier, he was not yet officially in charge. Pat Rice, the former Arsenal captain and long-time youth coach, was the placeholder until the Frenchman could take the reins on 1 October. But, as Wenger sat in the stands beside David Dein to observe his new charges take on Borussia Mönchengladbach in the first round of the UEFA Cup, he felt he needed to intervene.

Gladbach had won the first leg at Highbury 3-2, and the home side – playing at the stadium of their local rivals Cologne because their own ground didn't meet UEFA's standards – were bossing the second leg, too. An Ian Wright goal three minutes before half time meant the score was level at the interval, but still behind on aggregate, Wenger wanted to implement a tactical change. He stood next to Dein as the players – most of whom he'd not yet met – filed in. Then he stepped forward and instructed them to switch from a back three to a back four.

'That was the first time we met him,' Wright remembers. 'He came in and he was like he was always going to be from that day on: very cool, very calm. He was just really cool. I instantly wanted to make sure I played well. I was quite pleased with the way I played against Gladbach. At that time, I just wanted to make sure that I was in the team.'

Not everyone was impressed. Despite a Paul Merson goal early in the second half, Arsenal lost the game 3-2 and were eliminated. Tony

Adams felt Wenger's tactical intervention had served only to unsettle the side.

'I can't say I was overly impressed by Monsieur Wenger's initial contribution,' Adams wrote in his 1998 autobiography, *Addicted*. 'At half-time, he came into the dressing room, took over from Pat Rice and changed us from the 3-5-2 Bruce had introduced to a back four and we went on to lose the game 3-2 and the tie 6-4. I was not best pleased about being pulled off in the second half. At the end, Arsène said nothing before smartly disappearing.'

As Adams fumed post-match about the new manager's inglorious intervention, the captain's internal monologue echoed the widespread bemusement that had greeted Wenger's appointment: 'What does this Frenchman know about football?'

The Channel Tunnel might have begun transporting passengers between the UK mainland and Europe almost two years earlier, but Britain was insular and inward-looking in September 1996. The BSE crisis had led to the European Union banning British beef in April. Prime Minister John Major and the Conservative government clung to power, but Tony Blair and New Labour were on the rise, leading all polls. British culture was exploding. The Britpop phenomenon had crested in August when Oasis played to 250,000 people over two nights at Knebworth. The Spice Girls had burst on to the scene in July, spending seven weeks atop the UK singles chart with their debut release 'Wannabe'. And in the football world, the country had just rekindled its love for the game during Euro 96, the Continental championship held on home soil. The refrain of Baddiel and Skinner's anthemic hit 'Three Lions' was ubiquitous as England captivated the nation on their run to the semi-finals, where they lost to Germany on penalties at Wembley. Football had come home. British was best.

Except, to an extent, in the Premier League. The growing riches of the rebranded top flight was leading to a rapid influx of foreign players as clubs increasingly looked abroad for their on-field stars. In the summer of 1996, for instance, Chelsea signed Italian striker Gianluca Vialli from Juventus, the reigning European champions, and would add Gianfranco Zola in November. Previously unfashionable Middlesbrough were among Europe's biggest spenders, adding Brazilian duo Juninho and Emerson and signing silver-haired hotshot Fabrizio Ravanelli from Juventus for £7 million. In total, 120 non-British or Irish players would feature in the 1996–97 Premier League season, a 42.8 per cent increase on the previous campaign.

But foreign managers were still a rarity. As the new season began, Ruud Gullit, who'd succeeded Glenn Hoddle to become Chelsea's player-manager, was the only coach from outside the British Isles in charge of a Premier League side.

What made Arsenal's move for Wenger particularly befuddling was not merely that he was foreign but that he was also unknown. After Rioch's dismissal, Johan Cruyff was installed as the betting favourite to be Arsenal's next manager. The legendary Dutchman had recently departed Barcelona, where he'd won four La Liga titles and a European Cup. Alongside Wenger, Terry Venables, fresh from guiding England to the semi-finals of the European Championship, completed the billing on what was considered a three-way contest for the vacant Highbury post.

The *Evening Standard* was one of few publications to name Wenger as Arsenal's first choice among the three. 'I understand he has already been sounded out about taking over and has agreed,' wrote the journalist Steve Stammers. Yet that didn't stop the same newspaper placing bill posters around the city that read 'Arsène Who?' when the new manager's identity was officially confirmed. Inside that day's edition was a tutorial on how his name should be pronounced. 'If you are French, you will probably address him as Ar-senn Won-jair,' the article said. 'German? Ar-sehn Ven-ger, perhaps. But you are unlikely to be either if you inhabit the North Bank and read any of the four Arsenal fanzines.'

Nowadays, a young coach with a track record of player development, attractive, attacking football and who'd won a French title and reached a European final would be high on the wanted list of even the most casual supporter of a club in need of a manager. No pronunciation tutorials needed. But this was an era long before football fans in Britain had access to blanket coverage of European leagues. If it happened outside of Serie A or La Liga – covered by Channel 4 and Sky, respectively – it might as well have not happened. Nor was there any form of social media upon which short highlight packages of Wenger's teams could be shared and digested. Facebook and YouTube were still nearly a decade away, Twitter even longer. Only 4.1 per cent of the UK population had regular internet access. The bestselling mobile phone of the time, the Nokia 1610, didn't even include text messaging as a standard feature. Outside of ploughing through back issues of *World Soccer* magazine, Arsenal fans had little recourse for educating themselves about the mysterious bespectacled man set to take charge of their club.

'I remember being very underwhelmed,' says the Arsenal writer Tim Stillman. 'I'd never heard of Arsène Wenger. We'd been linked with Johan Cruyff and Terry Venables. I'd obviously heard of Cruyff, and Venables, after Euro 96, was considered a really good manager at the time. I remember there being some discussion among fans of whether we could accept Venables, because of his Spurs connection – "How would we feel about taking someone with a Spurs history?" But he was good, so it was, "But what if we take someone *good* from Spurs?" Wenger was unknown. After the Bruce Rioch season – which wasn't as bad as it's remembered – we were ready for something new, but just not *this* new.'

Most of the players were confused by the appointment, too.

'When I went to the training ground to announce that Arsène was going to be our manager, I said to the boys, "I've got an announcement. We have got our new manager. There will be a press conference shortly. It's Arsène Wenger,"' Dein says. 'And Ray Parlour piped up and said, "Who the fuck is that?"'

'No one really knew who he was,' says Parlour. 'We always thought it was going to be a British manager going forward. And then David Dein came out and said, "I've been following this guy for many, many years, at Monaco and Grampus Eight, and this is the time." First impressions, he was a little bit like a schoolteacher, the glasses. But as soon as he spoke and expressed what he wanted to do for the club, then there was a focus there. You looked at him and he really meant what he said.'

'His name was bandied around a short period of time before,' Dixon remembers. 'I'd never heard of him. Although I was a student of trying to learn my trade and of the game domestically, I wasn't interested that much in world football at the time, so I wouldn't have known Wenger. But his name had popped up in conversations about managers. I'd heard David talk about him, because he was key in bringing him to the club. He knew him very well and they were good friends. He had mentioned his name, and it was like, "Wenger who?" It seemed like a really weird name we hadn't heard, and also the fact his first name sounds a bit like the football club. It was a bit like, "Oh, that's a bit strange, he's obviously destined to manage the club." But no, I didn't really know much about Grampus Eight and what was going on over there.'

Not all of the Arsenal stars were completely unaware of Wenger, though. Ian Wright shared an agency with George Weah, the Liberian World Player of the Year Award winner who'd played under Wenger at Monaco. 'George Weah used to talk about Arsène Wenger,' Wright says. 'I knew George very well and he held Arsène in very high esteem.'

And David Platt had a minor historical connection with the Frenchman, having once turned him down. 'When I left Bari, Monaco were one of the clubs that wanted me,' he says. Platt decided to stay in Italy, instead signing for Juventus, but when he heard Wenger's name in connection with Arsenal's vacant post years later, he was on board. 'When you've got the chance to go out and get someone as thoughtful – and as in-depth thoughtful – as Arsène Wenger, you do it,' he says. 'It didn't surprise me that that was the decision they made.'

While he might not have boasted the name recognition among fans and the general public of a Cruyff or a Venables, Wenger was respected and admired within the game's inner circle.* Discerning consumers of the English football press might have recognized Wenger's name from a handful of reports earlier in the year that linked the Grampus Eight manager with the role of technical director of the Football Association.

---

\* George Graham, in fact, was of the belief that Wenger was the man to whom Arsenal should turn when replacing Rioch, a fact he confided to his barber, an Arsenal fan named Michael Michael. 'I used to cut George Graham's hair,' says Michael, who has cut the hair of dozens of Arsenal stars down the years and was a regular visitor to London Colney during Wenger's early years in charge. 'Around the time Arsenal were looking for a new manager, Johan Cruyff was one of the names linked. I remember saying to George, "Johan Cruyff is the one we need." And he said, "No, no, no. This guy Arsène Wenger – that's who you want. I've heard a lot of good things about him."'

Glenn Hoddle, England's new coach, played under Wenger at Monaco and has listed him as a tremendous influence. Hoddle wanted Wenger to bring his developmental skills to the FA's top administrative position. And, in addition to having been courted by Bayern Munich previously, Wenger had left an impression in Italy after he travelled to AC Milan's training ground to study Arrigo Sacchi's methods and exchange ideas with the great Italian coach.

'I had a really good impression of Arsène Wenger when he first arrived at Milanello,' Sacchi says. 'I thought that he was somebody who was very professional and a modest man. He was somebody who always tried to be better at the job he was doing. When we spoke to each other in that time, it was really about trying to get an understanding of each other's philosophies and to learn from each other. Wenger had been at Milanello for around ten days and when it came time to say goodbye, he said, "Let's say goodbye to the future champions of Europe."'

Sacchi likely saw something of a kindred spirit in Wenger. Like the Italian, Wenger was not able to count on a stellar playing career as a launchpad into the upper echelons of the coaching world. He grew up in Alsace in the east of France. The region borders Germany and has changed hands between the two countries several times across the course of history – hence Wenger's Germanic name; he was not fully fluent in French until around the age of seven. His parents, Louise and Alphonse, ran a bistro, La Croix d'Or, and Wenger and his brother, Guy, played for the local football team in their hometown of Duttlenheim.

Wenger recalls watching the FA Cup final on TV among his earliest and most vivid football memories. 'On the television at school, and later in the family bistro and at home, we used to watch the cup finals in the legendary Wembley Stadium,' he said. 'Television was still in black and white in those days but the ball stood out brightly against the grass pitch that looked so beautiful, perfectly mown and maintained, while we were still roughly cutting the grass on our pitch with our horses pulling the mower behind them. It is a dazzling memory: for me, it is the definitive image of football. I think that as a child I promised myself I would one day step on to that turf, a promise that of course I never voiced out loud, not even to myself. England and Wembley seemed to belong to another planet, another world.' Wenger also became fascinated with European competition after watching the great Real Madrid team of Di Stéfano, Puskás and Gento thrash Eintracht Frankfurt in the 1960 European Cup final at Hampden Park, a match a 19-year-old Alex Ferguson attended.

In his own modest playing career, Wenger was a gangly, one-footed centre half who lacked pace and athleticism, but he possessed a quick mind and a deep understanding of the game that enabled him to play at a strong amateur level before eventually making his professional debut with Racing Club Strasbourg, the club he grew up supporting, aged 29. Some of his most formative experiences as a young footballer came through watching, rather than playing. He'd accompany Max Hild, his coach from local amateur side Mutzig, to games across the border in Germany, studying the likes of Stuttgart, Cologne and Borussia Mönchengladbach. While playing for Mulhouse, a semi-professional club in the French second tier, Wenger earned around £50 per week and combined his footballing efforts with studying for an economics degree at the University of Strasbourg. His coach at Mulhouse, Paul Frantz, would have a great influence on Wenger, implanting within the future Arsenal boss a fascination with isometric exercises, an appreciation of nutrition and a belief in precisely timed high-intensity training drills. It was through a recommendation from Hild and Frantz that Wenger was hired as a player-coach for Strasbourg's reserves in 1978. It was in this dual role that he was occasionally called up to the first team, for whom he made just 13 appearances in total.

Wenger retired from playing aged 30 and quickly worked towards obtaining the relevant coaching qualifications to enable him to pursue a career in management. He also enrolled in a three-week English-language course at the University of Cambridge – 'I would never have become the Arsenal manager without those three weeks alone in an English city,' he said. He became the assistant manager at Ligue 2 Cannes in 1983 and the following year Aldo Platini, the father of legendary French midfielder Michel Platini, hired him to manage top-flight strugglers Nancy. Wenger mustered a mid-table finish from a substandard group of players in his first season by repositioning them into roles he felt better suited their skill sets and hiring a dietician to overhaul their eating habits. He kept them up the following season, albeit in less comfortable fashion, beating his former club Mulhouse in a promotion–relegation play-off. Nancy succumbed to the drop the next season after the sale of several key players, but Wenger's work had not gone unnoticed – Monaco, who'd made an unsuccessful approach to sign him a year earlier, hired him to be their manager in the summer of 1987.

Although negotiations in his Nagoya apartment between Wenger and the Arsenal directors had gone smoothly, he was not able to immediately begin work at Highbury. His contract with Grampus Eight did not expire until January 1997 and so an early release was negotiated between the two clubs. Grampus's Toyota overlords agreed to allow Wenger out of his deal ahead of schedule,* but he would still not be able to officially take charge in North London until 1 October.

Stewart Houston, who'd been assistant to both Graham and Rioch, was installed as caretaker manager to oversee the interregnum before Wenger's reign could officially begin. But Houston, understanding he would not be considered for the top job at Highbury, resigned five games into the new season to become Queens Park Rangers' manager. In an unusual reversal of roles, Houston hired Rioch to be his number two at Loftus Road, although it is said he would still occasionally slip into old habits and refer to his assistant as 'boss'.

After Houston's departure, Pat Rice took temporary charge until the new manager's arrival. Wenger kept regular contact with Rice and studied videos of every Arsenal match. Rice, meanwhile, harboured no illusions about keeping the hot seat.

'I was in the seat for half a dozen games,' he says. 'And we never lost any, except for Mönchengladbach. I'm Arsenal's most successful manager and no one knows that! When Stewart and Bruce left, the chairman called me in and he said, "I would like you to take over the team until our new manager comes. It will be Arsène Wenger. He'll be coming over from Japan."

'Arsène used to phone me up after every game. He'd say, "How did it go?" And I used to say to him, "I'll be bloody glad when you're here." I wasn't looking to be manager of the Arsenal. I was very happy to be number two.'

---

* Wenger was eventually replaced at Grampus Eight by Carlos Queiroz, the Portuguese coach who'd later spend two separate spells as Sir Alex Ferguson's number two at Manchester United either side of a short stint in charge of Real Madrid.

Arsenal won five of their eight Premier League games under Houston and Rice and lost just once, away to Liverpool on the season's second weekend. Meanwhile, the identity of the club's next manager became football's worst-kept secret.

The first major giveaway was the Gunners' transfer business in the days after Rioch's dismissal. Arsenal signed two French midfielders: 30-year-old Rémi Garde from Wenger's old club Strasbourg, and 20-year-old Patrick Vieira, a £3.5 million arrival from AC Milan. 'The Frenchman Arsène Wenger is the new manager of Arsenal,' said *The Guardian* on 15 August. 'The choice became clear yesterday when the Highbury club confirmed they had signed two French players.' *The Independent* claimed Weah would soon follow.

It would later transpire that Wenger had intervened directly to secure Vieira's signing, convincing the six-foot-four midfielder to reject a rival approach from Ajax. 'I managed to convince him and his agents Marc Roger and Jean-François Larios that he should come to Arsenal,' Wenger said. 'He had made a huge impression on me as a young player in Cannes when I was the Monaco coach.'

At Arsenal's annual general meeting of shareholders on 22 August, Hill-Wood let slip the thinly guarded identity of the next boss in comical fashion. Attendance was higher than usual for the AGM, with more than three hundred stakeholders crammed into an oak-panelled room within Highbury's North Bank. The majority of these shareholding fans were disgruntled by the manner of Rioch's sacking. The hostility was palpable throughout the 90-minute meeting, with security guards positioned at either end of the stage to protect the board members. Hill-Wood tried to assuage the anger directed towards him. 'We have acted in the best interests of the club,' he pleaded. 'We have identified a replacement of considerable reputation who has agreed to join us.

We cannot announce his appointment officially, as we have given an undertaking not to do so.'

'To whom have you given that undertaking, Mr Chairman?' came a question from the floor.

'To Arsène Wenger and his club, but I'm not officially allowed to say who he is.'

Wenger did a slightly better job of respecting the pact of silence. Speaking to BBC Radio 4's *Today* programme, he said, 'Arsenal are a big club and managing Arsenal is an exciting job.' He refused to say outright whether he'd accepted said job, but when asked whether he'd find an offer from Arsenal difficult to refuse, he admitted, 'Yes.' He took charge of his final Grampus Eight match on 28 August and, aware of the presence of a number of English journalists, he refused to engage with any questions about Arsenal in his post-match press conference. 'I have a confidentiality agreement with Grampus and I can't break it,' he said, 'so questions only about the game, please.'

Wenger's appointment was officially confirmed on Monday 16 September. 'It is my dream to manage a team in a top-level European league,' the Frenchman said at a press conference in Nagoya. 'And if I don't accept the offer right now I will miss the chance. I think Arsenal is a club with big potential. I think that English football is going up and that the Premiership is one of the most important leagues in the world now. So I think that it also was a challenge for me to be maybe the first foreign manager – and for sure the first Frenchman – to go there and be successful.'

The new manager's visage was first spotted inside Highbury later that evening, albeit only via the two large video screens at opposite corners of the stadium. The Gunners were hosting Sheffield Wednesday and an interview with Wenger was played to the crowd before kick-off. 'You sensed a new chapter was about to begin,' said the *Evening Standard*, and Arsenal fans in attendance and watching on television got a glimpse into this promising new chapter in the form of Vieira, who came on as a first-half substitute to make his debut for the club when Ray Parlour was forced off injured. Arsenal had just fallen behind to an Andy Booth goal, but the Senegal-born midfielder exhibited the drive, athleticism and invention that would soon become familiar. He was the catalyst for a 4-1 victory. After the match, Ian Wright, who'd claimed a hat-trick, was asked about the imminent arrival of Wenger. 'Who?' the striker replied, a tongue-in-cheek reference to the *Evening Standard*'s bemused bill poster.

Wenger arrived at Highbury in person to meet the press on 22 September. Wearing a white shirt and a tie embroidered with the Arsenal crest, he stood at a podium to take questions. Behind him, the club crest again, only bigger, emblazoned on a purple wall, and the motto '*Victoria concordia crescit*' – 'Victory grows out of harmony'. But the questions he faced centred around a perceived disharmony within the club. Arsenal had once been a bastion of stability. Before Graham's sacking, they'd had just four managers in 39 years – 5, if Steve Burtenshaw's 11-match spell as caretaker boss is included. Now, Wenger was their third manager in the space of a year and a half, and their fifth including Houston's and Rice's temporary stints. They'd begun to underperform both on and off the pitch, too. Perennial contenders for the first half of Graham's reign, the Gunners had become an unpredictable, inconsistent unit better suited to cup success than league challenges. With Dein one of the drivers behind the Premier League's formation, Arsenal ought to have reaped the commercial rewards the rebranded top flight brought, yet at the time of Wenger's appointment, their annual turnover was less than a third of Manchester United's and smaller even than the likes of Liverpool, Newcastle and Tottenham. And to add to the delicacy of the situation into which Wenger was to be thrust, the club captain, Tony Adams, had taken the admirable step of admitting to his struggles with alcoholism just two days before the new manager's appointment was announced.

Yet, when asked about the apparent turmoil, Wenger presented a calm, confident front. 'I had the feeling there was a big crisis here,' he said, 'but every time I had contact with the board they looked very strong and determined and the players appear to have been very positive, too. The crisis has been around the club but never inside the club.'

Wenger went on to talk about his desire to 'win over' the fans, his plan to 'keep the majority of the players English' and to develop talent, rather than splurge on star names. He outlined, also, his preference for an English-style 4-4-2 formation, as opposed to the 3-5-2 Arsenal had been utilizing – 'It's strange, really, because all over Europe clubs are turning to the old English system of 4-4-2,' he observed, 'while here you are just adopting the Continental system of three at the back.'

He'd rung all the right notes and the assembled press pack was suitably impressed. 'If Wenger coaches football as well as he talks about the game,' wrote Christopher Davies in the *Daily Telegraph*, 'Arsenal will have signed the most successful foreign manager to work in England.'


As Wenger walked through Highbury's famous Marble Halls for the first time since his appointment was publicly confirmed, he strode across the red cannon that adorned the floor, a reference to the club's beginnings as a factory team for a munitions manufacturer. Before he turned right and began to climb the stairs to the first floor, he noted the bronze bust of Herbert Chapman presiding over the art deco entranceway. Chapman was a visionary who, as Arsenal manager from 1925 until his untimely death in 1934, guided the Gunners to two league titles and an FA Cup while conjuring modernizing and influential innovations in tactics, training and infrastructure.

'When I came to Arsenal, I discovered this man's story,' he later said, 'his innovative techniques, his invention of the WM formation when the law of offside was changed, the way that he used physiotherapy, his ideas on training methods, numbered shirts and more modern studs, floodlighting, the list goes on.'

Wenger had his own list of modernizing changes to introduce at Arsenal. It was just as extensive as Chapman's. He hoped his would be equally successful.

# 3
# Stretch Goals

At 8am on 12 October 1996, the Arsenal players walked bleary-eyed into the function room of a hotel in Lancashire. They would play Blackburn Rovers at Ewood Park later that day in what was to be Arsène Wenger's first match as manager. Usually, on the morning of an away fixture, most of the squad would skip breakfast in favour of an extra hour or two in bed; then they'd amble down from their rooms and shake off the cobwebs with a gentle mid-morning stroll. This time, though, Wenger had instructed them to set their alarms for 7.30am and meet him promptly downstairs.

When they walked in, the Gunners' assortment of stars saw their new boss across a cleared floor space. He was wearing a T-shirt and a pair of shorts so high-rising and snug they'd have been much more in keeping in the previous decade.

'It was really strange, because everybody else in the room didn't know what was going on,' remembers Ian Wright. 'Then, all of a sudden, we're doing yoga stretches and Zen movements. You could imagine what it was like. When he was doing it, he was deadly serious. We were meant to have our eyes closed, but everybody's got one eye open, looking at everybody else. I remember him, while he was doing it, saying about the importance of being at one with yourself and being calm.'

'George Graham would have had his suit and tie on and be looking a million dollars in the corner,' says Lee Dixon. 'He wouldn't have his boxer shorts on and his T-shirt. The lads were saying, "What's this all about? Why are we stretching? Kick-off's seven hours away. Why are we stretching?" He was saying, "No, it's good for you."'

This stretching routine was a new addition to the players' match-day preparations, but they were already getting used to such limbering and conditioning exercises throughout the week. It had been almost two weeks since Wenger first arrived at Arsenal's training ground in London Colney, a leafy village in Hertfordshire around 15 miles north-west of Highbury. The Frenchman was dismayed at what he saw. The dated facilities fell well short of his standards and expectations. What's more, Arsenal didn't own the training ground. It belonged to University College London and the Premier League club had to share their practice sanctuary with students. The changing rooms were cramped and lacked any modern comforts. There was no office space for the manager. 'What is this?' Wenger kept asking rhetorically as he strolled the grounds ahead of his first session. 'I do not understand. This is not the Arsenal.'

Matters were complicated further shortly after when a fire at the training ground damaged the changing rooms so severely as to render them unusable. Instead, Arsenal's players began to assemble at Sopwell House, a nearby luxury hotel, to change into their kit each morning before being ferried to training by minibus. It was always understood that the cause of the blaze was a youth-team player misusing a tumble drier. Nigel Winterburn suggests in jest an alternative culprit. *Arson* Wenger, perhaps?

'Was it Arsène Wenger that did that?' Winterburn jokes. 'Because it certainly wasn't luxurious at London Colney. It was basically a college grounds. London Colney was quite a pokey little training area, in terms of facilities for getting changed. Going to a hotel to get changed and then jumping on a coach ten minutes down the road, it's not really much of an inconvenience. You just get on with it. Sopwell House is pretty nice, so I don't think too many players had a problem with it.'

There was a marked difference in Wenger's approach to training compared to Arsenal's previous managers. It was evident from his very first session, and it was the cause of some schoolboy snickering and back-row teasing from the players. Most notable was how hands-on the Frenchman was. He would later be joined by Boro Primorac, his assistant manager from Grampus Eight, who'd take a lead role in training exercises. A quiet character whose English was limited at first, Primorac, in contrast to Wenger, impressed the players with his ability with the ball. The former Yugoslav international, who was 42 at the time, five years Wenger's junior, had enjoyed a distinguished playing career with Hajduk Split, Lille and Cannes. When joining in with Arsenal's training sessions, he earned instant respect.

'He was brilliant,' says Pat Rice. 'His knowledge of football was fantastic. He was brilliant. He was very quiet. He was quite funny in the things that he said. He was just an all-around nice guy, but he could play. He was terrific in the air. Sometimes, if Arsène wanted to play six v six and someone had gone off injured, Boro would go in and play. His mind was just as quick as everybody else's.'*

---

\* Wenger might not have been as gifted a player as his assistant, but he was tremendously competitive whenever he dusted off his football boots and joined in. 'We used to play staff games at the end of the season, youth team against first team and stuff like that,' says club photographer Stuart MacFarlane. 'Arsène would always cheat. It would always be his throw-in or his free kick. I remember one of the kit men said to me that he was marking Arsène and Arsène said to him, "Fuck off on the other side of the pitch. I don't want you marking me," because he wanted to have a bit of space to be able to play. But that's what he was like.'

While Wenger waited on Primorac to join him in England, he relied only on the help in-house, with the coaches already in place and Rice as his number two. He believed strongly in the value of isometric exercises, designed to strengthen the body without adding bulk, and plyometric drills, where short bursts of activity aid explosiveness and dynamism. He'd had his players jumping over hurdles, tiptoeing across rope ladders and hopping from side to side. He'd demonstrate it all first, which amused his new charges no end.

'I think from the outset, the players realized that, even though he was an ex-professional, he wasn't the best with the ball at his feet,' says Adrian Clarke, who was a young midfielder with the club at the time. 'He'd like to have a little kick around with the players sometimes when you were waiting to do the session and he always looked a bit awkward. There were one or two giggles. But, overall, I have to say they were really receptive. I'd say it only took one session, maybe two sessions, and then all of a sudden it became normal and players were up for it.'

Wenger also strongly believed in the benefit of stretching. The Arsenal stars were, of course, accustomed to running through a few cursory limbering motions before taking to the field each morning. But this was different. Ten seconds or so stood on one foot while holding your other ankle behind your backside to awaken a sleepy quadricep wasn't going to pass any more. Wenger brought the science of injury prevention and recuperation to the players' newly expanded stretching regime.

'He did it all himself,' says Clarke. 'He'd get himself a mat. Everyone was gathered around in a semicircle. We'd all have mats and he would demonstrate all the exercises himself.

'There were a lot of laughs in the first couple of sessions, players moaning and groaning about body parts they'd never stretched before – "Fucking hell, what's this all about?" There was a bit of mickey taking behind the scenes about him as well. But the focus was on becoming more flexible, more supple, becoming willing to embrace stretching and yoga and dynamic exercises before training, which was something we'd never really done before. Prior to that it was sort of, "Go and have a jog and then we'll go into training." But here, we'd do a full-on Pilates session and then stretches and then a lot of bunny hops and jumping in and out of hurdles, sit-ups with medicine balls. All of this was relatively new to us at the time. Most players of that period discovered they had hip flexors. Up until that point we didn't really bother stretching that part of the body. He'd clearly heard some correct stories in regards to the way some members of the first team weren't looking after themselves at that point and decided to act on it promptly, which was really smart.'

Alien though these new exercises were at the outset, the players quickly noticed improvements in their flexibility. The post-training aches that had become a begrudging fact of life for many of the older members of the squad steadily began to fade, too. And while the terms 'mindfulness' and 'well-being' would certainly not be found in any football dictionary of the time, the players came to appreciate the change of pace the pauses for stretching facilitated on a daily basis. 'It was something that, after a while, you looked forward to doing,' Wright says.

'He was a revelation, really,' says Lee Dixon. 'We saw this bloke with glasses on and the patches on his elbows, looking like a geography teacher, telling us all this stuff. We literally stretched for hours in the day. We'd stretch before we went out for a warm-up. Before the warm-up started outside, we'd stretch a bit more. We'd do a warm-up and then stretch after the warm-up. We'd train, then we'd do some stretching.

We'd go in the gym and do some weights, then we'd stretch. It was like, "Jesus!" But we all bought into it. I think that's the important thing. That was the green light to go, "Right, we've got these new players, these guys we'd never heard of, they're not bad players. We can do something here." That was the start of it.'

The work on the training pitch differed from what had come before, too. The players – particularly the defenders – were well accustomed to unopposed shape drills from George Graham's tenure. They'd walk through imagined scenarios, with non-existent opponents, in order to fine-tune their formation, perfecting the spacing between each player and how the unit ought to move to cover every potential in-game scenario. It proved widely effective, with Arsenal's backline renowned and a central cog of their successes of the past decade. But the work was a slog. Wenger also utilized unopposed drills, but his were not designed to foster regimental defence. With training mannequins arranged around the pitch, players were instructed to pass and move through the spaces in between, tuning into one another's movements and perfecting swift patterns of attacking play. This was fluidity rather than rigidity. He even had a couple of basketball hoops placed on the training pitch that would be used for cool-downs after sessions; an influence, perhaps, from his partner, Annie Brosterhous, who was a former Olympic basketball player. 'It was a bit of fun,' says Matthew Rose, a young defender on the fringes of the first team at the time, 'but I also think he was a big believer in the passing and movement of basketball and how that could translate to football.'

'From day one, his training methods were superb,' says Ray Parlour. 'I always say the manager's job, for me, is Monday to Friday, to get you prepared for the game for the Saturday, and then it's down to you. But he was brilliant on the training field, absolutely fantastic, always helping you. Even if I said I'd stay behind after training to do a bit extra, he'd say, "I'll do it with you, no problem." You always respected him for doing that, because he could get anybody to do it, but he used to love staying. He just loved football. He just loved being out there and seeing you get better.

'Football was changing in that era, anyway. From '96, it was changing, when he first turned up. It was getting a lot more professional. More foreign players were coming into the Premier League. So I think the British guys just had to go with it, really. My eyes were wide open, thinking, "OK, I'll do it if it's going to make me better."'

Everything was timed to precision. A principle he had learned while playing under the coach Paul Frantz while a semi-professional in the French second tier, Wenger calibrated the workload of every session, every drill, and insisted on it all being timed with absolute accuracy.

'Everybody had a stopwatch,' Pat Rice says. 'The coaching staff had one, because all of a sudden there might be different games going on on different parts of the pitch. Everybody would have to be synchronized. I remember once we had a six-a-side. There were three teams playing and it was winner stays on. They were playing across two 18-yard boxes. I was refereeing the game and it was 1-1. You had people like Martin Keown and Nigel Winterburn, Tony Adams and Dicko [Lee Dixon] playing. Of course, they're all winners. I just kept on playing. Arsène had said the game should last 15 minutes. I just thought, "Keep going. Next goal wins the game." But Arsène turned around to me. He said, "Pat . . ." and then he just pointed at his watch. I said, "Boss – winning goal?" He said, "No." Afterwards, I asked him, "Why no winning goal?" He said, "They've had enough time to score the winning goal."'

There was one area of Arsenal's training regimen with which Wenger didn't venture to tinker. He understood the importance of a formidable defence – his Monaco side had routinely boasted one of the best defensive records in France throughout his time at the Stade Louis II. His early Arsenal training sessions revolved around unlocking his new players' creativity in attack, encouraging expression, improvisation and movement, but he was careful not to bulldoze the sturdiest foundation already in place. When it came to matters of defence, he stayed out of the way. He had no new tricks to teach the old dogs.

'We had our way of playing and it was hugely successful in keeping the ball out of the net, and Arsène saw that,' Dixon says. 'We did it as second nature. We didn't even think about doing it after doing it for nine years with George. It was just what we did. I think Wenger came and thought, "Wow, they're quite organized." He knew that because of the results we'd had and the things we'd won before. But to see it in action and to then put his flair on top of that, I think George should take a huge amount of credit. Arsène hugely benefited from what was at the club when he came, and he just put his flair on it. He's not a coach who could go into a team who are struggling defensively and mastermind a defensive, tactically aware team. I don't think that's his forte. When he came, he already had one in place.'

'I only trained once or twice, maximum, with him when I got a feeling at that time that that was something I needed to be part of,' says Nigel Winterburn. 'I pushed as hard as I could. I just loved everything that Arsène Wenger did. I felt so different. I quickly realized that I needed to be a little bit selfish and push, so he realized I was someone he would be considering to be part of the squad. The way that he talked to people, the way that he trained – his methods just seemed so different to what we'd done before, what we were used to. He gave you a freedom to go and play. We worked a lot on attacking options in areas of the pitch. He let us organize ourselves defensively, really. It was just a couple of training sessions and I knew that this was something that I was going to enjoy and needed to be part of.'

Wenger's methodological revolution wasn't limited to the physical work he asked of his players. It was all change in the changing room, too. Within the first week of the new manager's arrival at London Colney, players taking a pre- or post-training rest stop noticed a fresh sign placed above the toilet, a chart with coloured tiles progressing from white through to yellow and across to brown. The players could've been forgiven for thinking they were expected to pick out a paint shade from a 1970s colour palette.

'That was the pee chart,' the goalkeeping coach Bob Wilson explains. 'Every time you go to the toilet – in the morning, after training, in the afternoon – check your pee. If it's anywhere in that last three or four shades, you need to drink water. This wasn't just training-field stuff; this was professorial stuff.'

Professorial? Perhaps. Popular? Not universally. Uptake with the off-field changes was slower. English football was playing catch-up to the Continent when it came to the dietary practices of the time. Some old habits died hard. Sausage, eggs and beans was suddenly no longer deemed a suitable pre-match meal. Now only slight variations on a base of boiled chicken, vegetables and mashed potato were allowed. Carbonated water was banned, with Wenger believing the bubbles hampered hydration, and yogurt was recommended as a digestion aid before every meal. Sugary sweets and chocolate as pre-kick-off pick-me-ups were out. Instead, small sugar cubes laced with caffeine were passed around. Wenger introduced periodic vitamin B12 injections and creatine was provided to aid stamina. The players would joke that physio Gary Lewin, who was responsible for dispensing the various pills and powders, was their dealer. The science of supplementation had arrived and it was not wholly welcome.

'We went through a nutritional programme where you had a big main pre-match meal three hours before the game,' Lewin explains, 'and then leading up to the game, you would have what we would call "quick sugars". That would be jelly beans, jelly babies, a bit of chocolate, jaffa cakes. He was a complete opposite. Wenger's argument was, "If you have the right amount of food pre-match, you don't need quick sugars. Quick sugars are a short-term answer, where you get a big rush of sugar, but it only lasts five or ten minutes. We want the longer term." I would say the biggest resistance was the players getting used to the lack of sugar.'

'There was only one slight resistance from players that he didn't like,' Winterburn says. 'We used to travel by train and come back by coach or fly up and come back by coach. He didn't like players having chocolate on the Friday if we travelled. We used to go to the station. He'd usher everybody on to the train and he used to control what you could have and what you couldn't have when the food was coming around. I think he knew that certain players used to stop off in the little kiosk at the top of the platform and pick up a bit of chocolate. I think he was aware of that, but he was trying to let players know what he wanted to happen.'

In his pursuit of enhancing performance in any way possible, Wenger enlisted the help of experts from France. Philippe Boixel, a Paris-based osteopath with whom Wenger had worked at Monaco, would visit London Colney twice every week to help the players recover from the knocks and strains of Premier League matches. And Yann Rougier, a neuroscientist and nutritionist, spoke to the squad about nutrition. 'He came in and gave us all these speeches about what the body should be doing, how to refuel,' Dixon says. 'Obviously, 12 pints of lager wasn't on the menu.'

In the canteen, chips were off the menu, too. Ketchup was banned. 'It was a low-fat diet, which nobody really knew about back then,' says club chef Rob Fagg. 'I went down the library and read up about it. It was chicken, fish, broccoli. It was all grilled – plain food, no sauces. They were allowed Tabasco sauce, so they used to cover everything in Tabasco sauce. It started off as poached fish, but the players didn't like that, so we started grilling it. I used to say that if it was brown, they'd eat it.'

Hotel stays for away games offered a chance for players to rebel via room service. The Welsh striker John Hartson was chief among a number who'd order sandwiches and fizzy drinks to their room, until Wenger caught on and began asking hotel staff to inform him of any illicit food orders. Fagg would even facilitate the odd indulgence on home soil. He remembers sneaking a handful of the squad into his kitchen, where he'd cook bacon rolls for them to snaffle before the manager found out. 'Rob, are you cooking bacon?' Wenger said, sniffing the air as he walked into the canteen. 'Only for the staff, boss,' Fagg insisted. Fagg also recalls baking a cake for Dixon's birthday, which, courtesy of a Ray Parlour prank, the chef ended up wearing. 'The cream is off on this,' the curly-haired midfielder claimed. 'Here, smell it.'

'Arsène was very, very intelligent, very sensible,' says David Platt. 'What he knew was that he could control the dietary intake of the players while they were at the training ground, knowing that players when they leave and they go home for dinner can have what they want. And because they run around and burn off so many calories, it doesn't matter so much. What Arsène knew was that, really, it might not be ideal if you're having fish and chips at night and sticky toffee pudding and custard, but if you're doing that at lunchtime as well then you're compounding the problem, so why not control what you're having at the training ground?'

But, for the most part, the changes Wenger was introducing were recommended, rather than dictated. The players had the choice to opt out of certain aspects, to find what worked for them. Winterburn, for example, found some of the supplements upset his stomach, so he stopped taking them. And the full back was granted permission to continue to consume his regular pre-match meal of eggs and toast – provided he didn't add baked beans.

'I remember Dennis [Bergkamp] didn't like to take creatine,' Dixon says. 'We were told what it was supposed to do, but, for whatever reason, he said, "No, I don't want to take it." So all the lads, immediately that day, stopped taking creatine because Dennis wasn't taking it. We were like, "If it's not good enough for Dennis, we're not taking it." We abandoned the creatine. He was scoring worldy goals every week, so it wasn't doing him any harm. We gave Arsène something back. We'd take all the other stuff, but we ditched the creatine.'

Wenger was willing to compromise with his stretching routine, too. 'I don't know this, but I've got a feeling he was very clever, because, after a while, there were lots of changes – about timings, about food, all the supplements – and I think to avoid a rebellion, he did the stretching early on a match day and I think he knew we'd get sick of that,' Dixon says. 'We got hold of Tony Adams and said, "Tony, we can't be stretching at eight in the morning. This is ridiculous. We want a lie-in. The lads want a rest." He actually went to see Wenger and said, "Maybe we could make it later?" The boss changed it. We didn't do the stretching at eight in the morning. He gave us something back. The players felt as if we had a bit of player power, but I think he was always going to do that anyway. It wouldn't surprise me if that was his motive, because he seemed to give it up quite easily once we said we don't like it.'

It wasn't long before the players began to notice performance improvements in themselves and their colleagues, though. Wenger's methods were having the desired effect. The proof, it seemed, was in the lack of pudding. 'Players, within three or four weeks, started to feel sharper, started to feel better,' says Clarke. 'That was when they fully bought into this way. I went on loan to Rotherham around Christmas time and I came back in the new year. The difference in the players was unbelievable from earlier on in the campaign. They seemed to run faster, seemed more powerful, seemed to be just so much fresher when you played training-ground matches. It really struck me that he'd got them in better physical condition. I think a lot of that was down to the nutrition and the stretching and also the supplements. Players were running more powerfully. It was pretty startling.'

'He said, "If you take all this information on board, do the stretching, eat the food, take the vitamin tablets, then you will go on and play a couple of years longer than you otherwise would've," Dixon says. 'I was like, "Right, I don't want to stop playing. Let's do it." We took all the tablets and we did all the stretching.'

On the coach journey back to London after Arsenal had defeated Blackburn 2-0 in the new manager's first match in charge, Wenger sat at the front of the coach. The Frenchman basked in the contentment of a solid start to life in England and the Premier League – a gritty win against tough opposition and a satisfactory uptake of his ideas and philosophies. Behind him, his players sang a mischievous rebel chant: 'We want our Mars bars back! We want our Mars bars back!'

# 4

# Onside

Ewood Park's away dressing room was cramped. The Arsenal players were packed tightly together, shoulder to shoulder along the benches. Although they were leading Blackburn Rovers, 1-0 up thanks to Ian Wright's third-minute goal, they had trudged disconsolately down the tunnel at half time. They knew their first-half performance had left plenty to be desired, that their lead was fortunate. And as they sat in the dressing room, waiting for their new manager to speak, they knew what was coming. Each player was silent, his gaze fixed on the brown-tile floor.

'Every manager I'd been with before, they were coming in and the first thing they were doing was shouting and screaming,' says Wright. 'No one looked at the manager, because if you hadn't started well in that game or you hadn't played well, you didn't want to get eye contact with the manager. That was George Graham's favourite – if you got eye contact with him, he'd direct his whole team meeting at you when he was shouting.'

Then Arsène Wenger walked in, and the players' silence was reflected back at them. The manager uttered not a word. He shuffled into the adjoining medical room and back again. He consulted quietly with his coaches. The players barely twitched on the benches, anticipating the maelstrom of reproach to which they had grown accustomed.

It never came.

Ten minutes passed before Wenger finally addressed his charges. His demeanour was unchanged. His temper had not been tweaked. 'Keep doing what you're doing,' he encouraged. 'We've done great stuff in training – keep doing that and we'll be fine.'

Slowly, the astounded Arsenal players began to understand there was a strategy to the boss's silence. 'We stayed there for a while,' Wright remembers. 'No one moved. Then we started whispering to ourselves. We went on to realize what he wanted – for us to sort out what we think happened in that half. Five minutes before the end, when we were getting ready to go back out, he'd come and just give everybody love. That sticks in my mind because it was the first time I'd been in a dressing room where a manager – whether you'd played good, bad or indifferently – has not come in and blasted everybody, shouting. He just came in with the same calm, tranquil vibe. It made everybody just chill, think about what you'd done and sort it out among yourselves. When he came in at the end, he just said some lovely things and you went back out there. It was harmonious, beautiful.'

It was also successful. Arsenal doubled their lead in the second half through a goal that exemplified the freedom of expression with which Wenger wanted his team to play. After centre back Steve Bould broke up a fifty-first-minute Blackburn attack with a sliding interception, Patrick Vieira and Paul Merson exchanged a one-two to swiftly progress the ball through midfield. Vieira then swept a swishing, outside-of-the-boot pass to split the Rovers backline and put Wright through on goal. Such opportunities were manna from heaven for the veteran striker, and he duly dispatched the chance, lifting the ball over the on-rushing goalkeeper and into the far corner of the net. Arsenal had secured their sixth league win of the season, their fourth in a row, and the first under their new manager. The Wenger era had begun.

Wenger's communicative approach and response to subpar performances hadn't always been so even-keeled. Once, while in his first managerial post, with Ligue 1 strugglers Nancy in the mid-1980s, Wenger was so furious after a heavy defeat at the hands of Lens that he became physically sick. He had to instruct the coach driver to halt the team's homebound journey so he could exit the coach and vomit into a roadside ditch. 'He's learned to control himself more since,' Jean-Luc Arribart, one of Wenger's players with Nancy, told journalist Xavier Rivoire for his 2008 book *Arsène Wenger: The Authorised Biography* of the French tactician, 'but back then there was real anger when things did not go well.'

At Monaco, he could occasionally display hardline, dictatorial traits and an internal fire more reminiscent of Sir Alex Ferguson's Old Trafford reign than anything Wenger's Arsenal players would recognize in the Frenchman. Anyone transgressing the manager's steadfast rule that every player had to arrive into the dressing room at La Turbie, Monaco's training ground, a full 30 minutes before each session would receive his wrath. Brazilian midfielder Luis Henrique was once scolded in front of his teammates for that very reason, with the manager shouting and pointing to his watch to ensure the midfielder, who spoke little French, got the message.

On another occasion while Monaco manager, fuelled by a righteous sense of injustice, Wenger had to be restrained in the tunnel of Olympique de Marseille's Stade Vélodrome during a heated exchange with the rival club's controversial president Bernard Tapie. In 1993, Marseille were found guilty of match fixing. They were stripped of the Ligue 1 title they'd claimed that year and relegated to Ligue 2. But Marseille were not dispossessed of the four consecutive championships they had won prior to the 1992–93 scandal. Wenger felt his Monaco side would have won more than the sole title they'd achieved under his tutelage were it not for the slippery influence of Tapie. Indeed, Wenger's long working relationship with Boro Primorac stemmed not only from an admiration of the Bosnian's footballing know-how but also of his opposition to Tapie. While manager of Valenciennes, Primorac refused to throw a match at Tapie's request and later testified against the Marseille president in court.

With Wenger's assimilation to Japanese life and culture upon taking charge of Nagoya Grampus Eight in 1995, though, he mellowed. The newly minted J.League was gearing up for just its third season of existence. Its clubs were spending big to raise the profile of the sport in Japan, where football played, at best, second fiddle to baseball. Brazilian stars Leonardo and Dunga were signed by Kashima Antlers and Júbilo Iwata, respectively, and European coaches were lured east by more lucrative wages than were typically on offer back home.

At Grampus Eight, Wenger found himself in command of a desperately underperforming side who had finished bottom of the league the previous season. Compared with the likes of Glenn Hoddle, George Weah and Lilian Thuram, whom he'd managed at Monaco, his Japanese charges were footballing novices. But what they lacked in talent and top-level experience, Wenger discovered, they made up for in effort and application. Hamstrung by the language barrier and his new players' ability levels, he learned to simplify his instructions and to be more patient.

'The ability level was different,' says former Barcelona, Tottenham and England striker Gary Lineker, explaining the milieu of Japanese football into which Wenger arrived. 'Back in these days it was a new thing. Baseball is very much the main sport. Football – or *sa-ka*, as they'd call it – was just an up-and-coming thing, but it was very popular with the youth, especially with young girls. You'd go to a game and it would be like a schoolboy international, where the crowd was very high-pitched and there was a lot of squeaking.

'In terms of the players, of course, the level was much lower than I'd been accustomed to in Europe, but the players were very keen to learn,' continues Lineker, who finished his career with a spell at Grampus Eight the season before Wenger arrived in the land of the rising sun. 'They had a really excellent work ethic. For a coach like Arsène Wenger, who likes to improve players, I think that would have been a massive pull, in terms of doing that job. I'd played in that team the year before and we were pretty awful. I didn't play much, because I was injured pretty much for the entirety of the time I was in Japan, sadly, but when I saw what he was doing after I'd left, with the same team primarily that I was a part of, I was quite shocked. He was very quickly very successful over there.'

'Very quickly' might be a slight stretch. Grampus Eight were rooted to the bottom of the 14-team league after 2 months of their first season under Wenger. The Frenchman began to fear the club's Toyota owners were lining him up to be sacked. Instead, it was his interpreter who was replaced. With his pared-down instructions subsequently relayed with better clarity, and thanks to his newfound malleability as a coach, results began to trend upward. Wenger led Grampus Eight to triumph in the Emperor's Cup – the Japanese equivalent of the FA Cup – in 1995.

'On a footballing level, I learned things, of course,' Wenger said of his time in Japan. 'But I learned more on a personal level. I became more tolerant, more understanding than I had been. Before, I was too obtuse, too stubborn, too bad-tempered. Over there, I rediscovered my main motivation as a manager, without the bad sides. I learned to rediscover my joy for training, for guiding players and giving them what they need.'

Stuart Baxter recognized this shift in Wenger's man-management sensibilities. The veteran English coach was a friend of Wenger's dating back to his Monaco days. The pair managed opposite each other in Japan, with Baxter serving as boss of Sanfrecce Hiroshima and Vissel Kobe in the J.League's nascent years.

'When I visited Arsène in Monaco, he could dig people out and be quite aggressive,' Baxter says. 'When he came to Japan, he respected the culture. In Japan, you don't dig people out individually because they'll lose face, and then you've lost them. If you go there shouting and screaming, they switch off and think you're a barbarian who doesn't understand Japanese culture. You have to strike a balance, and that's what he developed there. I'm sure he dug people out at Arsenal, but it wouldn't have been what they were used to; it wouldn't have been teacups flying or throwing things around. But Arsène could absolutely enforce his measure of discipline. He was impressed by the culture and the respectfulness in Japan. I'm sure that helped him develop whatever personality he had as a coach at Arsenal. He enjoyed finding that harmony.'

Wenger was crowned J.League Manager of the Year in 1995, after overseeing the cup success and a rise to a second-place league finish. He added the Japanese Super Cup to his list of accolades attained out east the following year. More significant than any on-field success, when Wenger left Grampus Eight in September '96, he returned to Europe with a reshaped philosophy.

His ideas on how the game should be played hadn't shifted an iota. Expression and a commitment to cohesive, team-based attack remained his dogma. But he'd learned that a one-size-fits-all approach to delivering his message would fall down when crossing countries and continents. In Japan, he softened his language so as not to single out or humiliate his players. He accepted compromises in his methods of training and preparation to account for cultural differences. He allowed the Japanese players to continue to have hot baths before a game, for example, even though he believed it might be detrimental to their physical readiness.

Arriving in England, he knew immediately an overhaul would be required. Changes were needed in the way the players ate, trained and socialized if Arsenal were going to meet their potential. But he recognized, also, that he was once again depositing himself into a different football culture; it was foreign to him and, crucially, so was he to his players. His changes would have to be gradual – evolution rather than revolution. He would earn buy-in from the players by showing his trust in them. These were not the jumble of comparative novices and ageing stars he'd tutored in Japan. His Arsenal squad was constructed largely of experienced internationals and past title winners. He would treat them accordingly.

There was one member of Arsenal's English contingent to whom Wenger's laid-back man-management style felt perfectly natural. Former England captain David Platt had spent four years in Italy – with Bari, Juventus and Sampdoria – before signing for Arsenal in the summer of 1995. Platt had been content in Serie A and only left Sampdoria because the Genoese club's financial belt-tightening saw them accept Arsenal's £4.75 million bid. He returned to England – where he'd previously played for Crewe Alexandra and Aston Villa – at age 29 with the express aim of collecting winners' medals for the first time in his homeland. He felt Arsenal's stature and playing talent offered that, but he initially found the dynamic between players and the manager at the club – and, more broadly, in English football – had evolved little in the years he'd been away.

Wenger changed that. And Platt saw in the new manager traits shared with a Continental coach with whom the English football audience would become acutely familiar half a decade later. 'We're going back to what was an English style of coaching and managing,' Platt explains, 'which was work, energy, endeavour – if things are going against you then you work harder. If you need to have a rocket up your arse, you get a rocket up your arse. That, theoretically, gives you a stimulus to work harder and run faster. It's a little bit antiquated in many ways, because you are [already] working hard.

'My previous two years were under Sven-Göran Eriksson at Sampdoria. It was very, very similar to Wenger. You weren't going to get a rollicking. The fear factor of playing under these people is that they would leave you out. Your fear factor was your place, not that they were going to tear you off a strip if you weren't performing. And I think here was this almost respect that you aren't not working, that you aren't not playing well on purpose, that we're all in this together and the moment you stop performing for whatever reason, he'll get someone to go into your place and perform. It was very similar to Eriksson.

'It didn't surprise me that we would come in at half time and players would be sat there waiting for him to speak, and he didn't, because he was having a few minutes to collect his thoughts and think, "OK, what am I going to say to have the biggest impact in terms of performance and helping the team to win tactically?" Rather than just, "You're not playing well", giving you a rollicking and "You're going to work harder". That wasn't going to be of any benefit.'

Platt's Continental experience made him an outlier among the

English players in the Arsenal dressing room, though. Most of the others had been mainstays of trophy-winning teams under George Graham. An uncompromising, dictatorial style of management was all they'd ever known. A working life without daily bollockings and obey-to-the-letter instructions was a welcome new world, even if it required some adjustment at first.

'He was totally different than all my mangers I've had,' says Lee Dixon. 'I've had some strict disciplinarians over the years. You're almost told what to do and told how to play and you expand on those instructions, but they'd be quite rigid if you didn't do things right. There'd be lots of telling off and throwing teacups and angry moments. I didn't see much anger in Arsène. He was very placid. He'd talk to you. He never told me one thing to do on a football pitch. He trusted that I knew what to do and he basically said to me every week, "Just go and play." I was like, "What do you mean? Are you going to tell me what to do?" And he'd say, "No, just go and play. Express yourself." He had trust. I mean, I knew how to defend a goal better than he does. "You're a defender – just go and do it. Then, when you get the ball, just play football, do what you think." That, for me, was dreamland.'

'I think it was just the way that he spoke to players, as a group and individually, that you felt that there was something different about him,' adds Nigel Winterburn. 'I think it just shows the class of the man. If you think about all the players that left, there's nobody who's come out and had a real go at Arsène Wenger about the way he treated them. That just shows a lot of quality. Even towards the end of my career, when I was getting left out of the team, I didn't fall out with Arsène Wenger at all. He always tried to make you feel part of the squad, even if he was talking to you and telling you – which he was with me, particularly in that last six months of my contract – he needed to start switching things around defensively and I wouldn't be playing as much. But, on the flip side, he was saying, "I need you ready when I need you. You're an important part of the team still." In one way, he's sort of easing you out. In the next way, he's making you feel that you've still got a massive part to play at the club. I think that's why I've got so much respect for him, in terms of the way he treated me. It seemed to be like that with a lot of players.'

Wenger was more approachable than his predecessors, the players found. He'd often be seen walking a lap of the training ground in conversation with Paul Merson. The gifted playmaker had endured a turbulent period in the mid-1990s, battling addictions to cocaine, alcohol and gambling. He found an understanding ear in the new manager.

'It was the same with everybody,' says Adrian Clarke. 'He would be very, very charming in one-to-one chats, incredibly charming. I remember knocking on his door before I went out on loan in late November. I'd been sort of frozen out of the training group a little bit. I had arranged a meeting at Highbury in his office. It was the first time we'd had a proper one-on-one chat. I went in feeling a bit angry and annoyed that I was being frozen out. But he was so charming. He turned the conversation into wanting to find out about me and my background, what interests I had. He basically wanted to know everything about me as a person. For a manager to want to talk about random stuff like that was quite refreshing. I just found myself really liking him. By the end of it – even though he didn't make any promises at all, in regards to involving me – I couldn't feel like I didn't like Arsène Wenger. I felt like he was a really, really charming person, just able to sort of take conversations to different areas. I think at that time I was going back to my old school to do

A levels to get a back-up plan, educate myself, and he was particularly interested in that. He was excellent and made people feel good about themselves.'

It wasn't just the players who picked up on Wenger's more delicate form of delivery. Just as much of the squad had been in place during the regimes of Rioch and Graham, so too had many members of the support staff. Gary Lewin had been Arsenal's first-team physio for a full decade by the time of Wenger's appointment and had recently taken up the same role within the England set-up alongside his club duties. A confidant of sorts to many of the players, he instantly recognized the effect of Wenger's softer touch.

'The way he dealt with players was to treat them as intelligent people, to try and understand the game and what he wanted,' Lewin says. 'He would talk to them about situations in training or matches. They would go for a pre-match walk and you would always know when he had something specific to say about what's going to happen that day in the game, because he would walk with the player he would want to make a point to. One thing he did meticulously, all the time, was defend his players. Outside the club, it became a bit of a sport, taking the mick out of him. But players loved him for it. They loved the way he would defend them. The motivational side of it was playing for a manager that you felt cared about you, talked to you, shared in the decision making and how the team were going to play, and made you take responsibility for how you prepared and played.'

Old habits sometimes die hard. Wenger was changed by Japan, but that's not to say remnants of his old temper didn't occasionally simmer somewhere deep beneath the surface. Dixon remembers a rare example of the manager losing his temper early in his Arsenal reign. Down 1-0 at half time, Wenger entered Highbury's home dressing room sipping water anxiously from a disposable cup. His frustration was evident and he began to vent.

'He started shouting,' Dixon says. We were like, "Wow, that's a bit weird." He was saying, "It's not good enough. We haven't done what we needed to do." It was getting louder and louder and louder. Some of us English lads were quite pleased, because we always thought that some of the French lads needed that side of the game, to be told off sometimes. We would do it. We would say, "You're not doing it. You've got to do this. If you let me down and pull out of a tackle like that again then I'll tackle you. We need you to do this, this and this." So he was shouting at somebody. And as he got to the top of his anger, he screwed this plastic cup up and threw it in the bin as he stormed out. But as he threw it, it hit the edge of the bin and fell on the floor. He stopped, turned round, came back and put it in the bin, then walked out. It was like he was doing so well with anger, but he didn't really know how to finish it off.'

This kind of red-faced indignation had become as ill-fitting to Wenger as those oversized padded jackets with the zips he'd seem to wrestle with perpetually in later years. Half-time hollering had gone the way of the ketchup in the Colney canteen – it was off the menu.

Wenger liked to chip in with the grunt work ahead of training sessions. It became a common sight at London Colney for the manager to haul one of the large, netted, nylon bags of footballs out on to the pitch while Primorac guided the players through a warm-up routine. And, after doing so, he often enjoyed showcasing his modest ball skills. As the players jogged the perimeter of the training pitch, Wenger, bedecked in shorts and football boots, would run though a routine of keepy-uppies and Cruyff turns.

On one such occasion early in his Arsenal tenure, Wenger showcased an altogether different – yet equally frequent – display that would entertain his players much more than his ball juggling: the pratfall.

After dumping the heavy sack to the turf, Wenger attempted to extract one of the balls from within via a deft flick of his right boot, but his studs became entangled in the netted bag. As he attempted to free his foot, he tumbled over, sending the players, who'd witnessed the whole scene, into hysterics. 'He had about 12 balls in this net and he was trying to keep his balance,' says Dixon. 'All these balls were going everywhere. It was like an octopus caught in a net. It was just hilarious. And that would happen on a weekly basis.'

Wenger was evidently a highly intelligent man, an innovative thinker. He carried a natural air of authority, too, even after his man-management style had become more collegiate post-Japan. He was also strikingly clumsy.

This was an endless source of amusement for his players. Every slip and trip would elicit a chorus of snickers. Ray Parlour, the squad's resident joker-in-chief, coined a nickname for the new boss. 'I nicknamed him Inspector Clouseau,' Parlour says. 'I used to love those films growing up, Peter Sellers, *The Pink Panther*. If you look at Inspector Clouseau and what he did – getting his hand caught in doors – that's what Arsène Wenger was like. We all know he's very sensible, but there were a couple of times he'd trip over nets or fall down stairs. You'd see him on the sideline, struggling to do his zip up – stuff like that.'

When, during one preseason meal-time gathering, he attempted to let some air into the stuffy room by opening a side door only for the window above to crash down on his head, the players howled. In another slapstick scene, Wenger once fought a losing battle with an easel during a pre-match meeting at a Four Seasons hotel. 'He kept trying to put it up, but it would slip back down,' goalkeeper Stuart Taylor says. 'He'd get it to stay up for two minutes, then he'd put a pen on it and it would slip back down again. I remember Ray Parlour and Steve Bould just crying. They were in fits of laughter.'

During a preseason trip to Austria ahead of his first full campaign as Arsenal boss, Wenger arranged for the group to spend an afternoon at a local spa. Clad in a white dressing gown, he addressed his players by the side of the pool. 'There's public in here,' he cautioned. 'Let's be sensible. Don't get loud and stupid in here. Whatever rooms you want to go into, you go into them. Just enjoy it. Go and relax for the afternoon.'

'As he went to walk off, he slipped over and just went flying,' one player remembers. 'He landed flat on his back, right in front of everyone around the swimming pool. Everyone was just like, "Oh my God, this bloke." You couldn't write it.'

The most you-couldn't-write-it moment of slapstick hilarity involving Wenger occurred at a manor hotel near Birmingham, the night before Arsenal were set to take on Aston Villa. By and large, Wenger stuck to a similar dietary routine to the one he insisted his players follow. He did, however, enjoy the occasional dessert. When he spotted a piece of apple pie on offer at the dinner buffet, he couldn't resist. He slid a pristine slice on to his plate and, transfixed by a football match being shown on the catering room's television, distractedly headed back to his table. As he settled back into his chair, eyes still trained on the TV, he hadn't noticed that his chosen treat had slipped from his plate and splatted on the floor several paces earlier.

'He sits down and he's still watching the football,' Dixon laughs.

'Then he looks down at his plate and there's nothing on it. We all knew what was happening. And his face – he was looking under the table. How can that happen to him? It always seemed to be him.'

Wenger's clumsiness never undermined his authority, though. If anything, it served only to further endear him to his new players. He was the consummate professional and the unquestioned figurehead, but he was much more approachable than the typical manager in English football at the time. He didn't insist on being called 'gaffer' or 'boss'; 'Arsène' would do just fine. George Graham, the manager under whom many of these Arsenal players had spent most of their careers, was always immaculately turned out and suitably reserved. He never would have committed such clownish calamities. But if ever the fiery Scot were to have fallen foul of a Wenger-esque faux pas, he wouldn't have taken kindly to snickering from his subordinates. Yet the laughter at Wenger's trips and tumbles was seldom one-sided.

'The big thing about Arsène Wenger: he always laughed at himself,' Parlour says. 'If he does something stupid – and it was stupid at times – he would always laugh at himself and have a good time. He didn't mind doing that. Some managers might have thought, "Don't laugh at me!" It was always a nice atmosphere.'

'We've had many a laugh at his expense,' Dixon adds. 'He laughs along the way as well. He has a great sense of humour. He would laugh his head off. He'd say, "Did you see me then?" And we'd say, "Yeah, we did see you, gaffer." He had a laugh at himself. He had to – it was quite a regular thing.'

Lee Dixon walked through Highbury's famous Marble Halls, across the red cannon mural on the entranceway floor, past the bust of Herbert

Chapman and upstairs. The 32-year-old wasn't sure why Wenger had summoned him to Highbury. He entered the manager's red-walled office and perched on a leather chair embossed with the Arsenal crest. Wenger sat on the other side of his mahogany desk. Behind the new boss was a vast bookcase stocked with leatherbound tomes that included a detailed history of the club, charting its beginnings as a workers' team for a munitions factory in Woolwich in 1886.

Wenger explained why he'd called in the full back. 'I've been looking at everybody's contracts,' he said. 'I just want to apologize for your lack of financial reward over the years. Here's a new contract.'

The Frenchman had reviewed the club's pay structure and found it to be stingy in comparison with their Premier League contemporaries. Past managers had penny-pinched. Driven not only by an admirable sense of fairness, Wenger spotted an opportunity to satisfy the old guard. Buy-in from the club's influential veterans would be essential to his grand plans. A few overdue pay rises could comfortably be absorbed.

Captain Tony Adams had been given a new contract shortly before Wenger arrived. Manchester United wanted to sign the England defender – 'I always thought Adams was a United player in the wrong shirt,' Ferguson wrote in his 2015 book, *Leading* – and the Arsenal hierarchy had tripled his wages, up to £20,000 per week, to fend off their rivals. But other members of the famous backline remained grossly underpaid.

'He called me and Nigel in virtually on the same day and said, "I've been looking at everybody's contracts,"' Dixon says. 'When Dennis [Bergkamp] came, the wage structure went through the roof. There was a ceiling on wages, then all of a sudden Dennis turns up, and I think maybe Wrighty had a parity contract. Arsène started to look at the contracts and was quite embarrassed when he saw mine and Nigel's. He more or less doubled our wages overnight. That was a nice day. I remember that day quite high up in my memory bank.'

Bob Wilson, the club's veteran goalkeeping coach and mainstay of Arsenal's 1971 Double side, approached Wenger one morning explaining he might have to step down from his role. He'd been offered £50,000 a year to coach one day a week at another London club.

'I don't understand,' Wenger said. 'Do you not get paid here?'

Wilson explained that, no, he was not on the club's payroll. His position was voluntary, with his only compensation being a small stipend to cover the travel expenses he incurred driving back and forth from London Colney to Television Centre in the west of the city, where he worked as a sports presenter for the BBC.

'So he sorted a little salary for me for my last two or three years before I retired,' Wilson says.

The changes Wenger was implementing at Arsenal in the autumn of 1996 were revolutionary in scope. The new diet, the routine of stretching and finely tuned physical preparation, the precision-timed training sessions and the energy boosting supplements were all alien within the outdated routines of English football at the time. His success in applying these new methods was aided by the fact that he introduced them gradually, rather than wholesale, and that they were suggested, not dictated. But the almost unanimous uptake of Wenger's ideas among this group of high-level, high-performing stars was aided most by the manager's amiability, by the calm respectfulness of his messaging and by the harmony he sought to cultivate.

'It started with us, this hugging each other on the training field and on the pitch, and you saw it with those who came after us, even in the

Invincibles,' Wright says. 'That love, that's what he gave us. He brought that feeling of togetherness and love.'

There remained a bigger cultural reset Wenger was intent on instituting, though; one that would be more essential to this gifted group of players reaching their potential than cutting chips from the lunch menu or pre-match Pilates sessions.

Getting the players onside wouldn't be easy. Fortunately for Wenger, he could count on a new commitment from his captain.

# 5

# Goodbye, Boozy Tuesdays

Arsène Wenger and Tony Adams sat together beneath the morning sunlight on 30 September 1996 on a bench at London Colney and began a frank exchange of views.

'You jeopardised our entire season by doing what you did,' Adams said.

The captain was referring to Wenger's interjection at half time of the UEFA Cup defeat to Borussia Mönchengladbach just five days earlier. Adams explained that he understood the manager's affinity for a 4-4-2 formation and a flat back four; it was, after all, a shape with which the Gunners enjoyed their period of success under George Graham. But Adams felt Wenger's timing was poor in attempting to revert from the 3-5-2 that Bruce Rioch had introduced the previous season.

'We're doing all right. We're fourth in the table,' he continued. 'There's a time and a place for everything, so why don't we wait until next season?'

Wenger listened. He agreed. There'd be no disruptive tactical changes for the time being. The manager then went on to ask Adams about the club, about his teammates, about himself.

Just two weeks earlier, Adams had publicly admitted to a battle with alcoholism. He'd begun attending Alcoholics Anonymous meetings in an effort to end his drinking. Wenger offered a sympathetic ear.

'I was six weeks clean and sober and going to meetings,' Adams wrote in *Addicted* (1998). 'It was great having someone that understood. Maybe not empathised but sympathised. His mum and dad had a pub near Strasbourg, he saw the way that alcohol changed people. He saw the way that gambling changed people. Subtly, more different, but he did see the psychological effect. He's not an idiot, that guy. It's one of his strong points, the psychology. He is an amazing man.'

It was on Friday 13 September that Adams gathered the team together at the training ground to open up about his struggles. He was four weeks sober at the time. With the club yet to confirm Wenger as manager, some of the players thought Adams was about to announce that he was now the new boss. Instead, Adams explained that he had enlisted the help of Alcoholics Anonymous and asked that they showed him the same support they'd shown to Paul Merson, who had battled alcohol, cocaine and gambling addictions. 'I always thought you had bottle,' Ian Wright said after. 'Now I know.' The defender Andy Linighan quietly approached the captain with words of encouragement. 'You've cracked it, Tone,' he said. 'You've taken the first step.'

The news of Adams's admission leaked to the press and, after training the following morning, he decided to tackle the headlines head on by facing journalists' questions.

'I'm not living a lie any more and I feel better for it,' he told reporters. One hack from the *News of the World* began hurling monetary figures in Adams's direction, insinuating he could earn huge sums for selling his story to the tabloid. 'This is for me,' the Gunners' skipper replied as he drove away. 'It's not for money.'

Adams's dad, Alex, was a keen amateur footballer in Essex. He was a tough-tackling centre half with a proclivity for heading the odd goal from a corner – the apple couldn't have fallen much closer to the tree. Once young Tony showed an interest in the game, Alex enrolled in coaching courses to best equip himself to guide his son. He started a Sunday-league club, Dagenham United, for whom Tony played. They won everything locally for five years and Tony began to attract attention from local professional clubs for his obvious talent.

Despite his early success on the pitch, though, Adams was something of an awkward kid. 'I always felt inadequate and a loner,' he said. He experienced panic attacks as a pre-teen and was teased at school for a minor speech impediment, cruelly labelled 'the Wheelie Kid' for his inability to properly pronounce the word 'really'. 'I was ridiculed and felt useless,' he said.

At 13, he was rejected by the England Schoolboys team after attending a trial at the FA's national centre in Lilleshall, Shropshire. He was angered by his omission and resolved to funnel his fury towards manifesting a professional career in the game. He signed for Arsenal at 14 and, just four weeks after his seventeenth birthday, he made his first-team debut in November 1983. 'Tony might be young, but he's more than ready,' said Arsenal coach Don Howe. 'We've no worries whatsoever. He's a great prospect, a big tall athlete and a very mature young man.'

Adams's singular dedication to his craft saw him purchase a computer as a young player on which he stored information about opponents. Decades before websites loaded with statistical data on teams and players became accessible with a couple of swift clicks, he stored notes on, for instance, the tendencies of attacking players he'd come up against, which foot they preferred to shoot with and how he'd fared against them in past encounters. Aged 20 years and 4 months, he became the youngest centre back to debut for England since Bobby

Moore. He was voted the PFA Young Player of the Year for the 1986–87 season and in the following campaign he became the youngest captain in Arsenal's history.

He had proven himself to be a talented and committed footballer, but he was shaping up to be an equally prodigious drinker. For the young Adams, it was an aspirational pursuit.

'I wanted to become a proper drinker because all the people I liked, the ones I wanted to be like, enjoyed a drink,' he said. 'They were confident and funny and outgoing, all the things I wanted to be. I had to work at liking alcohol. It was the effect, not the taste, I was after.'

He began, at 17, drinking bitter shandy – ale mixed with lemonade – before progressing to light beers and later worked at acquiring a taste for Guinness, which would remain his tipple of choice. He rarely drank spirits, except when he'd tip a measure of brandy into his pint for an extra kick.

At first, he'd drink only on a Saturday night, after a match, a well-earned release after a week's work. 'Only another forty-five minutes, boys, and then it's job done,' he would say to the fellow drinkers among his teammates at half time. 'Then we can have a beer.' Soon Sundays, provided there was no Arsenal fixture to scupper his plans, were filled with all-day drinking sessions.

'I could drink four pints in an hour,' he said. 'A session would probably be about twenty pints. In the evenings I could do a couple of bottles of wine on top. My mates would say that it was because I was an athlete that my capacity was so high, that I had a fast system and that my body could deal with it. I thought wetting the bed, which was becoming more frequent for me, was also my body's way of dealing with it. In fact, I welcomed it because I thought it was not rotting my stomach and that I was getting rid of it ready for Monday training.'

He'd also wear a plastic bag under his shirt or extra layers of kit once he'd arrived for the following week's first training session in an effort to sweat the alcohol out of his system.

Adams's drinking didn't have an obvious detrimental effect on his football. He led Arsenal to First Division titles in 1989 and '91 and was, by all accounts, the consummate captain.

'I remember being 16 years old, coming into Colney for the first time as a trainee player with a group of others,' says midfielder Paul Shaw. 'He came into the changing room, sat us all down and said, "Listen, whatever happens here, if you need to talk to anybody, come and talk to me. If you have a problem with other players or coaches, you can talk to me. I'm always here for you." As a group of 16-year-olds coming into the club, that went a long way. It meant an awful lot and made us feel part of the club straight away.'

'He was the perfect captain,' Adrian Clarke adds. 'He was aggressive in the dressing room. He'd wind players up and get the juices flowing. He was old school in terms of getting psyched up for games. But on the pitch, he was always in control of that aggression. He was a great character. He could muck around and have a laugh, but he could also berate anyone in the squad and they'd listen. He was a lad's lad, but also someone you didn't want to mess with and someone you really wanted to please. Tony Adams was, in effect, a manager on the pitch. You didn't want to let him down. You didn't want him to give you a verbal volley on the pitch in front of everybody. You wanted him to be the one to say, "Clarkey, that's brilliant. Keep it going."'

In the summer of 1988, Adams was selected for England's European Championship squad. The Three Lions gravely disappointed at the tournament in Germany, losing all three games to finish bottom of their group. In a 3-1 defeat to the Netherlands, Adams was tasked with marking the world's best striker, Marco van Basten. The AC Milan superstar scored a hat-trick and Adams, despite still being just 21 years old, was scapegoated. England's Euro failure brought about a scathing national assessment of the quality of English players compared to their apparently superior Continental counterparts. European defenders were considered more sophisticated and skilled in possession than English centre halves. Adams was deemed lumbering and rough-hewn by comparison. The following season, opposition fans around the country targeted him for abuse, labelling him a donkey and chanting 'ee-aww' from the stands. The *Daily Mirror* depicted Adams with donkey ears the day after he scored at both ends in a 1-1 draw with Manchester United in April 1989. At Middlesbrough's Ayresome Park the following month, home fans threw carrots at the Arsenal captain.

'Privately, in all honesty, it hurt like hell,' he said, 'and the only way I knew how to deal with that pain was to get drunk and get on with the next game; drink and football, my two saviours.'

Adams's alcohol consumption became increasingly dangerous and destructive. One night out on the booze in London's West End finished with a fight in which the Arsenal skipper broke a crutch over another man's head. His party piece had become smashing pint glasses over his own head. And his head required 29 stitches after a drunken fall down a flight of stairs at a nightclub.

The most egregious incident landed Adams in jail. On the evening of 6 May 1990, Arsenal were due to fly from Heathrow to Singapore for a post-season tour. Adams had spent the day on a drinking session. While at the pub drinking he was invited to a barbecue nearby, where the alcohol continued to flow. After a drunken game of cricket in the host's back garden, Adams reluctantly left for home, where he intended to pack a suitcase before heading to the airport. He strapped into his Ford Sierra and set off, but in his inebriated state he careened across a dual carriageway at 80mph, clipped a telegraph pole and crashed into a wall on a residential street just yards from where he had begun his wayward journey. When breathalysed, his blood alcohol level was found to be more than four times the legal drink-drive limit.

Adams appeared at Southend Crown Court on Wednesday 19 December 1990 to face a drink-driving charge. The Arsenal players' Christmas party was scheduled for that evening. The captain had told his teammates he'd see them there. He would not. He was ordered to serve four months' jail time and transported to Chelmsford Prison.

One of the warders tasked with taking Adams from the court to the prison asked for an autograph. Adams was prisoner number LE1561. On Christmas Day, he spent 23 hours locked in his cell as there weren't enough prison staff on duty to supervise the inmates being out on the block.

He received sympathetic messages from friends and colleagues on the outside, including the new England manager, Graham Taylor, and the man Taylor had replaced, Bobby Robson. He also received a letter from Manchester United manager Alex Ferguson.

'What I do know about footballers is that you can't leave your character in the dressing room,' Ferguson wrote. 'It goes out on the field with you and whatever you see of a footballer on the playing field is a true representation of his life. That being the case, Tony, you have no problems.'

The most gratifying correspondence was pushed through the door of Adams's cell in early February. It informed him that his sentence was to be commuted and that he'd be released on the fifteenth of that month. His four-month sentence was reduced to fifty-eight days.

But, while he was overjoyed to be released ahead of schedule, prison had not proven to be the anticipated wake-up call in regards to his drinking.

'Going to jail had little effect on my drinking or my perception of it as any sort of a problem,' he said. 'In fact, though I lost my driving licence, I gained a drinking licence, because I didn't have to worry about the car any more, I could get drunk more often and get people to drive me about.'

It is said that an addict must first reach 'rock bottom', the pit of their despair, before they can truly confront their illness and begin to work towards recovery. For Adams, that moment arrived in the wake of Euro 96.

The England manager, Terry Venables, had made Adams captain for the first time in October 1995 and, despite a knee injury that had required surgery the following February, the Arsenal centre back was determined to be fit for the European Championship on home soil in the summer. He'd remained sober since the end of the club season and was receiving painkilling injections into his injured knee before every game he played after April. While many of the England players made headlines for their drunken behaviour during a pre-competition Far East tour, Adams was not involved.

After England's semi-final exit at the hands of Germany, Adams began to spiral. The disappointment of England's Euro 96 run ending was compounded by Adams's personal circumstances. He had separated from his wife, Jane, who had recently entered recovery for cocaine addiction. After the Euros, he sought solace at the bottom of a pint glass. He drank near constantly for seven weeks until, at around 5pm on Friday 16 August, he took what would be his last taste of alcohol.

At a social club near his home in East London, Adams sat behind an empty glass.

'You alright, Tone?' the barman asked.

'No,' Adams replied, 'I'm not.' He began to cry.

At training the next day, Adams approached Paul Jacobs, a friend of Paul Merson's who'd helped the Arsenal midfielder with his recovery.

'I've got a drink problem and I need to go to Alcoholics Anonymous,' Adams said.

He attended his first AA meeting the following Friday, in Fulham. And at his second meeting, this time in St Albans after training and accompanied by Merson, Adams found the courage to stand and speak.

'My name is Tony,' he said, 'and I'm an alcoholic.'

Around another one hundred meetings followed over the next three months as Adams's sobriety hung firm. On days when he felt down and in need of respite, he'd call into the club to tell Pat Rice that he wouldn't be at training that day. He was never questioned.

With his spare time no longer consumed by consumption, Adams embarked upon a period of self-discovery and self-intellectualization. He read classic literature and self-help books. He discovered an affinity for poetry. He attended the theatre. He took piano lessons and studied French. He even, with the help of Arsenal-supporting magician Marvin Berglas, began to learn some close-up magic tricks. The following April, he joined a friend from AA on a sky dive.

One afternoon later in the season, Adams sat with Wenger at Sopwell House. The pair chatted over a coffee.

'Tony, I cannot believe it,' said Wenger. 'I cannot believe how you achieved everything you have with the way you abused your body and your mind. You have played to only seventy per cent of your capacity.'

\*

The Football Association professed to be so concerned with the drinking culture ravaging the game in 1996 that, just days after Adams's admission of alcoholism, it was announced that breathalyser tests were to be introduced for all professional players. Random tests were to be conducted after training and matches; any player found to be above the drink-drive limit of 35 micrograms of alcohol per 100 millilitres of breath after matches or training would face disciplinary action.

Yet such handwringing did not prevent football clubs and governing bodies from taking money from major breweries to promote alcohol to the game's millions of followers. England's top division at the time might have officially been known as the FA Premier League, but for sponsorship purposes it was branded the FA Carling Premiership, owing to a money-spinning deal with the Carling Brewery. In the 1996–97 season, five of the league's twenty clubs bore the logo of a brewing company as their primary shirt sponsor.

English football has a long and uncomfortable history with alcohol. A few beers after training or a match was long seen as being more beneficial to team bonding than it was detrimental to physical conditioning and well-being. Some of the game's greatest talents have battled alcohol issues throughout their careers and later life – from Jimmy Greaves to George Best to Paul Gascoigne. By the late 1980s, days-long boozing sessions became endemic as increasingly wealthy players sought recreation, release and entertainment – 'win or lose, on the booze' was the mantra. The rise of lad culture, the burgeoning nightclub scene and the heightened public profiles of the game's stars thanks to the rabid popularity of the Premier League only exacerbated the issue. This drinking culture was as prevalent at Arsenal as anywhere else.

'After a game, once George Graham had finished his debrief, the old kit man, Tony Donnelly, used to come in and put three crates of beer on the bench in the changing room,' says the midfielder Ian Selley. 'Win, lose or draw, there'd be 48 cans of lager sitting at the front. Fifteen minutes after the game, you're opening a can of beer. You'd have another can after you'd had a bath, then you'd get your suit on and go to the players' lounge where there's a free bar. Within an hour of playing a match, you've probably had five pints. And then you're in the middle of London, so you leave your car at the stadium and go out and about on the town. It's crazy when you look back on it. Even on away trips, there'd be booze on the bus. George would be sat at the front and the boys would be getting stuck in at the back.'

It wasn't just after matches that the alcohol would flow, either. Due to their having to share a training facility with University College London, Arsenal did not typically train on a Wednesday, with the university having exclusive use of the facility on that day. The heavy drinking element within the squad utilized the scheduling quirk as a chance for a midweek session. The boozing capacity of the self-proclaimed 'Tuesday Club' became well known.

'Most Tuesdays, the boys would finish training and then go to a pub around the corner,' says Selley. 'You could drive out of training and, before you get on to the motorway, you could see the pub with all the lads' cars parked there.'

Wenger was aware of the alcohol habits of his new players and was keen to curb them. In the newly sober Adams, he found an ally. Adams's teammates were supportive of his efforts to quit drinking and acquiesced when the captain suggested that booze no longer be served in the Highbury players' lounge after matches for a year, with soft drinks and sandwiches instead made available. He asked that there be no drinking on the team coach during return journeys from away games, too. The changes stuck.

'Tony and Arsène had discussed and said, "We'd like to take the alcohol out of the players' lounge after the games. We don't think it's appropriate to have alcohol after a sporting event,"' Dixon says. 'Arsène was loving that. He liked a glass of wine, but we're talking a glass of wine – five or six pints of lager is slightly different. So that stopped literally overnight. The lads were furious. You'd be in the players' lounge with your family, who'd come to watch the game, and your wife or your dad wants a drink but there was no alcohol; it was tea only. The lads rebelled a little bit, I have to say. But it stayed like that.'

Booze wasn't outlawed outright. The players continued to enjoy a few extracurricular beers – Adams would even get upset about not being invited to social meet-ups after beginning his recovery. But the combination of the captain leading by sober example and veterans within the squad not wanting to compromise the physical improvements they had begun to feel under Wenger's new training regime meant the inclination towards regular binge sessions dissipated.

'I will not ban beer completely, because one pint helps relax people,' Wenger told the media. 'But I do not want the players drinking fifteen beers, because that is bad. A footballer's body is his work. If he then destroys that with bad habits like drinking, it's silly. My players will have to change their social habits.'

# 6

# Three-Nil to the Arsenal

There are a handful of theories surrounding the origin of the 'One-nil to the Arsenal' chant that reverberated regularly around Highbury during the latter part of George Graham's reign. One hypothesis is that the song, sung to the tune of the Village People's 1979 hit 'Go West', was first belted out by Gooners in the latter stages of a 1-0 victory over Manchester City in 1992. The Wikipedia page dedicated to the chant, however, claims Arsenal fans first sang it during the 1994 Cup Winners' Cup final in Copenhagen, when a first-half Alan Smith goal was enough to see Graham's side triumph over Parma.

But the most feasible – and, in some ways, romantic – theory of the chant's origin suggests it was birthed in Paris, during the first leg of that year's Cup Winners' Cup semi-final. Arsenal were leading 1-0 at half time at the Parc des Princes when the stadium DJ played the Pet Shop Boys' 1993 cover of 'Go West'. The Paris Saint-Germain fans picked up the tune and sang 'Allez, Paris Saint-Germain', while the travelling supporters responded with 'One-nil to the Arsenal'. In the event, David Ginola equalized early in the second half, but the Gunners won the return leg 1-0 to book their place in the final, in which the same scoreline was repeated and the song was reprised.

It was also around this time that Arsenal fans began to sing 'Boring, boring Arsenal' in ironic riposte to criticism from pundits and opposition supporters of the risk-averse, defence-first playing style Graham espoused. The fact that the Gunners' success under Graham had been achieved with a brand of football that irked rival fans only added a further element of pride for Arsenal supporters. But as an entertainment product, even in periods of triumph it made for uninspiring viewing. When success waned, the football was hard to stomach. Seven of Arsenal's eighteen Premier League wins in the 1993–94 season were by virtue of a 1-0 score, with another three single-goal wins in Europe and one more in their short FA Cup run. There were also seven 0-0 draws in the league and five defeats in which they did not score. Although the Gunners finished fourth in the table, ten top-flight clubs boasted a higher tally of total goals than their modest return of fifty-three, including fifteenth-placed Spurs.

'George Graham had stylish teams and he's harshly judged at times, but in his final season it was horrific,' says journalist John Cross. 'It was so boring and so dull. Arsenal had gone back to being really turgid to watch.'

After battling to a 2-0 victory over Blackburn in Wenger's first game at the helm, Arsenal then drew 0-0 at Highbury against a Coventry City side who'd won just once in their previous nine games and would escape relegation by a single point at season's end. It wasn't the most auspicious beginning. But if Arsenal's performances in these games didn't signify an immediate stylistic sea change, Wenger's third league game in charge – with a familiar face in the opposition dugout – revealed the revolution afoot.

George Graham was given a standing ovation by supporters in all four stands at Highbury when the club's most successful manager ever returned on 26 October, now in charge of Leeds United having served his one-year FA suspension. The fans who lauded the homecoming of the former boss could not have asked for a greater display of the contrast between the football he once oversaw to the new style being cultivated by Wenger.

It took just 44 seconds for Arsenal to strike first. Patrick Vieira burst through the Leeds midfield before sliding a pass across the penalty area to find Lee Dixon on an uncharacteristic gallop into the opposition box. The veteran full back side-footed a confident finish into the net.

It was 2-0 four minutes later, when Dennis Bergkamp capitalized on a defensive mix-up. Ian Wright completed the scoring in the second half after left back Nigel Winterburn wandered forward and stroked a delightful pass in behind the Leeds defence. It was a second period that also saw centre backs Steve Bould and Tony Adams spring into the kind of forward forays rarely glimpsed previously. The words 'Allez les Rouges' flashed across Highbury's video screens. Arsenal were emboldened. They were also top of the table.

It wasn't all smooth sailing over the following months. The resounding win over Leeds was followed by a 2-2 draw with Wimbledon and a 1-0 defeat against champions Manchester United at Old Trafford. There was a run of four games without a victory to round out the calendar year, too, and a 5-2 thrashing of First Division Stoke City in the League Cup was followed by a 4-2 elimination at the hands of Liverpool. Wenger's Arsenal were still evidently a work in progress, but the signs of that progress were clear.

'People still underestimate the change that Arsène instigated,' says Cross. 'He didn't disrupt the tactics at first. He kept the back three. The guy is a genius in terms of getting stylish football. All of a sudden, you were seeing players like Steve Bould, Tony Adams and Martin Keown opening up their bodies and playing a different way. It was pass and move. It was triangles. It was glorious. It was like night and day.'

'There was certainly more flair,' adds the Arsenal writer Josh James, who was a 14-year-old Highbury season ticket holder at the time. 'That was the main issue at the end of the George Graham era, how stale the team had become. It was just, give it to Ian Wright or Paul Merson and hope they can make something happen. You didn't have goal threats throughout the team. Arsène Wenger thought, "This back four is great. They know what they're doing. I'll leave that alone and rejuvenate the rest of the team." The midfield became so much more dynamic. We won games in midfield. We weren't used to that level of play in the middle of the park. It was much more exciting.'

It hadn't been Wenger's intention to keep the backline as it had previously been constructed. After observing September's UEFA Cup defeat to Borussia Mönchengladbach, he returned to Japan. Back at his apartment, he met with Boro Primorac and Damien Comolli, a young coach he'd taken under his wing at Monaco who'd later join him at Arsenal as a scout before going on to become director of football at Liverpool and Tottenham. 'I'm not comfortable with the system,' Wenger told his two confidants. 'I'm going to have to change it.'

But he was convinced to rethink his plans after his discussion with Adams when he arrived at London Colney. Wenger also realized that switching to his preferred 4-4-2 formation would mean dropping one of the veteran centre backs and foisting an increased running load on those who remained in the line-up, with four defenders to cover the defensive zone rather than five. He resolved to stick with 3-5-2 for the remainder of the season at least, and to let the well-established backline take care of themselves.

'Under George Graham, there was a very, very strict way of playing and defending as a team – showing opponents inside and don't let anyone beat you on the outside, all over the pitch,' Dixon says. 'It was almost our blueprint. That was so driven into our psyche, that you cannot be beaten around the outside. When you're standing, facing an opponent, you cut the line off, you show him inside, all over the pitch. I remember George shouting it on the first day of training when I arrived – "Inside! Inside!" I was like, "Why do they keep shouting 'inside'? I don't even know what they're talking about." Dave Rocastle said to me, "Look, when you go to the winger, you cut the line off and show him inside. When he goes inside, Tony Adams comes out, then he shows him inside to the other centre half, then he comes out. You just funnel them into the middle of the pitch, where all your players are." That was fundamental in how we played. We were drilled in that on a daily basis. We had our way of playing and it was hugely successful in keeping the ball out of the net and Arsène saw that.

'We did it as second nature. We didn't even think about doing it after doing it for nine years with George. It was just what we did. I think Arsène came and thought, "Wow, they're quite organized." He knew that because of the results we'd had and the things we'd won before.'

'That back four, we did a lot of work together with George Graham, a lot of tactical stuff, just walking around the pitch, no ball on the pitch sometimes,' adds Winterburn. 'When you look back, you think, "Boy oh boy, I don't know how I did some of that." But it moulded us into the back four and gave us the understanding of what George was trying to achieve, individually and collectively. And then Arsène Wenger took that on. There were rumours floating around that he had been told that that back four would need to be disbanded and he would need to look to replace certain players, but I'm pretty pleased that he made his own decisions and we managed to hang around for a little while longer.'

And in his position as referee for training matches, Pat Rice took the executive decision to continue to foster a level of aggression and physicality among Arsenal's players that would combine with their newfound free-flowing play to define the style of Wenger's Gunners. He would use his whistle sparingly.

'Whenever there'd be a bit of kicking in training, I'd leave it there,' he explains. 'If anybody said anything, I'd say, "What do you think is going to happen on Saturday? Do you think Roy Keane is going to be nicey-nicey to you?" They knew that if they showed any kind of weakness then, boy, that goes round football like wildfire – "All you've got to do is make contact with him and he goes out the game." That's the last thing you want.

'When you've got a back five of Bould, Adams, Keown, Dixon and Winterburn, and then you've got David Seaman behind, that in itself could sometimes play seven-versus-five or something like that. Not only were they organized; their reading of the game was something else. They were all really intense players who didn't want to lose. They treated every training game as though it really meant something to them. The reputation they had as bad losers was true, because they could ruck among themselves as well.'

A short purple patch straddling November and December highlighted the positive direction of travel at Highbury. The side's grit was on display when, after losing Tony Adams to a red card after just 22 minutes for clumsily dragging down a goal-bound Alan Shearer, they managed to beat Newcastle 2-1 at St James' Park. 'I can probably count on one hand the amount of times we lost at home over that three or four years,' says Newcastle midfielder Robbie Elliott. 'It wasn't expected. It was very telling. Not many teams came to St James' and turned us over, especially with a man down.' Dixon was again a surprise scorer, this time thanks to a spectacular diving header.

Another indicator of Arsenal's evolution was the fact Wright, so often a single-minded predator in previous seasons, provided the assist with a fine cross from the left. The England striker then showed his newfound creativity had not diminished his poacher's instincts as he calmly rolled home the winner. 'I was pessimistic,' Wenger said, 'but then I saw the team at half time. They did not want to give up. It showed the legendary spirit of our team.' A 3-1 win over Southampton in a midweek fixture on 4 December put the Gunners three points clear at the top of the league.

The game that best encapsulated Arsenal's stylistic shift under Wenger had come ten days earlier, though, and there could've been no better opponent against whom to showcase it. The battle for Premier League supremacy in North London up to this point had, at best, been even on the judges' scorecards. In the first four seasons after the top flight rebranded in 1992, the Gunners had finished ahead of Tottenham twice, and vice versa. The head-to-head exchanges read less favourably for the red side. Prior to Wenger's arrival, Arsenal had not beaten Spurs in the last five North London derbies; Tottenham were unbeaten at Highbury in their previous five league visits. But when Arsenal hosted their bitter rivals on 24 November, a knockout blow was struck. The Gunners won 3-1, with goals from Wright, Adams and Bergkamp. The captain's booming left-footed volley to put the home side ahead in the second half evidenced the team's commitment to all-out attack. It would be two decades before Spurs finished above Arsenal again.

'I am blessed with strong leaders,' Wenger said post-match. 'A good team without them would go nowhere but my aim is to keep Arsenal challenging for trophies. My team constantly surprise me because they are better technically than I ever believed and we made a very strong finish. Winning against Tottenham is the best moment of my time at Highbury so far.'

'The time it really dawned on us that the playing style was changing was the North London derby a couple of months after Wenger took over,' says Arsenal fan and writer Tim Stillman, 'when you've got Tony Adams hitting a left-footed volley into the top corner. We'd seen Tony Adams score a winner against Spurs three years earlier in an FA Cup semi-final, but it was a much more traditional Tony Adams goal, a header from a set piece. This was open play. It wasn't from a corner. Adams was in the box. You thought, "Wow, Adams has just scored a left-footed winner in a North London derby. What's going on here?" And the third goal from Bergkamp – it wasn't so much that Bergkamp had scored; it was that Ian Wright had put the cross in for him. Already you're getting a sense of this total football.'

And it was total football achieved without totalitarianism on the training pitch. Arsenal's players found it was an absence of strict tactical diktats and overbearing coaching that encouraged their adventurousness. It was about what they were allowed to do, rather than what they were told to do.

'He was very similar to Sven-Göran Eriksson,' suggests David Platt. 'If you asked me whether Arsène Wenger was an exceptional coach – he was a good coach who knew what he was doing, don't get me wrong – but in terms of actual coaching, teaching play on a training pitch, somebody like Terry Venables was streets ahead in that sense. What Arsène did was provide an environment and training regime that taught you what he wanted. It was not him saying, "Stop! You do this, you do this and you do this." It was the environment. So all of a sudden, where you'd had a back four who'd been taught to defend – you head it, you kick it, you clear your lines and things like that – Arsène was now very much encouraging them to play, to pass into midfield, to hit a 40-yard ball. There was an introduction of belief in players to say, "You can do more than just defend."'

'He seemed to get the best out of people with the way he coached the quality out of them,' adds Rice. 'Sometimes you've just got to let players go out and express themselves. And the more they play together, the more that you ask them to pass and move, pass and move, the more they actually do it and you see the success that comes through it.'

Arsenal's new free-flowing football wasn't just easy on the eye, either. It was easy on the lens, too. Stuart MacFarlane, the club's long-time official photographer, found himself busier than ever before.

'I'd been so used to George and with that back four that, when photographing games, if I missed the picture of the goal, I thought, "Let's just pack it up," because we'd only ever score one goal,' he says. 'I knew we wouldn't concede. And then when Arsène came in, all of a sudden I started to get lots of really nice pictures of players running with the ball. We'd score three or four a game. Just the atmosphere in the stadium, the way that the players played and the excitement from the fans, it was fantastic. We all loved the way that George played, but I think we knew the creativity was quite limited. As soon as Wenger came in it was still the same old backline, but it was just one of those feelings that we'd never concede and we'd always score.

'And they were just monsters. At Highbury, by the players' tunnel there was a little room called the Halfway House, where we used to go and have teas and coffees at half time. Sometimes I used to stand in there before the game, because the players would line up in that really narrow tunnel. So I used to stand in there and with a wide-angle lens, try to photograph the players as they came down, shoulder to shoulder.

I remember an opposition player shouting to get his teammates going, "Let's give it to them in the first twenty minutes." I think we were two or three up after twenty minutes. Our lot walked down the tunnel and the smallest guys were probably six foot. They were just monsters. All big and physical and technically fantastic.'

Big, physical and technically fantastic – also an accurate description of Arsenal's most impactful new recruit that season. 'In Vieira Arsenal at last seem to have found a midfielder capable of aiding defence and prompting attack with equal aplomb,' wrote *The Observer*'s Amy Lawrence in her match report of October's 3-0 victory over Leeds. 'He is exactly the type of player Graham's Arsenal cried out for.'

Patrick Vieira was born in Dakar, Senegal, in 1976. His love of football blossomed out of an upbringing of meagre means. He and his friends would play with makeshift balls. Piles of discarded clothes marked the boundaries of their dusty pitches and the breadth of their imagined goals. At the age of eight, he moved with his parents to France. By 15, his talent had become evident, and just two years later he made his professional debut for Cannes in the French Ligue 1. He was so prodigious a prospect and so mature a dressing-room figure that he captained the side aged 19.

What ought to have been Vieira's big break soon followed, when he signed for Serie A champions AC Milan in 1995. There, he developed a deeper tactical understanding thanks to the coaching of Fabio Capello, while examples set by Marcel Desailly and Demetrio Albertini provided a blueprint for his burgeoning midfield mastery.

But Vieira made just five senior appearances for Milan in his first year at the San Siro. With a World Cup in his home nation two years away, he felt he'd have to move on in search of regular game time to boost his international hopes.

In January 1996, Wenger visited Milan. He was a guest of George Weah, his former Monaco player who, on Christmas Eve, had been awarded the Ballon d'Or, the award crowning the best player in Europe each year. Wenger had been a great admirer of Vieira's since, as Monaco manager, first coming up against the young midfielder in France. He spoke with Vieira at half time of a Milan game he attended. Wenger found the youngster disconsolate at his lack of playing time in Italy, unable to dislodge the established and experienced midfielders ahead of him in Capello's pecking order. 'Hang on in there, my friend,' Wenger told him. 'You'll get there in the end, and this is AC Milan, after all.'

Wenger was still managing in Japan at the time, but by the early stages of the following season, with Vieira on the cusp of joining Ajax, the French tactician was biding his time before he could officially take over at Arsenal. He called Vieira and convinced him to divert from Ajax to Arsenal, where the coach would soon join him.

Like the mysterious new manager, Arsenal's players knew next to nothing of Vieira. He was just 20 years old and, while he'd appeared regularly for France at under-21 level, was not yet a full international. What's more, with his tall, sinewy frame and underwhelming early outing on the training pitch, he didn't look much like a footballer – until match day arrived.

'When he first came in, he got nicknamed Bambi because he was all legs and arms,' says Gary Lewin. 'He came on for Ray Parlour against Sheffield Wednesday to make his debut. I remember him coming on and everyone thinking, "I wonder what he's going to be like," because he hadn't really stood out in training. After the game, everyone came off the pitch thinking, "Wow, what a player you've found there." He was so aggressive. He was so athletic. It was incredible.'

'He's got quite an awkward running style, Patrick,' Dixon says. 'He seemed quite gangly. He was skinny and tall. So he looked quite an awkward footballer when he first came, and he had a knee injury, so we were like, "Who has Wenger signed here? Nobody's ever heard of this bloke. He can't really run. He's got a dodgy knee." He didn't train with us for a while. Then he came on against Sheffield Wednesday and it was like, "Wow, I didn't see that coming." From then on, he played every game. He was always moaning about his body, that he wasn't fit, that he had a knock. You're thinking, "This guy is going to be retired by the time he's 25. His body is falling apart." But he was an absolute hero on the pitch.'

Vieira was described in *The Times* as a 'thinking man's Carlton Palmer' after that imposing debut performance as an early substitute inspired a come-from-behind 4-1 win over Sheffield Wednesday in September. It was a line intended as praise, but it would prove far too conservative an appraisal of a unique and dominant talent. Vieira combined size, skill, athleticism and energy at levels rarely seen. He was a thundering tackler whose telescopic limbs enabled him to snatch possession from opposing players when they least expected it. Those lamp-post-like legs would carry him through the middle of the pitch at rapid speed, too, yet his gangly six-foot-four frame lacked nothing in deftness of touch and delicacy of execution.

'I remember going back to San Siro and the Milanese said to me, 'What on earth have you done to us, taking Vieira? How could we have let that guy go?"' Wenger said in 2005. 'We soon got the feeling we had achieved a real coup by signing Patrick. He was so strong, so dominating. He could destroy, direct and distribute the ball, often all in one go. Whatever one says, there weren't dozens of players of that calibre playing in Europe – there still aren't.'

One area in which Vieira was lacking initially was communication. His English was limited. He could converse fluently in French with the manager, of course, and he and Platt would speak Italian with each other thanks to their common experience in Serie A. But he made up for deficiencies in the mother tongue of his new home with a sheer ferocity that quickly endeared him to his English teammates.

'He was battle-worn and he'd fight for every single ball,' says Dixon. 'He absolutely epitomized that character and that heart that we had in the team. He was a huge part of that. And, obviously, he went on to be captain of the club in some of its most glory-filled years. It was always obvious that at some point when Tony left, he was going to take over.'

'He didn't speak much English but he had an aura straight away,' says Adrian Clarke. 'Plus he was really hard. That helps. Kind of like a Roy Keane character – just being a hard player gives you instant respect and instant kudos in the dressing room.'

'He was the French Roy Keane,' Lewin concurs. 'He was a quick settler. He loved the English players and their attitude. He had that will to win. Everyone understood what a powerful person he was. Once he established himself in the team, that then became very apparent.'

Vieira scored his first goal for Arsenal in a 2-2 draw against Derby County on 7 December, connecting with a sliding cutback from Adams to lash in a last-minute equalizer from 20 yards. The Frenchman had also collected his fifth yellow card of the campaign earlier in the match, meaning he'd serve a two-game suspension. It was no coincidence that Arsenal struggled in his absence, losing 2-1 to Nottingham Forest and drawing 0-0 with Sheffield Wednesday.

He returned to the line-up for a 2-2 draw with Aston Villa on

28 December, springing the attack that led to Ian Wright's opening goal with a snapping tackle in midfield. A 2-0 win over Middlesbrough at Highbury on 1 January 1997 meant Arsenal began the new year second in the Premier League, just two points behind pace-setters Liverpool and having played one game fewer. They also had the best goal difference in the division, with only Aston Villa having conceded fewer goals than the Gunners and only reigning champions Manchester United having scored more. For better or worse, they would finish the season without a single 1-0 victory. 'One-nil to the Arsenal became three-nil to the Arsenal,' Dixon says. 'And you're not going to beat us from there.'

# 7

# Cold Fury

On the afternoon of 7 November 1996, Arsène Wenger took a taxi to Highbury. The Arsenal manager had been officially in post a little over a month and was en route to watch the club's reserves take on Chelsea when he received a phone call from David Dein.

'Arsène, I'm afraid there's a lot of press waiting for you when you come in,' the vice-chairman said.

'What's the problem?' Wenger asked.

'There are some ugly rumours going around. When you come in, come through the back door, go into your office, and before you meet the press, let's discuss it.'

Wenger arrived at the stadium at around 1pm. He hurried to his office, where he met with Dein and Clare Tomlinson, the club's new press officer.

'Look, there's a group of journalists downstairs and there's been a very, very ugly rumour floating around,' Dein confided.

'What about?' Wenger said.

'It's about your private life.'

'David, you've known me long enough. You know about my private life.'

The internet was very much in its infancy in 1996. The sound of dial-up modems cranking into gear inspired a tinge of excitement and – with the advent of social media still the best part of two decades away – email was revolutionizing the way people connected and shared information. The 'information superhighway' was also aiding the prevalence of misinformation and the speed at which falsities could be spread – *plus ça change*! Wenger discovered he'd become the subject of a chain email detailing vicious and entirely false accusations about his personal life.

'I had to tell him what it was all about, because he'd been doorstepped when he came in,' Tomlinson says. 'He thought the taxi driver had been a bit odd with him, as well. I knew his English was good, but "paedophile" is quite a difficult word to say. I don't remember exactly what I said to him, but he went white. He was so furious. It wasn't like a red anger; it was a cold fury.'

The rumour was supposedly started by a Tottenham supporter working for a financial institution in the City of London, based on nothing more than Wenger's appearance. As it was circulated wider and wider, it began to be alluded to on radio and television. In an online equivalent of Chinese whispers, the falsehood swelled and mutated. It was said to be the reason why Wenger had left Japan and a major UK tabloid was threatening to publish the story the following day. At 10.10am on the morning of the otherwise uninteresting match between the second strings of Arsenal and Chelsea, a news agency called Cityscreen ran a story claiming Wenger was about to be sacked. The erroneous report was taken down just a minute later, but it had already been widely read. At 10.15am, someone purporting to be Arsenal's marketing manager contacted a host of national newspapers claiming Wenger had been fired earlier that morning.

'I had to keep him in his office while I explained to him the slander laws in England and that he had to get the journalists to say what they were accusing him of in front of witnesses,' Tomlinson says. 'I explained that they would ask to speak to him in private and that he must say no. He listened. He was as good as gold. We went down and I remember saying to him, "There's a TV camera there now. What you say now will last for ever. Just please try to be calm."

'He was unbelievable. So intelligent and clever about it. He said all the right things. The journalists were all saying to me, "We need to speak to him in private." I said, "No, if you've got something to say that stands up, say it out here. If it doesn't stand up, you can toddle off with your horrible rumours." It was a really vile day.'

Once Tomlinson had finished briefing the manager, Dein said, 'This rumour, I'm afraid you're going to have to deal with it. The press are downstairs in the Marble Halls.'

Before Dein could finish his sentence, Wenger rose from his chair and headed to confront the assembled gaggle of journalists. He would face the rumours head-on, through a quiet indignation and with nothing to hide. At the top of the steps outside the Marble Halls' entranceway, he held an impromptu press conference.

'Sir, Mr Wenger, are you aware of the nature of the allegations?' the first reporter asked.

'No,' Wenger replied.

'Mr Wenger,' another chimed in, 'the questions are being asked because there is a rumour rife that a publication tomorrow is going to include some pictures and some stories about your private life.'

Wenger, wearing a grey blazer and gold tie, with his mouse-brown hair slightly unkempt, cracked an incredulous laugh.

'What have you, concrete, from my private life?' he said. 'What do you know of my life, concrete?'

'We don't know anything.'

'Thank you very much,' Wenger said, waving away the journalists as he turned and walked back inside.

'They printed some stuff the next day that kind of hinted at it, and because everyone knew the rumours, everyone knew what it meant,' Tomlinson says. 'He phoned me. He'd spoken to the lawyers and the lawyers had said there was nothing they could do. He said, "You're the only one who seems to have a handle on this. I don't understand why I can't sue, why nobody seems to be doing anything about it." I had to say, "The lawyers don't think there's anything and there's nothing I can do about it. It's just stupid English law."'

Cityscreen issued an apology addressed directly to Wenger that was published in Arsenal's match day programme for the League Cup tie against Stoke City on 13 November. It read:

*Dear Mr Wenger*

*I am writing to express our very sincere apologies to you and your club for the news item about you on Cityscreen on the 7th November. Out item read that you were leaving Arsenal and our source of information was Sky News.*

*The news item resulted from an editorial misunderstanding in our office and we wholly accept that Sky News had not reported that you were to leave Arsenal (we have advised you of the original source of the misunderstanding) and that we had no reason to believe that to be the case.*

*We do regret the embarrassment and stress which has been caused to you by the news items and by the way in which our mistaken items were further misreported and referred to in the media.*

*You do of course have our assurance that we will not be repeating this mistaken item about you.*

*Yours sincerely,*
*Neil Morgan*
*CITYSCREEN UK Ltd*

Arsenal chairman Peter Hill-Wood issued a statement that was printed alongside Cityscreen's apology in the programme:

*We were determined that those responsible for the misinformation that sparked the ugly rumours of last Thursday apologised publicly, not only to Arsène Wenger, but to the Club and the fans for the hurt and anger they have caused.*

*We have insisted upon an undertaking that such an error is never repeated by them and also that the source of the rumour be disclosed to us.*

*I know all Arsenal fans were disgusted with the events of last Thursday and the appalling way in which Arsène Wenger has been treated. He is a man of great integrity and his position here has never been in doubt.*

Soon, Wenger would move into a house in Totteridge, near to the Deins, but at the time he was still staying at a hotel. His partner, Annie, who was pregnant with their first child, had not yet joined him from France and his chief confidant, Boro Primorac, was still in Japan. He admits to feeling isolated after the episode on the steps outside Highbury. But the poise with which he faced up to the spurious whispers and insinuations displayed a strength of character that belied the perception of him as a weedy football boffin.

Wenger might not have fitted the mould of the hollering, bawling manager *du jour*, but he was no pushover.

# 8

# A Rivalry Ignited

Going into the 1996–97 season, United and Arsenal each boasted ten top-flight titles between them through their respective illustrious histories. In terms of prestige, success and support base, only Liverpool could claim a place on par with, or in excess of, either at the top of the English football food chain.

Yet the historical triumphs of United and Arsenal had rarely overlapped. The 1950s was the only decade in which both sides claimed top-flight titles. There had been acrimony between the two clubs down the years, most notably with the 'Battle of Old Trafford' in October 1990, when a mass on-pitch scuffle led to a two-point deduction for Arsenal and a one-point penalty for United.

But while Arsenal went on to become First Division champions at the end of the 1990–91 season despite being stripped of a couple of points, United had been dominant since the Premier League's inception in 1992. Arsenal had beaten United just once in the Premier League era up to 1996–97, a 1-0 win at Highbury in November 1995 when Dennis Bergkamp seized on an underhit Denis Irwin back pass to score the game's only goal.

They'd fared even worse at Old Trafford, where they hadn't won since Anders Limpar scored with what was either a mishit cross or a canny near-post finish before the brawl had erupted that afternoon in 1990. The Gunners hadn't even scored at the Theatre of Dreams since the Premier League was founded. When the two sides first met in the 1996–97 season at Old Trafford, United had once again edged them out, this time by virtue of a Nigel Winterburn own goal.

The animosity of the fixture was rekindled that November day, with Ian Wright and Peter Schmeichel at the centre of what would whip up into a maelstrom of controversy. It started when Wright, who'd never scored against the Dane in a competitive match, slid to challenge the United keeper for a ball he felt entitled to contest. Schmeichel thought the striker's lunge was late and dangerous. The two players clashed in the tunnel at half time.

It was only when rewatching the incident on television later that evening that Wright came to believe he had witnessed Schmeichel racially abusing him after the incident. 'He grabbed the ball,' Wright wrote in his 2016 autobiography *A Life in Football*, 'jumped up and yelled at me, "You fucking black bastard."'

When United travelled to North London for the return fixture on 19 February 1997, Wright pounced on an opportunity to exact revenge. In the seventy-sixth minute, he launched into a two-footed challenge directed at the United goalkeeper's shin. Referee Martin Bodenham consulted with his assistant before deciding to take no action.

There was little public sympathy for Wright, who was garnering a reputation as the misbehaving bad boy of English football for his ill-discipline in a season that would see him score 30 goals. He'd been sent off in a costly 2-1 defeat to Nottingham Forest in December. 'It is time Ian Wright behaved properly and became more mature,' said Wenger. 'We lost because he was sent off. It is difficult to play with just ten men.' The same month, Wright was the subject of an FA hearing for calling Sheffield Wednesday manager David Pleat a 'pervert' after he'd scored a hat-trick against the Owls in September. He was warned about his future conduct. And the striker had been fortunate to escape sanction in October when, during a 0-0 draw with Coventry at Highbury, he lashed out at Steve Ogrizovic, breaking the goalkeeper's nose. Wenger, in an evasion tactic he'd repeat regularly in subsequent years and for which he'd be routinely mocked, claimed he did not see the incident. The man the Arsenal players nicknamed 'Windows' needed a shammy cloth taking to his rimless specs.

As the press pilloried the striker for his dangerous, studs-first challenge on Schmeichel, Wenger took to his player's defence.

'Do you want me to give him sleeping pills?' he said. 'Of course he would then act differently. But he would not score goals. I have seen many tackles and punches that have not been judged or seen by the referee and then nobody talks about them. I can show you 30 worse tackles since the beginning of the season in the Premier League that nobody spoke about. Is it the foul or is it the personalities of the two players involved, or is it the game? I think there is a little bit of all of that, more than the foul. I think it looked worse than it was.'

Inevitably, Alex Ferguson went to bat for his player, too. 'We can categorically deny any racist remark whatsoever from Peter Schmeichel, I can assure you of that,' the United boss told Sky Sports. 'There is no question of that, so it's very disappointing to read that. We place great store on our reputation, so it's a big slur on us.'

The spat meant the result of the match was reduced to a sideline issue. It was not a positive one for Arsenal. Another defeat. Going into the United match, Arsenal had dropped 16 points over their last 10 games, with just 3 wins in that period. During that spell they played George Graham's Leeds twice in four days in early February, drawing 0-0 at Elland Road in the league and losing to a single Gunnar Halle goal in an FA Cup fourth-round tie at home – Graham was still a master of grinding out 1-0 wins at Highbury, it seemed. With Eric Cantona suspended, United started a strike duo of Ole Gunnar Solskjaer and former Arsenal player Andy Cole for their visit to Highbury. Both scored in the first half, before a Bergkamp strike halved the Gunners' deficit but completed the scoring.

In the second half, Stephen Hughes – a half time replacement for the injured Tony Adams – struck Schmeichel's crossbar. Wright turned in the rebound, only for his first goal against his nemesis in the United net to be ruled out for offside. It was a sign that Arsenal were growing closer to United under Wenger but were still not quite at the champions' level. Their latest result versus United left them five points behind the Red Devils in the table, having played one game more than the league leaders.

The brewing hostility between the two clubs continued long after the final whistle. Proving himself no shrinking violet in the furious face of United's long-tenured manager, Wenger engaged in a heated verbal battle with Ferguson that played out in the press. With United's Champions League run extending to the semi-final stage, uncharted territory for them at the time, Ferguson angled for the FA to ease his side's pending fixture congestion. 'It's wrong the programme is extended so Man United can rest and win everything,' Wenger remarked in April 1997.

Ferguson had been irked by Wenger dating back to the coverage around the Frenchman's appointment the previous September. 'They say he's an intelligent man, right? Speaks five languages,' he said in response to the framing of the new Arsenal manager as a superior intellect to the average British manager. 'I've got a fifteen-year-old boy from the Ivory Coast who speaks five languages.'

The Scot was regarded as a master of mind games, baiting his rival managers into emotional reactions by seeding close-to-the-bone digs via his comments in the press. It had worked a treat just the previous season. United were chasing down Newcastle at the top of the table, with the Magpies' lead up to 12 points at one stage. As United reeled in Newcastle and assumed the momentum in the championship chase, Ferguson insinuated that Nottingham Forest, an upcoming opponent of Newcastle's, would lie down for the Magpies. Kevin Keegan, Newcastle's manager, famously lost his temper at the accusation during a live television interview. 'I'll tell you,' Keegan said, jabbing his finger towards the camera lens, 'I will love it if we beat them. Love it.' United wrapped up the title on the last day of the season.

Wenger seemed too cool, too smart to fall for such antics. Instead, it was the Arsenal manager who elicited an overemotional response from Ferguson. 'He's a novice,' Ferguson shot back after Wenger's complaining about United's request for a fixture reshuffle, 'and should keep his opinions to Japanese football.'

Tellingly, Arsenal's trip to Old Trafford in November 1996 was the last time the two sides played a Premier League fixture at 3pm on a Saturday, when matches cannot be televised live in England. Clashes between Arsenal and United – and, by extension, Wenger and Ferguson – had become box office.

After falling short against United, Arsenal lost again four days later. A first-half goal from Vinnie Jones was enough for Wimbledon to record a surprise victory at Highbury. Wright missed a chance to rescue a point when he hit the post and the Gunners left the field to boos at the final whistle. It was Arsenal's third home defeat of the month. They'd slipped to fourth in the table. Wenger blamed fixture congestion as he conceded that a title challenge was likely now beyond Arsenal's grasp.

'The Premier League schedule is not right,' he complained. 'We played Manchester United on Wednesday; Wimbledon played on Tuesday. Everyone should play on the same day. It means if we have four bad days like we have had, we are out of the race. The title is now an impossible dream.'

A place in the following season's Champions League, however, remained an achievable goal. The premier Continental competition was expanding. Whereas the 1996–97 edition had room only for league champions from around Europe, the format for 1997–98 would include an additional eight teams – swelling from sixteen to twenty-four – with runners-up from the biggest nations' top divisions offered the chance to qualify. Much like the Premier League's money-spinning emergence post-1992, the European Cup had received a new lick of paint the same year, rebranded as the Champions League. With its new logo of coalescing stars wrapping around its bespoke match balls, and with its grandiose anthem boomed over stadiums public-address systems ahead of every floodlit midweek fixture, the Champions League was tapping into football's increasing thrust towards theatre in the era of big broadcast contracts. It was estimated that qualification for the group stage alone was worth £2.6 million to each club. A run to the final could net upwards of £11 million. These might be modest figures by modern standards – 2023 Champions League winners Real Madrid, for example, netted around £76 million in prize money – but a modest run to the knockout rounds could fund a significant summer of transfer spending in 1997.

Heading into March, Liverpool occupied second spot and, just one point behind United, had their gaze fixed firmly on a potential first title since 1990. But the Merseysiders began to falter, with just three wins over their next eight league fixtures. Third-placed Newcastle began the month poorly, too. They'd finished runners-up the previous season after surrendering a lead over eventual champions Manchester United that was once as wide as 12 points. A run of one win in nine games led to manager Kevin Keegan resigning in January. His replacement, Kenny Dalglish, had steadied the ship. A shock 1-0 home defeat to struggling Southampton on 1 March was the first loss of his St James' Park tenure. Another quickly followed, this time against the club where Dalglish was a legend as both player and manager – Liverpool. In a remarkable repeat of a seven-goal thriller from the previous campaign that's still regarded as one of the most dramatic matches in Premier League history, the pendulum of momentum swung back and forth in the dying moments at Anfield, with three goals in the last four minutes. Robbie Fowler's ninetieth-minute strike settled the engrossing doppelgänger of a game.

Newcastle drew three of their next four games. With the Magpies and Liverpool stuttering, United raced clear at the top. They'd end the season as champions again, by a comfortable seven-point margin. Inconsistency among the chasing pack also opened the door to Arsenal.

A bizarre refereeing blunder could have kiboshed the Gunners' top-two hopes on 24 March. Liverpool were the visitors to Highbury and, with the away side leading 1-0, referee Gerald Ashby awarded a penalty after Robbie Fowler tumbled in the box when challenged by David Seaman. The Liverpool striker immediately popped up to his feet and began to wave his arms, indicating Seaman hadn't touched him and that the penalty decision should be reversed. Ashby ignored his and Arsenal's appeals and stuck with his erroneous call. Fowler, sportingly, rolled a lame spot kick that was parried by Seaman, but

Jason McAteer scored from the rebound. Wright scored in the second half to halve Arsenal's arrears, but they couldn't recover. 'Everybody knows it was not a penalty,' Wenger seethed. 'It killed the game.'

It didn't kill Arsenal's momentum, though. They'd won three in a row prior to the Liverpool loss – all by 2-0 scorelines. They smashed Chelsea 3-0 at Stamford Bridge and then recorded another 2-0, this time away to Leicester, in their next two fixtures.

There was controversy again at Highbury on Saturday 19 April. This time Blackburn were the opposition. Arsenal led 1-0 for much of the game, with David Platt having scored in the eighteenth minute. As the final whistle neared, Stephen Hughes sat on the turf awaiting treatment for an injury. Arsenal put the ball out of play so Gary Lewin could come on to attend to the young midfielder. Custom dictated that, after the resultant throw-in, Blackburn should return the ball to the home side. They did, but Rovers' striker Chris Sutton, weary of allowing the Gunners to run down the clock, blurred the lines of etiquette.

'In my view at the time, they were faffing around and time wasting,' says Sutton. 'And that wasn't just my view. We were in a bit of a relegation battle. As a team, we'd agreed to launch the ball back into the corner. I was the closest player. I pressed Nigel Winterburn, who gave away a corner, and then all hell broke loose. There were scuffles and shoving. Patrick Vieira and Martin Keown were irate. They switched off at the corner and Garry Flitcroft hit a wonderful half volley into the top corner. Then all the threats were coming from Vieira and Keown.

'I played the last three minutes on the left wing, by the tunnel. The final whistle blew and I was straight up the tunnel. Keown was trying to get into our dressing room after me. I was in the toilet with my feet up against the door. I probably shouldn't have done what I did, but in the heat of battle you do what you can. Keown has never forgiven me.'

The next match, again a disappointing draw against relegation-threatened opposition, ended with another Arsenal defender chasing an opponent into the changing rooms. It was a midweek fixture at Highfield Road and, after the pair engaged in a full-blooded challenge for the ball, Coventry's 40-year-old player-manager Gordon Strachan taunted Adams by gesturing as though he were sipping from a pint glass. Adams, Keown and Vieira all confronted Strachan, towering above the diminutive Scot. It was 1-1 at full time. Dion Dublin had capitalized on some comical Arsenal defending to put the Sky Blues ahead in the first half, before Wright and Ogrizovic renewed their duel in the second period, with the Coventry keeper bringing down the Arsenal striker in the penalty area. Wright converted his twenty-eighth goal of the season from the spot.

After the final whistle, an irate Adams sought out Strachan in the home dressing room.

'I need to have a word with you,' the Arsenal captain said, pointing at the Coventry boss.

'Come into my office,' Strachan said, before wisely apologizing.

'I had wanted to hit him, but he had taken the wind out of my sails,' Adams later reflected. '"Right, well don't do it again," was all I could say.'

Despite having dropped four points in back-to-back encounters with inferior opponents, Arsenal entered May with the Champions League in reach. In the penultimate game of their season, they hosted fourth-placed Newcastle at Highbury. Liverpool were third, one point behind the Gunners but with an extra game still to play. Newcastle were a further four points back but still with four matches on their schedule.

It would be a face-off between two of the country's most thrilling attacking sides. Wenger's expressive style of play continued to beguile, while Newcastle had been labelled 'the Entertainers' for their swashbuckling commitment to attack as they challenged Manchester United's supremacy the previous season. Their frontline was made yet more potent by the world-record £15 million signing of Newcastle-born Alan Shearer from Blackburn the past summer. An instant local hero, the England striker had also become a national icon after scoring five goals at Euro 96, after which he usurped Adams as the Three Lions captain.

In the event, it was not a match befitting of the two sides' footballing reputations. Instead, it was a scrappy and ill-tempered affair, with nine bookings in total. In a game of few clear-cut chances as the teams appeared to wilt either beneath the heat of the May sun or the pressure of the occasion, Newcastle midfielder Robbie Elliott headed the only goal in stoppage time at the end of the first half.

Post-match, Wenger and Dalglish agreed that, on the balance of play, Arsenal had been the better side and Newcastle were fortunate to escape with the crucial three points. That will have been of little consolation to the Gunners, likewise the admiration they'd earned from their opponents on the day.

'They were incredible at that time,' Elliott says. 'When Wenger came in, you saw the shift in the athleticism of the players. They were athletes. When you stood beside them in the tunnel – the likes of Vieira, Adams, Keown – they were immense. And it was a really small pitch at Highbury. You'd have your second wind after about 15 or 20 minutes at Highbury because they were relentless. When you were on the pitch against them, you knew they were doing something a little bit different. Arsenal were up there for a reason. They were a phenomenal side.'

Liverpool beat Spurs 2-1 the same afternoon to briefly reclaim second spot, only to fade in their final two fixtures, losing to Wimbledon – despite a 17-year-old Michael Owen scoring on his first-team debut – and drawing with Sheffield Wednesday. Newcastle faced three games in the space of six days to close out their campaign. Arsenal hoped for a capitulation. They almost got it. The Magpies drew the first two fixtures, a pair of goalless stalemates with West Ham and then Manchester United.

On Sunday 11 May 1997, the Premier League season's last batch of games all began at 4pm. Liverpool, starting the day second, would drop to fourth. Arsenal and Newcastle were locked on 65 points, with an identical goal difference. The Magpies were ahead by virtue of having a higher goals total. Liverpool's draw in the end meant Arsenal needed a better result away to Derby than Newcastle could muster at home to already-relegated Nottingham to clinch second. The Gunners gave an admirable effort, winning 3-1 in the final game at Derby's old Baseball Ground despite an early red card for Adams. But Newcastle's own East Midlands opposition provided even less resistance. Dalglish's side won 5-0, snatching a goal-difference advantage and the disputed Champions League berth as the three second-place contenders remarkably all finished level on 68 points. Arsenal had to settle for third.

And so a season that began with upheaval and internal turmoil but then came to promise so much ultimately ended limply. It would be the UEFA Cup again for Arsenal the next season. But the players were not despondent. Progress had been made. A bright horizon was creeping into view. 'I don't remember any disappointment,' Platt says. 'I think it was just a case of, "We've got better. We've qualified for Europe again." I didn't feel there was a sense of disappointment at finishing third.'

'It was all new,' says Dixon. 'We knew it was going to be a new era. At the start of it, you're not going to knock the lights out. We were more than happy with what we'd seen so far. I was really happy with how Arsène was getting us to play and the new players that were there. It was an exciting time. I didn't feel let down or disappointed. It didn't last long if I did. It was like, "Right, let's have a real go at next season."'

# 9

# Assembling Arsène's Army

In June 1997, Emmanuel Petit travelled to England to discuss a transfer to the Premier League. The Monaco midfielder had worked with Arsène Wenger while a young player at the Stade Louis II. He'd begun his career as a left back, but now, aged 26, he'd evolved into a combative, physical midfielder with an impressive range of passing. After seven full seasons in the Monaco first team and with thirteen senior appearances for France under his belt, he was ready for a new challenge.

A move to North London seemed an obvious next step, yet the club leading the race for his signature was not the obvious one. Petit, who was also wanted by Rangers, went to White Hart Lane to meet with Alan Sugar, the Tottenham chairman.

As soon as Wenger learned of Tottenham's pursuit of Petit, the Arsenal manager contacted his former player and urged him not to commit to Spurs just yet. After his meeting with Sugar, Tottenham arranged for a taxi to collect Petit and take him back to his hotel. But the Frenchman had another destination in mind. Spurs inadvertently ferried him to their rivals – and footed the bill.

'As soon as I came into the cab, the cab driver asked where I wanted to go,' Petit says. 'I gave him the address. It was Arsène Wenger's home. It was not at the stadium or in the offices. So I went straight over there.

After two hours talking with David Dein and Wenger, I gave my word to them and I signed the contract.'

A £3.5 million deal was agreed with Monaco and Petit's Arsenal switch was ratified on 1 July. In Petit, Wenger saw a central midfielder who'd complement Vieira and allow the manager to reshape the Gunners into the 4-4-2 formation he preferred and had always envisioned unleashing at Highbury. With the six-foot-one Petit next to the six-foot-four Vieira, Arsenal's midfield duo would have the requisite physicality to cope with the bustle of the central third of the pitch in England's top flight without the need of an additional man in the middle.

'Arsène knew me very well,' Petit says. 'He knew that I was having a meeting with a Spurs representative. I knew that Arsenal were interested in me because I'd had Arsène on the phone. I spoke with him a couple of times before I came to England. He took me from the Monaco academy when I was 17 years old. I went straight to the first team and I never left. I remember when he was sacked from Monaco. He went to Japan and then after that to England. That's when we got connected again.

'He knew that I was becoming a different player. I was changing my position on the pitch. I used to play left back, centre back, central midfielder, holding midfielder. I used to play a different position on the pitch. I think this is exactly what convinced him to ask me to come to England, because in terms of the physical strengths, it's completely different when you play as a central defender to when you play as a holding midfielder. I really developed myself mentally and physically. I became a different player who can play a different position. I think this is what Arsène was looking for with me.'

On the day he was presented to the press out on the Highbury pitch,

Petit wore a pale blue suit jacket and trousers with his long blonde hair pulled back into a ponytail. Wenger was pictured with his right arm over his compatriot's shoulder. Under the manager's other arm was another new arrival who'd prove equally vital to his plans of unleashing a dynamic 4-4-2 system.

Marc Overmars had first become an Arsenal transfer target two years earlier, with George Graham keen to sign him. The rapid yet diminutive Dutch winger had been one of the stars of Ajax's 1995 Champions League triumph, but a cruciate knee ligament injury later that year sidelined him for eight months and threatened to rob him of his most outstanding attribute – his pace.

'I had a bad knee injury the year before with Ajax,' Overmars says, 'I'd just come back from injury and I needed to prove I was still the player that I was before the injury. In that period, there were only two clubs interested. The other was Real Betis. I knew that Arsène Wenger had come over to see me play in the Ajax Arena. I think he wanted to double-check whether I was still as good as before the injury. I think he was given some information from agents that was quite negative, saying, "He's not back on his old form." I'm grateful that he saw me play and that he could see that I was on my way back and that I was fit. It's not easy for a coach to take a gamble for 14 million gilders. He was also looking at a player from France, Ibrahim Ba. I think that was his first choice, but he went to AC Milan. That was good for me. That transfer didn't go through and they took me. I was happy with that. After all, I think they made the best choice to sign me.'

Convinced that Overmars was back to his pre-injury best, Wenger signed off on a £7 million deal to take the 24-year-old Netherlands international from Ajax. Although right-footed, Overmars would play on the left flank in Wenger's 4-4-2. His speed and goal-scoring instincts would add a new dimension to the Gunners' attack, while his adventurousness would be counterbalanced by Ray Parlour's industry and discipline on the other side of midfield.

Other big-money arrivals were mooted in the media. George Weah, Wenger's former Monaco striker, was said to be a £10 million target. A £7 million move for Derby County's Dean Sturridge was also reported.* Graeme Le Saux was another player supposedly on Arsenal's radar, but Wenger ruled out a bid for the Blackburn and England left back – 'I think he is over-priced,' the Arsenal manager said. 'It just shows there is a huge difference between the Continental market and the English market.'

Rather than make another superstar purchase, though, Arsenal opted to apportion the rest of their transfer budget to strengthening Wenger's squad around the margins. In addition to Petit, two more players were signed from Monaco – 22-year-old Liberian striker Christopher Wreh, a cousin of George Weah's, arrived for £300,000, and 27-year-old French utility player Gilles Grimandi, who'd made his professional debut under Wenger in the principality, came in for £1.75 million.

They bought the speedy and direct winger Luís Boa Morte from Sporting Clube de Portugal for another £1.75 million, while 20-year-old Austrian goalkeeper Alex Manninger joined from Grazer AK. And although the Gunners were pipped to Champions League qualification by Newcastle the previous season, they exacted a modicum of revenge

---

* To give an illuminating snapshot of the Premier League's burgeoning finances and newfound appeal to foreign stars: Derby were said to be lining up none other than Ballon d'Or winner Roberto Baggio as Sturridge's replacement.

over the Magpies in the transfer market by snapping up one of the most promising young defenders in the country.

'It was between Arsenal and Newcastle, who'd agreed with Luton,' Matthew Upson explains. 'The manager, Lennie Lawrence, pulled me in and said, "We'd like to sell you." He handed it over to me to decide what direction I wanted to go down. To have interest from Arsenal – and Newcastle – was a big deal to me. I decided to go to see Arsenal first. Once I did that, my mind was made up.

'The chief scout Steve Rowley was the person behind me going there. I think they were looking for a young centre back to follow on from the great centre backs they had at the time in Keown, Adams and Bould. I was the right age. It was almost like doing a degree, going to learn off those three. It had massive challenges in terms of playing on the pitch, but in terms of being able to train with them and tap into their knowledge it was too big an opportunity to miss.

'I went and met Arsène Wenger at Sopwell House with my mum and dad. I didn't have an agent at the time. We got a great feel for the club. It just made total sense.'

Arsenal paid £1.2 million to sign Upson, who was just 18, from third-tier Luton. In total, they made eight new signings ahead of the 1997–98 campaign at a cumulative cost of £16.75 million. Evidence of the club's faith in Wenger and their desire to adequately equip the manager ahead of his first full campaign in charge, it was the most they'd ever spent in a single off season. In the Premier League that year, they were outspent only by Newcastle, whose whopping 20 new arrivals came at a cost of £24.6 million. The Magpies were spending to merely tread water, though – most of their outlay was offset by major outgoings such as the sales of David Ginola and Les

Ferdinand to Spurs for £8 million in total and Faustino Asprilla's £6.2 million return to Parma. Arsenal's transfer splurge signified a renewed ambition.

'That changed the whole squad,' Pat Rice says of Arsenal's summer of spending in 1997. 'All of a sudden, from being a good squad, it then became a really, really good squad. The guys that came in and played, they were already joining a squad that was on the up and up, and they just raised it even more. I always say that to know whether your team is good or bad, just look at the bench.'

It wasn't all about incoming in the summer of 1997. Wenger was operating a revolving-door policy at Highbury.

John Hartson had been the first major departure of the Wenger era the previous February. Arsenal received a bid from West Ham for the bustling centre forward. Hartson had been in negotiations over a new contract at Highbury when the offer arrived and, despite the Welshman not being an obvious fit for the style of play the new manager was introducing, Wenger insisted he wanted the striker to stay. But Hartson understood he could not usurp Ian Wright and Dennis Bergkamp in the pecking order. The offer of more game time at Upton Park, he felt, would boost his chances of leading the line for Wales at international level. The fact the Hammers were offering a £12,000 weekly wage, compared to the £10,000 on the table with Arsenal, convinced him to move on. A £5 million deal was agreed.

'Arsène Wenger could not have been kinder or more complimentary,' Hartson later said of his departure from the club he'd joined from Luton as a 19-year-old in 1995.

If the sale of Hartson, even if Wenger professed a reluctance to lose him, made sense in respect of the way Arsenal were evolving, Paul Merson's move to Middlesbrough surprised many.

'I thought Merse was his type of player,' says Lee Dixon. 'I don't know whether that was a money thing. I don't know Merse's situation, whether he felt as if he needed more money. I don't think it was based on talent, because he was hugely talented. Maybe Wenger thought he couldn't get the best out of him because Merse was the type of player who needed constant geeing up. I was a bit surprised.'

Although an avid Chelsea fan, Merson had been with Arsenal since he was 14. He'd experienced a turbulent life off the pitch in the mid-1990s, battling alcohol, cocaine and gambling addictions, but as a footballer the England international was sublime. With the versatility to play out wide, in midfield or as a withdrawn forward, Merson possessed a deftness of touch and an inventiveness in the final third rarely found in English players of his generation. He'd been voted the PFA Young Player of the Year after breaking through at first-team level under George Graham and was key to the title wins of 1989 and '91. He'd been a regular starter for Wenger, too, and the Frenchman was keen to keep such a mercurial talent ahead of the 1997–98 campaign.

But, Dixon suspects, it may have been a 'money thing'. Merson was flattered to have been identified as a transfer target by legendary England midfielder Bryan Robson, the manager of recently relegated Boro. The £4.5 million fee on offer for the 29-year-old represented a record figure for a club outside the top flight, while Merson would double his wages at the Riverside Stadium, earning £20,000 a week. The deal was wrapped up six days after Petit and Overmars had been paraded around Highbury.

'The rest of the players who left probably didn't suit Arsène's style of play, so I wasn't really that surprised,' Dixon says. 'I was just pleased I wasn't one of them.'

With the exception of 29-year-old Dutch winger Glenn Helder, who returned to Holland with NAC Breda, the other departures were made up of young players whom Wenger deemed not of the level to match his ambitions for the team. Adrian Clarke joined Southend on a free transfer. Matthew Rose and goalkeeper Lee Harper both headed to Queens Park Rangers for around £750,000 combined. Ian Selley went to Fulham for half a million and Paul Shaw signed for Millwall in a £300,000 deal. And while Wenger exhibited a ruthlessness in trimming the squad of those he considered short of the new standard, he applied a typically collegiate and sensitive man-management approach to soften the blow for the exiting youngsters.

Shaw, a 23-year-old attacking midfielder, had played 9 games the previous season, scoring 2 goals – both, coincidentally, against Southampton, with one at Highbury and one away at The Dell. He'd been with the first team throughout preseason, but Wenger was open with him about his prospects of further senior involvement in the upcoming campaign. After training one morning, Wenger took him aside at Sopwell House.

'We've brought in a few players in your position and we're planning to bring in more, so we're going to be listening to offers for you,' the manager said. 'But what I want to do – every bit of interest we get, I want to sit down with you and discuss it.'

'I remember two or three times he sat down with me and told me there were clubs interested in me,' Shaw says. 'There was one in Switzerland, FC Zürich. But he said, "I don't think this is right for you." So it wasn't a case of, "Well, we don't need you any more. You go and train over there and that's it; you're off on your own." I still trained with the first team. We turned down a couple of offers that he didn't think were right for me. Then Millwall came in. We spoke about it again. He said the club had accepted the offer and that he thought it was a good move, but he said, "But if you don't think it's right, don't do it. You're more than welcome to stay here." I accepted it and moved on, but I thought that was pretty unique. We had started preseason. I left around September. He kept me involved and I left on very good terms. That doesn't always happen. It made me feel valued.'

The ruthless efficiency with which Wenger was reshaping his squad extended to the optimization of his backroom staff, too.

Twice the previous season, tension had arisen involving the kit man, Bobby Armitt. One of the incidents came late in the campaign when Armitt asked Ian Wright to resist giving away his shirt to fans at the end of matches as stock was running low. Armitt had been a teammate of Wright's at non-league level and the pair ordinarily got along well. But when the kit man questioned the centre forward's decision to gift another of his red number 8 jerseys to a delighted supporter after one game, a storm brewed.

'Wrighty, where's your shirt?' Armitt said once the player had returned to the changing room.

'I threw it into the crowd,' Wright responded. 'What are you going to do about it?'

'I ain't going to do nothing about it, mate. You've just got no more fucking shirts. It's as simple as that.'

The two met in the middle of the changing room, bumping chests. With star striker and kit man on the brink of exchanging blows, other players intervened.

'I certainly wasn't going to back down to him,' says Armitt. 'Bouldy and Tony held him back. David Seaman held me back and took me into the other part of the dressing room. I was quite upset about the whole situation. I'm not sure if that scenario was part of my downfall.'

The first flashpoint that likely contributed to Armitt's downfall came earlier in the season, when Arsenal were preparing to head north to take on Newcastle. After a rain-soaked training session concluded at around 12.30pm on Friday 29 November, the day before Arsenal's appointment at St James' Park, the team coach took the players back to Sopwell House to shower and change. From there, they headed to Stevenage train station. The original plan had been for the squad to take a short flight to the North East. That idea was nixed at the last minute and arrangements to go by train were made. Armitt scrambled to take the wet training kit back to the hotel before getting on the coach to the train station. By the time he had finished making arrangements for the afternoon's used training kit to be washed and securely stored, the team had departed without him. But in Armitt's pocket was the key to the hopper containing the players' match-day kit that was already on board the coach. He took a taxi to the station instead. When he got there, he saw the team bus, but the squad had departed without him. Fuming, he boarded the coach and travelled the four-and-a-half-hour journey by road.

When Armitt arrived at the hotel that evening, he could barely contain his frustration as he confronted Wenger.

'I got to Newcastle about eight o'clock that night,' he says. 'I had a face like thunder when I got down to dinner. Wenger could see I was upset. That was when I said to him, "What you did today was out of order. I understand you've got a train to catch, but come and let me know and I can do something about it without it leaving me there. I nearly went home with the keys and you wouldn't have got the kit at all. You'd have been fucked."

'He said, "Why are you upset?" I said, "I'm either part of the team or I'm not. I was only doing my job. If you came in on Monday and the kit had been stolen, you'd be up in arms about that as well – I can't win. I do my job, I get left behind. I don't do my job, the kit gets stolen."

'I wasn't rude to him, but I basically said, "I'm either part of the team or I'm not part of the team. If I'm not, that's fine. Just let me know."'

Wenger did let him know.

Two days before the first preseason training session the following July, the manager's secretary called down to the changing room and summoned Armitt to Wenger's Highbury office.

The kit man was unsuspecting. He arrived thinking the Frenchman wanted to chat about the upcoming season.

'Bobby, we're getting rid of you,' Wenger said.

'Why?' Armitt asked. 'Have I done anything wrong?'

'No, I just don't want you to be the kit man any more. If you go to see Ken Friar, there will be some compensation for you.'

Armitt had to hand over his keys. Friar, the club secretary, offered a £3,000 severance package, which Armitt rejected, later launching a civil case for unfair dismissal. The two parties settled out of court.

Wenger was a football obsessive. When he wasn't at Highbury or London Colney working with his players and searching for marginal gains, he'd be at home, watching obscure games from around the globe. Once he'd settled into his Totteridge home, he had an elaborate satellite TV system installed so that he could pick up broadcasts of football matches far and wide. Such a deep fascination with the game meant he was well versed in the habits and characteristics of rival teams. It also meant there were few players with whom the Arsenal manager was not familiar from afar. He was always watching. Always scouting.

'When I went first to pick him up from the West Lodge Park hotel, in his bedroom there must have been 150 games, all on cassettes,' Pat Rice remembers. 'He'd watch football in the afternoons and at night time. Arsène would come in and say, "Did anybody see Düsseldorf versus Berlin?" or some obscure game, and you're thinking, "What the hell has he been watching?" He never stopped watching games. In the afternoon, he'd watch the game that we'd played the Saturday before, three or four times – at home and at work. Annie, his wife, she must have thought, "Christ, not another." Especially if we'd lost – "Why did we lose?" [a line Rice delivers with a well-honed Wenger impersonation]. When he first came, he watched all these games so that he knew all the players we'd play against. He wanted to familiarize himself with the players we were going to play against, what tactics they were going to use and what system they'd play. You had to do your homework with Arsène.'

The success Vieira had enjoyed in his first season at Highbury and the promise shown by teenage striker Nicolas Anelka, who'd been plucked from Paris Saint-Germain the previous February, evidenced a discerning eye for unheralded, under-appreciated or simply unheard-of talent. But Wenger was not infallible when it came to spotting young prospects ready for Premier League stardom. Alberto Méndez was a case in point.

Méndez, a 22-year-old midfielder, was playing semi-professionally in Germany's fifth tier when Wenger made the trip to watch him play at the end of the 1996–97 season. Despite the humbleness of his surroundings, Méndez was not a complete unknown within football circles. Wolverhampton Wanderers and Coventry City had sent scouts to assess him and he'd even met with the latter's manager, Gordon Strachan. Bundesliga side Freiburg had made an offer to sign him, but his club, SC Feucht, rejected it.

Méndez and Feucht had already secured promotion by the time Wenger arrived in the small market town near Nuremberg. With the pressure off, Feucht lost to ESC Nürnberg Rangierbahnhof in the game the Arsenal manager had gone to observe, standing among 150 spectators, and Méndez played poorly. He didn't know Wenger was there. Feucht informed Méndez of Wenger's presence the next day. The Frenchman was undeterred by Méndez's underperformance. Perhaps he saw something of himself in the young German, who was combining his semi-pro career with studies towards a degree in business economics at Nuremberg University. Méndez hadn't even considered a professional career in the game prior to Freiburg's interest. Now, the young midfielder, who still lived with his parents, was being told the mighty Arsenal wanted to sign him.

Shortly after, he flew to Birmingham, where he met with Strachan again. Then he travelled to London to visit Highbury and meet Wenger.

'When I arrived at the Marble Halls, I saw all the old pictures of historic games and the history of the club,' Méndez says. 'I fell in love. It was quite easy then for Arsène Wenger to sign me.'

Méndez had only one question for Wenger before he could commit to signing for Arsenal: 'Why do you want to sign me? I played so badly in that match.'

'I think I saw some things that were very special,' Wenger told him. 'I just want to try it out.'

Although he had been hesitant to leave Germany and to forgo his studies in pursuit of the Premier League dream, Méndez settled quickly into life in North London after a £250,000 transfer was brokered. He initially stayed at Sopwell House, in a room next to Marc Overmars, and he impressed in early training sessions. 'I was doing quite well in training and the players couldn't believe I wasn't a professional before,' he says.

Once the adrenaline of those first heady days as an Arsenal player began to wear off, though, Méndez found the game more hard-going.

'After the first two or three weeks where I was performing really well in training and even Arsène Wenger said he was impressed, I felt my body was not keeping up to that level.'

He made his first-team debut on 14 October, in a League Cup tie against Birmingham City at Highbury. A youthful Arsenal side laboured against their second-tier guests. Birmingham scored after 20 minutes and had several opportunities to extend their shock lead before Boa Morte equalized after the hour mark. It was only in extra time that the Gunners finally broke down their opponents, with a David Platt penalty and a second for Boa Morte. Then, in the one hundred and thirteenth minute, came Méndez's moment. Taking the ball 25 yards from goal, the German midfielder, with his jet-black hair gelled carefully, lashed a low, left-footed shot past David Bennett and into the bottom corner of the Birmingham net.

'I didn't sleep much before the game because I was quite nervous,' Méndez says. 'But when I scored, I wasn't walking on the earth any more; I was walking on air. I slept well that night.'

He was rewarded with a Premier League debut four days later, replacing Ray Parlour for the final 18 minutes of a 0-0 draw with Crystal Palace at Selhurst Park. He played again in the next round of the League Cup, a 1-0 victory over Coventry, before making his first start in the English top flight the following week, away to Sheffield

Wednesday. He lasted just 54 minutes at Hillsborough, though. An injury forced him from the field and kept him out until April. He'd make one more appearance that season.

'Wenger saw me after a few weeks and said, "You look tired. You look like you need to go home for a weekend,"' Méndez says. 'I was missing home a bit at that time. He gave me two days off. I went to see my parents and my friends and when I came back I got injured again.'

After appearing just five times during the first half of the 1998–99 season, Méndez was sent on loan to AEK Athens to finish the campaign. The next season he was loaned to – deep breath – Spielvereinigung Unterhaching back home in Germany and he spent the entire 2000–01 term on loan with Racing Ferrol in the Spanish La Liga 2, the second division. As his loan odyssey took him further – figuratively and geographically – from Arsenal's first team, Méndez came to understand his future at Highbury was limited. He was sold to Ferrol in 2002, before spending much of his later career back in the German lower leagues.

'My dream was always to come back and have a real chance to compete for a place at Arsenal,' Méndez says. 'I never wanted to leave the club.'

After Méndez had returned to London Colney from his loan spell in the Bundesliga in 2000, he felt he had finally grasped the physical demands of top-level football. He spoke with Wenger before going back out on loan with Racing Ferrol.

'Now you are in the shape you should have been in when you arrived,' the manager said.

'Yeah,' Méndez replied. 'But now it's too late.'

*

In the summer of 1997, Arsenal announced a seven-year kit deal with Nike thought to be worth £10 million. The *Evening Standard* described the agreement as 'one of the most lucrative and comprehensive kit sponsorship deals in the history of football'. Arsenal were at last showing signs of closing the commercial gap to Manchester United. After spending heavily to bolster and reshape their squad ahead of Wenger's first full season in charge, they were hoping to do the same on the pitch.

But Wenger – who, one can only assume, had been listening to rapper Notorious B.I.G.'s posthumous single released that July – insisted the Gunners' hefty transfer outlay did not in itself guarantee success. It could be a case of 'Mo Money Mo Problems'.

'We have a new group and that means a bigger risk to find a stability and a new expression,' he said.

'My first target is to build a team, but there is no doubt that we have the ambition to do better than last season when we were third.'

# 10

# Hands Across the Channel

Upon returning to Sopwell House after one of his first training sessions as an Arsenal player, Emmanuel Petit showered, changed and headed to his car. As he walked out of the hotel entrance and towards the car park, the gravel path crunching beneath his feet, he lit a cigarette.

A handful of Arsenal's English contingent clocked the Frenchman sucking on a Marlboro Red as he stood next to his brown Mercedes 300 SL. They were astounded by the sight of the new midfield recruit smoking.

'You're an athlete, what are you smoking for?' one protested.

Although the weekly Tuesday Club binge sessions had become a thing of the past thanks to Arsène Wenger's influence and Tony Adams's sobriety, the drinking culture prevalent throughout English football had not been entirely eradicated. Many of Arsenal's long-tenured players still enjoyed the occasional overindulgence. Petit picked up on the hypocrisy of his teammates' abject opposition to his tobacco habit. He'd heard of how they'd have no such regard for their athletic capacity when throwing back pints in the pub. He'd seen how their culinary choices, though much improved up to that point under Wenger, still lagged behind their Continental counterparts when it came to match preparedness.

Petit cracked a smile as he shot back.

'You lot are going out once a week and having ten pints,' he laughed. 'You think that's OK, but I can't have a cigarette?'

'English players used to have bad habits when they were preparing for games, especially with the food, the drinks,' Petit remembers. 'They used to eat beans and sausages three hours before a game. They used to eat chocolate bars on the way to the stadium, an hour before kick-off. They used to drink a lot. It was kind of tradition. But when you want to play high-level football, you have to follow certain things. This is why Arsène had to fight with some players for weeks and weeks. Us, the French players, the foreign players, it was not very difficult to do that, because we were already doing that. But for the English players, it was a little bit difficult and different, in terms of their culture. This is why it took a while. But, at the end, some players understood – especially the English players – that it was for their own benefit and the team benefited as well.'

It wasn't only in the Arsenal players' extracurricular activities that the cultural chasm between the British core and the overseas imports was apparent. Petit also found himself falling foul of his new colleagues in the changing room.

It was customary for any player entering the changing room – be that at Highbury, Sopwell House or London Colney – to greet his teammates. Sweep the room with a hearty 'hello', eye contact, a nod.

Petit's demeanour, initially, was more businesslike than congenial. He'd walk in, take his seat, begin to change. In silence. No 'hello'. No nod. It was noticed. But this was not a case of the France international being arrogant or unwilling to mix. The new arrival was simply accustomed to a different way of operating. Once one of the old guard joked that they might have to cut off Petit's ponytail if he refused to partake in the pleasantries, the Frenchman quickly adopted the team ethos.

It was a similar story with another of the recently arrived Frenchmen. Nicolas Anelka would later be labelled 'Le Sulk' by the tabloid press for his sullen manner. He'd come to be perceived as moody and disruptive by the time he forced a departure from the club for Real Madrid in 1999. But when he signed for Arsenal in February 1997, just a few weeks shy of his eighteenth birthday, the gifted young striker was thought to be shy and, understandably, somewhat intimidated by his new surroundings.

'He was very, very shy,' Lee Dixon explains. 'He was a kid. He was in a scary, horrible dressing room full of cynical, old English blokes.'

One of those 'cynical, old English blokes', Tony Adams, made a point every morning of shaking hands with each of his teammates before he'd get dressed for training. Anelka had made just four Premiership appearances in the 1996–97 season and was still scoreless in senior football. But his talent was evident and, by the summer of '97, with Ian Wright ageing, Wenger had earmarked a significant role for the teen in the coming season. That meant more exposure to the first-team environment. And more uncomfortable morning greetings from Adams for the reclusive prodigy.

'He always used to go up to Nicolas and say, "Morning, Nicolas,"' Dixon says. 'And Nicolas was like, "Who is this freaky guy in front of me saying 'good morning'?" And Tony would make him say "good morning" to him every day. It was kind of like a ritual. "He's in our dressing room now; he's got to say hello." He pestered him every day.'

*

Sweden had been Arsenal's destination of choice for recent preseason camps, but Wenger decided to station his team in the small Austrian spar town of Bad Waltersdorf in preparation for his first full season in charge at Highbury. Situated in the south-east corner of the country, Bad Waltersdorf offered few distractions. It had just two hotels, one football pitch and a population under four thousand. What it did offer, though, was elevation. At nearly 1,000 feet above sea level, the thin air would raise the players' red-blood-cell count in readiness for the arduous season ahead.

Previous preseasons had been treated as a time for hard work and equally hard play. Dennis Bergkamp was shocked during his first preseason with the club, a tour of Scandinavia in 1995, when he and his wife, while out for a stroll, happened upon a group of his new English teammates deep into a boozing session. And even in Wenger's carefully selected Austrian oasis of tranquillity, many of the usual suspects were determined to uphold tradition.

Wenger green-lit an evening out for the players towards the end of their stay in Austria, a reward for their work. A number of the English group immediately plotted a trip to the nearest pub. All the French players opted for a quieter time, meeting at a nearby coffee shop.

All except one.

'Do you mind if I come out with you guys tonight?' Gilles Grimandi enquired of his new English teammates.

'Yeah, come out with us,' replied Ray Parlour. 'You will have a much better time.'

Reconvening in the hotel reception at 6.30pm, the group of six pub-bound players, Grimandi in tow, then strolled 100 yards or so down the street before folding into the nearest watering hole. The Englishmen asked their French companion what he'd like to drink. 'A small glass of wine,' was the curly-haired midfielder's modest request.

Steve Bould strode to the bar to order the first round.

'Thirty-five pints of lager and a small glass of red wine, please.'

Confused, Grimandi looked around. 'Who else is coming?' he asked. The English lot laughed and got to work on their seven-pint starting course.

'The likes of a Gilles Grimandi helped the situation massively,' David Platt remembers of the French player's role in harmonizing the new overseas imports with Arsenal's established English core. 'There was certainly a . . . divide is the wrong word, but Patrick was a strong character. Emmanuel was a strong character. I think they felt they had the backing of the professionalism of Arsène, that this is what you do in terms of eating and drinking. What the English guys had was, "We've been here for years. We know what the club's about and we are diehard together."

'There was the fitting together of two cultures. Somebody like Gilles Grimandi was right in the middle of that. He didn't gravitate towards the French. He understood that the two cultures could meet and prosper. From my point of view as well, I wasn't somebody who was going to go out after lunch on a Tuesday and have a big drink. I think by that time it had stopped a little bit anyway. But if they had a Christmas night out, then you'd go and you'd have a drink. There was this cultural coming-together at the time, but it didn't really manifest itself in a bad way.'

After a thorough sampling of Bad Waltersdorf's finest ale – or at least its most readily available – and a moderate swill of the house red, the Arsenal players embarked on a bleary-eyed navigation of the short trip back to the hotel. On their way, they passed the French boys stationed outside the coffee shop, enjoying company, conversation and, for some, a cigarette in the mild, mid-July night.

'Lads,' Parlour began to wonder aloud, 'how the hell are we going to win the title this year? We're all drunk and they're all smoking!'

'I can't remember who exactly was smoking, but it seemed like that was a bit of their culture,' reflects Nigel Winterburn. 'And occasionally, even with Arsène Wenger, we used to have a beer. I think they thought that was a bit weird. That's just the way it was. I didn't really worry about it.

'I don't know if I'd call it a divide, but I think it's natural. When you are close to certain players and a new culture comes in, you tend to stick a little bit to what you know and you're a little bit fearful of crossing the divide. A lot of the French players stuck together and socialized together, and a lot of the English players came together. But I've always said that I didn't feel as if there were any problems whatsoever.

'The biggest thing for me was that when we went out on to the pitch, everybody was together. That was the most important thing. Yes, a lot of the French players did stick together and so did the English players. But there wasn't a divide, there wasn't a split. There couldn't be, because we'd never get the results we got with a split within the team. It's impossible.'

'There was always a really good atmosphere,' Parlour adds. 'No problem at all. Everyone got to know each other very quickly. I think the British guys were very good as well with the foreign guys. We made them really feel at home and got involved with everything. In the end, that's why I think a lot of them stayed so long, because they enjoyed it.'

The change of scenery wasn't the only deviation from previous

Arsenal preseasons that Wenger sought to implement. The manager's methods on the training pitch, just as they had been during the midst of the last season, proved distinctly dissimilar from what the players were used to under previous regimes.

In the past, during George Graham's reign and Bruce Rioch's short stint in charge, preseason training sessions would consist almost solely of gruelling cardiovascular work. Chiefly lots and lots – and lots – of running. The squad might be a week into their preseason schedule before they'd even see a football. Mornings might bring miles and miles of jogging along the roads and countryside surrounding their training base. Afternoons might see the players lace up their boots and walk out on to the training pitch, but only to compete against one another in shuttle sprints and the dreaded bleep test, a back-and-forth sprint drill in which participants have to outrun an ever-faster sequence of bleeps. The simplistic theory behind the arduous work was that it was the best – the *only* – way to bring players to the required level of physical fitness for the long season ahead.

Had the Arsenal players got wind of Wenger's plans for double and triple daily training sessions throughout their time in Austria, there'd have been some fearful gulps and sweaty brows. But the Frenchman had markedly different plans for how to prepare his charges for the 1997–98 campaign.

'Preseason we might start off with a cup of coffee and a croissant at eight o'clock and then go for a twenty-minute jog through the woods, come back and have more of a breakfast,' remembers Platt. 'Then at eleven o'clock, come back and do an hour's physical work, then come back at five o'clock and do your football work. Although there were three training sessions, if you actually added up the minutes, it was more like a double training session. I'd had four years of that regime in

Italy. In many ways, I was one that was perfectly happy and controlled in the whole situation. I was never worried in the slightest.

'It was something I was very used to – training, resting. I think there would have been a case under Bruce and in England when I was there before that the first two weeks of your preseason were extremely heavy and you were almost physically ready for the first preseason game, but almost at the risk of missing some of that preseason because of going too quickly.'

The work under Wenger was still intense. But it was, in typical fashion, planned and timed with precision. The manager broke up the preseason schedule into three blocks. The first would entail a hefty workload but nothing overly demanding, so as to allow the players' bodies to acclimatize to the physical workload after their summer holidays. The intensity would increase gradually through the final two blocks, with friendly matches incorporated latterly.

The biggest difference of all? Balls.

There would be pattern-of-play and skills drills mixed in with short plyometric sessions – jumping through hoops, over hurdles, etc. Most of the heavy cardio work even incorporated a ball. Shuttle runs along the sideline might culminate with a cross into the penalty area, for example.

The added technical elements and the precision-planned nature of the training was a joy for the players, compared with the sapping sessions of past preseasons. But from within Wenger's coaching staff, there was scepticism.

Assistant manager Pat Rice was from the old school. The former Northern Ireland international spent 13 years at Arsenal as a player, the starting right back in the last Gunners side to win the Double, in 1971, and later the club captain. He retired from playing in 1984 and had worked as a coach at the club ever since. His long and storied time in the game had cemented within him a singular definition of what preseason training meant.

'Arsène, I don't think they've done enough hard work,' Wenger's number two told his boss. 'I don't think they're going to be ready for the season.'

Seeking to allay Rice's concern, Wenger explained the premise behind his preseason plans. He was training footballers, not marathon runners. The old way might have fostered high fitness levels, but it likely came at an eventual cost of injuries and burnout.

'His fear was, if you overtrained them, you lost them in the latter part of the season,' club physio Gary Lewin says. 'And that was probably the biggest thing that he changed and had to change in people's attitudes.'

Still, partway through the trip, the players evidently felt they'd worked hard enough to deserve a reward. After one friendly match, some got together and approached Adams. 'Ask the gaffer if we can have a beer after the game,' they said. The captain, though now teetotal, agreed to forward the request to Wenger.

Adams returned with welcome news: 'The gaffer said you can have a beer.'

Back at the hotel that evening, the staff and squad gathered for dinner. The players sat across three tables: the older English lot on one, the foreign players on another and the youngsters on the last. Adams felt a nudge at his side – 'Tone, can we get that beer?'

'Arsène, is it all right if we get that beer?' the skipper asked.

'Yes, no problem.'

A few minutes later, a waiter approached the table of excited veterans. He was carrying a service tray, on top of which was a single bottle of beer. As he plonked it down on the table, the bemused group of players looked over to their manager.

A wry smile cracked across Wenger's face. 'You asked for *a* beer, you got *a* beer,' he said and chuckled to himself.

'That's what he was like,' Dixon says, smiling at the memory. 'He had a really dry, cutting sense of humour, and I loved him for that. He wanted to be one of the lads quite a lot of the time.'

Wenger's approach to preseason was new to the Arsenal players whose time with the club predated the manager's. It was not revolutionary to the new signings. What did strike the recent arrivals as unusual, though, was the intensity with which the English players attacked the sessions. Although the work under Wenger was different – more football-focused, less punishing – than in years past, the Arsenal stalwarts approached it with customary vigour. The reason they particularly enjoyed their preseason drinking sessions was because they felt they'd earned the right to blow off some steam after expending such effort through the day. Dennis Bergkamp was surprised and inspired by the ferocity and competitiveness of his teammates during his first preseason with the club, in 1995, and the '97 crop of new signings felt similarly. The players – old and new, sublimely skilled and, well, otherwise – bonded around this ethic of grit and grind.

'The great memories I have are of the personalities of the players, how great they were all the time,' Petit says. 'I really wanted to come to England for that, to live the passion, the relationship with the fans. I wanted to live that. But I discovered a different world in the dressing room – the way the players trained, the way they prepared for games mentally, the way they prepared in general. I think it was different with what I lived in France. I loved it.

'The personality of Ian Wright, Tony Adams, Martin Keown – it's brilliant. I had so much pleasure being in the dressing room. It was a free dressing room. It was based on responsibility, but they were respecting our character and personality. When you look at this team, you know every single player is so different. At the same time, we were a unit, a team. For me, that's the beauty of sport and the beauty of football. It doesn't matter who you are, what kind of personality or character. At the end, if we are all focusing on the same target, we can make miracles.'

Arsenal's results over preseason were broadly positive, if not portentous of a miraculous campaign ahead. Before heading to Austria, local lower-league sides St Albans and Leyton Orient were dispatched 4-1 and 1-0, respectively. On the Continent, trips to take on Stade Nyonnais in Switzerland, Strasbourg in France and PSV in Eindhoven, the Netherlands, had been arranged across a ten-day period. The fixture at Strasbourg's Stade de la Meinau carried particular significance as it marked a return for Wenger to the club at which he'd both culminated his playing career and taken his first steps into coaching almost two decades earlier. Twelve thousand fans watched as the homecoming Alsatian manager guided the Gunners to a 2-1 victory. Petit assisted a second-half winner for Wright, after Grimandi had equalized a first-half strike from the home side's David Zitelli, who'd played under Wenger at Nancy in the mid-1980s.

Three new signings were on the scoresheet in the opening game of Arsenal's preseason tour, with Alberto Méndez, Luis Boa Morte and Marc Overmars netting before Bergkamp – whose fear of flying meant he travelled up to eight hours by car to participate in each friendly –sealed a 4-0 win over Nyonnais. And the trip was capped with a disappointing and ill-tempered 1-0 loss to PSV, in which Vieira and Matthew Upson were both sent off. Vieira had little cause for complaint, having kicked out at goal scorer Tomek Iwan. Upson, though, was an unfortunate victim of mistaken identity, inexplicably sent off after Boa Morte's red-worthy challenge on Igor Demo.

Arsenal rounded off their preseason preparations upon returning from Europe with a 6-2 thumping of Norwich City. The summer had seen an influx of new signings, all but one arriving from the Continent and many representing instant qualitative improvements. This squad of disparate backgrounds, experience levels and nationalities had begun to foster a harmony and unity of purpose. The direction of travel of Wenger's first ten months was evident – the bookmakers William Hill named the Frenchman the Premier League's 'safest manager', with 16-1 odds of being sacked during the coming campaign; Alex Ferguson was a 10-1 shot. Arsenal were building towards a challenge to Manchester United's supremacy.

But if a title charge was brewing, the players didn't yet have a sense of how quickly.

'I thought we'd be competitive, but you never really know,' says Dixon. 'You think, "We're pretty good." We'd got Nicolas Anelka, who was unplayable. We'd got Petit and Vieira, who were a brilliant shield for us lot. We knew what we could do. We won't let many goals in. We've got the best goalie in the league. These two in front of us are brilliant. We've got pace on either side and Nicolas Anelka can kill anyone from a pace point of view. And Dennis and Wrighty were still there.

'It was all new. We knew it was going to be a new era. At the start of it, you're not going to knock the lights out. We were more than happy with what we'd seen so far. I was really happy with how Wenger was getting us to play and the new players that were there. It was an exciting time. It was like, "Right, let's have a real go at this season." It was his first preseason. All that was new. And it set us up for a brilliant season.'

'Not really, because Manchester United were flying back in the day,' Petit says of whether he envisaged a title challenge in his first season at Highbury. 'They were the team to beat. It was a lot of pressure on us, but we were very confident. When you have players like Tony Adams in your team, David Seaman, when you have Patrick Vieira, Nicolas Anelka, Dennis Bergkamp, Marc Overmars as well, I think, if you are honest with yourself, you have a team to compete with Manchester United. Maybe we don't have the bench, but we at least had fifteen, sixteen very good players.

'We can do *something*.'

# 11

# The Non-flying Dutchman

Of all the various accolades and achievements of Dennis Bergkamp's football career, there is one in particular that will likely never be equalled.

On 27 August 1997, the Dutch maestro scored a hat-trick in a 3-3 draw with Leicester City. So far, so impressive yet attainably repeatable. Just four days earlier, he'd scored twice in a 3-1 win away to Southampton. Five goals in four days – again, heck of a feat, but it's been done.

What is remarkable about Bergkamp's purple patch at the end of the 1997–98 season's opening month is that his strikes were so consistently and variously spectacular that the Arsenal striker single-handedly dominated the *Match of the Day* Goal of the Month competition, which had not happened before and has not happened since. The BBC's flagship football highlights programme would present viewers with the ten most eye-catching goals at the end of each month, from which a panel of pundits would select the top three. In third place for the August '97 edition was Bergkamp's first strike against Leicester, a curling, swirling effort from the corner of the penalty area that precisely picked out the far top corner of Kasey Keller's goal.* In

---

\* Keller must have felt Bergkamp's performance was personally uncharitable. The American goalkeeper will have been sleep deprived after his wife had given birth to twins the night before the game.

second place, one of his strikes against the Saints, a determined solo effort finished by a tidy cutback and emphatic finish.

There was a slight hollowness to his hat-trick against Leicester. It ought to have clinched a victory in a tricky trip to the Midlands against Martin O'Neill's plucky Foxes. Instead, after the Dutchman put the Gunners ahead in the ninety-third minute, just one minute after Leicester had drawn level, Arsenal conceded again. The disappointment of the draw detracted nothing from the artistry of Bergkamp's hat-trick strike, though. It was a goal of maximum majesty.

When David Platt picked up possession near the centre circle, Bergkamp began to pull away from his marker. He darted into the penalty area. Platt chipped a pass high and dipping into the number 10's path. Bergkamp pulled the ball out of the sky and killed it dead with his unmatched deftness. Matt Elliott, Leicester's bruising centre half, was quick on the scene, suffocating the striker with close attention. But with his second touch, one perfectly calibrated tap from his left boot, Arsenal's artist in residence evaded the defender and created a clear sight of goal for himself. Then, opening out his shoulders, he curled a nonchalant shot across the goalkeeper and into the far corner of the net. If the goal's artistry were to have been judged in the manner of an Olympic high dive or a figure skating routine, it would have been assessed the highest degree of technical difficulty, yet Bergkamp made it look so easy, breaking neither stride nor sweat.

A masterpiece of touch, anticipation and execution, it was not only deemed the best goal scored in the Premier League that August but the finest of the season. Bergkamp, now playing the best football of his career, was also voted Player of the Month for August and September.

'The third one was, for me, very special,' Bergkamp said of his treble at Filbert Street, 'because as soon as the ball came I had in my mind what I wanted to do and that exactly came true. The first touch was to control the ball and keep it in the air. The defender was coming and I tried to get it past him, which worked. And the third touch was the shot on goal, and it was a goal.

'You don't realise in the moment how it looked, what it was like. When you looked at it on television after, you realised, "Yeah, that's exactly what I tried to do." That's what made it quite special.'

The final move of that goal, the shift on to his right foot and the measured curl into the far corner, became Bergkamp's trademark. It was a technique he repeated to great success several times throughout his career, ordinarily from around the edge of the penalty area. He'd done so the previous season to score against Sunderland, then he did it twice against Barnsley – poor Barnsley! – in 1997–98 and again versus Port Vale in the FA Cup in January.

'Dennis had that little drop of his shoulder and then a side-foot shot to guide the ball into the far corner,' says club photographer Stuart MacFarlane. 'So time and time again at away grounds, I'd go and put myself in that position. And as soon as the ball came over and got to him, I always knew where it was going. It was a sixth sense. I knew what he was going to do.'

But, of course, from an opponent's perspective, it was one thing to know what Bergkamp was going to do; stopping him doing it was a different matter.

'Dennis Bergkamp was ridiculous,' remembers Barnsley defender Darren Barnard.* 'He picked the ball up 25 yards from goal. He didn't

---

* At the time he was interviewed for this book, Barnard's Twitter profile picture was a shot of him marking Bergkamp at Barnsley's Oakwell Stadium in April 1998.

even beat the player. He just used his marker as a wall and bent it around him into the top corner both times. You just couldn't stop it.'

'Dennis Bergkamp that day was just unplayable,' adds Barnsley midfielder Neil Redfearn. 'I remember when we prepped that week, we worked a lot on losses in transition and how dangerous they were when Bergkamp dropped into space. He had this thing where he would take it down the left-hand side and then check back and curl it with his right foot. His first goal was exactly that. We'd lost the ball in midfield and it went to Bergkamp. Eric Tinkler was up against him and we were shouting, "Keep him on his left foot." I was right behind it. As soon as he opened himself up, it was inevitable. He curled it right into the top corner. He must have rehearsed this finish thousands of times, because not only did he do it against us, he did it against loads of teams better than us.'

Thousands might be a conservative estimate. Bergkamp began to pursue footballing perfection from an early age. He was born in Amsterdam in 1969 and grew up in a working-class suburb of the city, the youngest of four sons in a devoutly Catholic family. Named after former Manchester United striker Denis Law, a fondness for sport was as inevitable as those trademark goals would later become. His father, Wim, was an electrician who played football locally and his mother, Tonnie, had been an accomplished amateur gymnast in her youth. Bergkamp would play football with his three older brothers in the streets around the apartment block where they lived. He credits his outstanding balance to the fact they'd play on concrete and were thus incentivized to stay upright to avoid painful scrapes and bruises. He was fascinated with geometry as a young boy and his interest in angles bled into his passion for football. He'd spend hours kicking a ball against the wall beneath his bedroom window, experimenting with applying spin to the ball or aiming for a specific brick and working out the various ways it would bounce back to him.

'I'm not sure why, but the thing that always interested me most was controlling the ball, especially when it was in the air,' he said in his autobiography, *Stillness and Speed* (2013). 'I wasn't interested in dribbling or doing tricks or scoring goals. Control. That was my thing.'

Bergkamp would watch English and German football on television. His preference for passing and control manifested in his selection of a favourite player: he would study Tottenham and England midfielder Glenn Hoddle. He thought deeply about the art of passing and creating for others.

'In my mind the idea is, "Make it a fantastic pass." But what is the best pass? For some people it's get it over the defender and the striker can receive the ball. To me that's not good enough. No, I have to beat the defender, and make the goalkeeper think he can get it, so he comes out, leaving space. And I have to get the ball in front of my striker or on to his head so he can put it into the corner. It's a different way of thinking.'

When Arsenal paid a club-record £7.5 million to sign Bergkamp in 1995, there was a sense of shock that they'd managed to attract one of the most skilled and sought-after players in Europe. He'd signed for Ajax at the age of eleven. There, he developed into one of the most gifted players ever produced by the Dutch club's famously productive academy. He scored 122 goals in 237 appearances for Ajax, where he'd been crucial to a domestic title and a UEFA Cup triumph, before joining Internazionale in 1993. He was well known to the English football audience for his part in the national team's bleakest moment of the decade. He'd scored at Wembley when England hosted Holland during the qualification campaign for the 1994 World Cup. Then, he scored again – dribbling past Tony Adams and finishing beyond David

Seaman – in the return fixture in Rotterdam that sealed England's failure to qualify for USA '94.

'I was a football geek, so I knew all about Dennis Bergkamp and his exploits for Holland and in Italy, and before that in the Netherlands with Ajax,' says Adrian Clarke. 'I couldn't believe Arsenal had attracted a player of his ability in his peak. I think the signing of Dennis Bergkamp is as important in the history of Arsenal Football Club as the appointment of Arsène Wenger in many ways. To get a player like Dennis, for that kind of money, it took Arsenal to a different level and showed we meant business.'

Arsenal fended off rival interest from Bayern Munich and Barcelona to land Bergkamp. But that they even had a chance of signing the Netherlands superstar was down to the fact that his two seasons in Serie A could hardly have gone worse.

Bergkamp's Inter spell was not entirely without success. He claimed a second UEFA Cup winners' medal in his first season at the San Siro, scoring eight goals in the Continent's secondary competition. He struggled domestically, though. He claims Inter president Ernesto Pellegrini had promised him the club intended to adopt an attack-minded style of play before he elected to move from Ajax. AC Milan had recently enjoyed tremendous success under innovative coach Arrigo Sacchi and with Dutch stars Marco van Basten, Ruud Gullit and Frank Rijkaard. They'd pressed and passed their way to back-to-back European Cups in 1989 and '90. Bergkamp, who signed alongside Ajax colleague Wim Jonk, was expecting Inter to replicate their rivals' formula. The promise was not kept. Inter played a reactive, defence-first style, often leaving Bergkamp isolated in attack. In his second and final season in Italy, he scored just three goals in twenty-one league games.

For someone seeking to escape the shackles of defensive football, Arsenal in 1995 did not appear the obvious destination. Bergkamp had been oblivious to the Gunners' miserly reputation under George Graham, though, and the club were attempting to inject a degree of adventure into their play with Bruce Rioch at the helm. From the moment he stepped on to the training pitches of London Colney, his new teammates recognized a transformative talent.

'From Monday to Friday he's doing stuff you've only seen on the telly,' says Lee Dixon. 'You see pieces of Lionel Messi and all the brilliant players throughout the years, but we got to train with him every week. It was like, "Wow! Did he just do that? How did he do that?"

'He was so instinctive of the moment and of his balance and body position and where the opponent was. As opposed to a thought process, it's more a feel process. It's about how his body is and where the ball is, all of that stuff that's alien to me. I've got a slight understanding of brilliant, skilful players, but sometimes you've got to stand back and don't try and work it out. Just enjoy it.'*

'He made everyone around him better, whether that's with how

---

* Flash forward to 2 November 2002 – Newcastle vs Arsenal at St James' Park. Arsenal winger Robert Pires feeds a low pass into Bergkamp on the edge of the penalty area. To escape the close attention of his marker, Nikos Dabizas, the Dutchman flicks the ball around the defender with his left foot before spinning in the opposite direction and collecting it on the other side of the Newcastle man. From there, he calmly slides a low finish into the net. It is remembered as one of the great Premier League goals. It has also been the subject of debate ever since – did Bergkamp mean to do what he did with that magical touch? Could he have meant it? Lee Dixon: 'I looked at him in the dressing room after the game and I said, "Dennis . . ." He looked at me. I said, "Did you mean that?" And he gave me a look. I'll never forget it. It was like, *Why are you asking me that? Of course I meant it*. He didn't say it; he just looked at me. I went, "Yep, fair enough. I retract the question."'

good his touch was in making your passes look better or how he'd pass the ball to you in the perfect place for you to receive it,' Clarke says. 'He was a perfectionist.'

While Arsenal's established stars marvelled at Bergkamp's magic in training, the club's youngsters identified an example to follow. When Bergkamp first broke into the first-team set-up at Ajax, he'd watched the side's senior players – Van Basten in particular – and studied their technique, their work ethic. At Arsenal, he embraced the opportunity to pass on pearls of wisdom. After his hat-trick against Leicester, for instance, he gathered the club's under-18s squad and talked to them about the importance of honing a cushioned first touch.

'He was a role model for the younger players,' remembers Ian Selley. 'He'd stay behind after training and do 50 or 60 free kicks. It used to be a bit frowned on if you went in early or stayed late, like you were creeping. But he changed all of that. Us younger lads thought, "OK, we can do this now. We won't get frowned upon."'

'I remember thinking it was impossible that somebody could be that good at football,' says Alberto Méndez. 'It gave you a lot of confidence on the pitch, because if you got into trouble you knew you could give him the ball and he would get you out of trouble.

'I remember in one game, I got into a bit of trouble. I had three or four players around me and I didn't know where to go. I saw him, I thought, "Ooh, there's Dennis. I'll get the ball to him." But I kicked the ball too hard and it arrived at him neck high. But he let the ball pass and lifted his foot to control it. He killed it with one touch. I thought, "Oh, my God."

'Everyone knew how good his first touch was, how skilled he was and what a good scorer he was. But I don't think anyone really knew how fast he was. He was so fast. He was big, he was tall, he was strong and he was really fast. You only realized it when you played against him.'

Later, when fellow Dutchman Robin van Persie joined from Feyenoord, the young forward was inspired by Bergkamp's dedication to perfection. After one training session at Arsenal's new training facility, Van Persie sat in a Jacuzzi and watched through a window as Bergkamp put himself through extra work, a drill involving receiving a pass and shooting at goal. The youngster decided he'd stay among the bubbling water until he saw Bergkamp take an errant touch.

'My hands got all wrinkled in the bath but I just stayed there,' he said. 'I sat and watched and I waited, looking for one single mistake. But the mistake never came. And that was the answer for me. Watching that training session answered so many questions I had. I can pass the ball well, too. I'm a good football player as well. But this man did it so well and with such drive. He had such total focus. I found myself thinking, "OK, wait a minute, I can play football well enough, but I've still got an enormous step to take to get to that level." And that's when I realized, if I want to become really good, then I have to be able to do that, too. From that moment on I started doing every exercise with total commitment. With every simple passing or kicking practice, I did everything at 100 per cent, just so I wouldn't make mistakes. And when I did make a mistake I was angry. Because I wanted to be like Bergkamp.'

Bergkamp was three years into his senior career with Ajax before he learned how to be like Bergkamp. He broke into the first team of the historic Amsterdam club as a speedy, touchline-hugging winger, given a debut in 1986 by then manager Johan Cruyff. In 1989, with Ajax managed by the German Kurt Linder, he was demoted back to the youth team along with future Barcelona midfielder Richard Witschge.

'These two are useless,' Linder angrily told the youth coach, one Louis van Gaal.

Van Gaal disagreed. The enigmatic tactician had an inkling that Bergkamp was being misused. He redeployed the young forward as a number 10, operating in the space between midfield and attack. The young player was revitalized. When Van Gaal took over the first team in 1991, he installed Bergkamp as his attacking fulcrum. Bergkamp was subsequently named Dutch Footballer of the Year in successive seasons.

'Dennis Bergkamp was a right winger and I was a left winger,' remembers Scottish wide player Ally Dick, who played with a young Bergkamp at Ajax. 'We used to play in the reserves a lot together. I never knew he'd be a centre forward. If you'd have asked me who would be the next great world-class player, I never would have said Dennis. He was a great player, but I never thought he'd do what he has done, especially as a centre forward.'

'I suddenly felt completely free in my game,' Bergkamp said of his switch to a central role under Van Gaal. 'I could use my two-footedness and show I could score goals. Everything I had learned playing for the juniors and what the fans didn't yet know about me, could manifest itself in that position. Being the number 10 gave me that wonderful tension again. It was new, it was exciting. I didn't hesitate for a moment, wondering where I should run to. It was all automatic. Suddenly, something amazing happened to me.'

When Ian Wright heard the rumours that Arsenal were interested in signing Dennis Bergkamp, he hoped they were true. Wright was a poacher, a born goal scorer who lived on the shoulder of the last defender. His craft was bursting in behind opposition backlines and sniffing out scoring opportunities. After he was repositioned by Van Gaal, it was difficult to draw up a more perfect foil for Wright than Bergkamp, who enjoyed creating goals for others as much as Wright relished making nets bulge.

One afternoon in June 1995, as reports of Arsenal's move for the Dutchman gathered steam, Wright was driving home from training. On his way back to his house in Croydon, South London, he pulled off the M25 motorway and into Clacket Lane Services to refill. The combustible striker grew annoyed at the driver in front who occupied the nearest of the petrol station's two pumps, angered the unmindful motorist in front hadn't pulled forward into the vacant spot ahead. Wright gestured as he manoeuvred around the stopped BMW 7 Series and complained to his wife, Debbie, in the passenger seat. Then he caught sight of the disruptive driver.

'Debbie, look! It's Dennis Bergkamp!'

Bergkamp had just inked the contract that made him an Arsenal player and was on his way home to Holland, via the Channel Tunnel. Wright ran over and wrapped his new striker partner in a hug. Once they met again on the training pitch, they quickly got to work cultivating a devastating on-field relationship. Over the next three Premier League seasons, Bergkamp would assist more goals for Wright than for any other player during his time with Arsenal.

'Because he's world class, and I know that I'm very studious,' Wright says, explaining what made his partnership with Bergkamp so productive. 'When you get a player of that calibre, who can exploit space, and you've got myself, who can create space to run into – I can exploit the space and Dennis can create the space for me. It's going to work if you work at it. When you get a player of Dennis's calibre, you just fit yourself into him. Find the part of you that fits into his piece of the puzzle and clip yourself on, because he's going to create. He can get the ball to me no matter how tight the defender is on me, no matter how tight the gap is that he has to squeeze it through. Dennis will get it there.

'When we used to do stuff in training, it was like, good luck to anybody that's playing against me and Dennis. We hit it off because he's a fantastic player. And I know that I was doing the right things in the way I was trying to make myself a better player, all the way through my career, so I can end up playing with someone like him. In any situation where he gets the ball at his feet, I make my run and the ball will get there.

'Once you get into a situation where Dennis has made his move and broken through the midfield, and I'm running alongside the centre half, you make the move like you're going to go across [the centre back] – and he has to go with you – then you go back the other way and you've got 5 yards of space instantly. I'd have already said to Dennis, "Put it in to my left, because I'm going to run him over to the right." By the time he recovers, you're in on goal to get your shot off.

'People ask me the best player I've played with. Most of us will say it's Dennis. He's the greatest signing we've ever made. He changed everything about our club. It's no secret or coincidence that success came not long after him and continued all the way through his Arsenal career. I can't even tell you how much of a privilege it was to play with someone like that, and to call him my friend.'

As in sync as they became on the pitch, in Bergkamp Wright had found a partner in crime when it came to dressing-room pranks, too. Nicknamed 'The Ice Man' for his steely, unemotional demeanour, Bergkamp's hard-earned reputation as one of the chief jokers within the Arsenal squad might surprise many fans. His dry wit was as sharp as his eye for a defence-splitting pass and he had a penchant for a practical joke.

'Off the field, he loved a wind-up, loved all the banter,' says Ray Parlour, someone for whom wind-ups and banter are specialist subjects. 'People don't know that. He was a real good laugh in the dressing room.'

'They called him The Ice Man and he had that stern face,' says Stuart Taylor, a young back-up goalkeeper at the time. 'You would never know what he was thinking. I remember in some of my early training sessions with the first team, he would say something to me, having a bit of a go at me, and I'd be thinking, "Oh, no." But then he'd crack a little smile and I'd realize he was joking. He was actually a really funny bloke.'

When Wright and Bergkamp combined on their wind-up missions, Martin Keown was their favourite target. The defender was an intelligent, deep-thinking individual, but he was also fiercely intense and short-fused. The strikers knew they could get a rise out of him. Bergkamp tended to disapprove of Keown's fashion sense – or lack thereof – and would surreptitiously hang his clothes from the dressing-room ceiling after the players had changed into their kit. One time, he conspired with Wright to have the England striker dress head to toe in Keown's clobber. Keown only caught on to the ruse when Wright approached him for a hug. Just as the fearsome centre back figured out what was happening, Wright darted to the swimming pool.

One time, after Arsenal had moved into the state-of-the-art training ground they opened in 1999, Bergkamp teamed up with the club chef, Rob Fagg, to play a prank on Sean O'Connor, the grounds manager. The pair told O'Connor they'd seen someone fishing out on the small lake within the training ground. They'd even set up a tent next to the water. 'Sean went mad,' Fagg laughs. 'He was chasing down the lane after nobody. We'd set him up.'

Arsenal only learned of Bergkamp's fear of flying once a deal to sign him had already been agreed. It was something that began to develop in 1994, when he'd become panic-stricken before flying home from the World Cup. The issue worsened upon his return to Inter, as the team regularly flew on small, rickety propeller planes for away matches. After one especially stress-ridden trip to Florence to take on Fiorentina in February 1995, he vowed never to fly again.* David Dein, rather matter-of-factly, insisted the club would put the player through a course, run by British Airways, aimed at curing aviophobia. At the end of the two-day tutorial, participants would sit alongside a pilot in the cockpit as they were flown over London.

'No, Mr Dein, you don't understand,' Bergkamp said. 'I don't fly.'

His refusal to fly meant that Bergkamp missed a great many away ties in European competition. He'd occasionally travel by train and car to commutable Continental fixtures, likewise any domestic jaunts for which the rest of the squad took to the air. On such occasions, Vic Akers, the club's kit man who also served as the manager of Arsenal's hugely successful women's team, was his travel partner. The two developed a close relationship, one based in no small part around banter and piss taking.

'Vic and him were very close,' says Stuart MacFarlane. 'They were like a little double act. We were in Austria for preseason one year and obviously Dennis didn't fly. We were staying in a place called Bad

---

* Tony Adams also suffered a fear of flying, something the Arsenal captain sought to ease through alcohol prior to his 1996 sobriety.

Waltersdorf and I think we were playing in Switzerland. So the team flew on a plane for 45 minutes. Myself, Dennis, Vic and our head of comms at the time got on a coach for seven hours. It was one of the funniest seven hours of my life, with Vic and Dennis bouncing off each other, telling jokes. You wouldn't expect it off Dennis, but he was a great character. He really embraced the Englishness of the team and the sense of humour. He really came out of his shell with that group and everyone loved him.'

Akers was also the victim of Bergkamp's favourite – and perhaps most childish – prank. A handful of saleswomen had visited the training ground to proffer a range of grooming products. As the team walked back into the canteen area after the morning's session, Bergkamp spotted Akers leaning casually against a doorframe, chatting with the young women. The striker crept over and whipped down the kit man's shorts.

'People were laughing about it for weeks afterwards,' Bergkamp said. 'You know, I've won some trophies. And I've scored some nice goals. But this may be the highlight of my career.'

'He took the piss, Dennis,' says Pat Rice. 'He was in among all of them. And because you've got that impression [of him as quiet], you don't think it's him, but he's done the dirty trick – hiding people's shoes, kids' stuff.'

Bergkamp wasn't all lightness and laughs. There was an aggressiveness to his game and a competitive streak within him that often walked on a razor's edge between healthy physicality and downright nastiness – to which his record of 45 yellow cards and 4 reds in his Arsenal career attests. His vision and wit were sharp; so too were his elbows.

'He was a proper competitor in training,' says Dixon. 'He loved being involved in our club when he came because he loved a bit of competitive football. We used to kick lumps out of him and he used to kick lumps out of us back. He enjoyed it. He was a good trainer, a really good trainer. He was very feisty. We used to put Martin Keown on him all the time, to have a proper tear-up with him. The amount of times the both of them nearly got injured on a Friday, say, before playing Tottenham on the Saturday and Wenger was like, "Oh, my God." He was competitive and we loved that about him. You ask all the players who played against him – the likes of the United players – how many kicks they've had off him and how nasty he was, because if he needed to put his foot in, he did.'

'I was never worried about getting stuck in in training,' says Omer Riza, a young striker who'd begun to train with the first team during the 1997–98 season. 'I remember one time, I'd gone in on Dennis and I was on the floor. He trod on me on purpose, with his studs in my leg. That was a little wake-up call for me to say, "These guys mean business." He was a nice guy off the pitch, but on the pitch he was a different animal. He needed to be. With the qualities he had, if he didn't have that streak in him he would've gotten abused.'

'Some people said Dennis was too nice,' said Patrick Vieira. 'I can't agree at all. Dennis is not a nice sweet guy. I would not want to play as a defender against him, because he's really clever. He looks like "the good son-in-law" on the field, but he's not just there to play football and the beautiful game. He has a nasty side which he can dig out when he needs it.'

With that physical edge added into his vast technical skill set, it's little wonder Bergkamp was a success in England. His assimilation to life in the Premier League was not instant, though. He was scoreless through his first six games as an Arsenal player. Away fans chanted

'What a waste of money' and *The Sun* newspaper wondered which of North London's flopping new forwards would break their duck first – Bergkamp or Tottenham's Chris Armstrong. 'Arsenal supporters are beginning to view a goal by Dennis Bergkamp in much the same light as a small child regards Christmas,' said *The Independent*. 'They know it is coming, it is just the wait that is unbearable.'

He finally broke his barren streak at the seventh time of asking, netting a brace in a 4-2 win over Southampton at Highbury on 23 September 1995. He ended his first season in England with a modest return of 11 league goals from 33 appearances. Goals alone could never measure the full impact of Bergkamp on the pitch, but there was a sense the Dutchman was yet to fully deliver prior to Wenger's arrival. On 30 December 1996, *The Independent* published their yearly rundown of the top players in the Premier League. Bergkamp was fortieth, ranked lower than Saša Ćurčić, Aljoša Asanović and Mark Draper.

By the early weeks of the 1997–98 season, Bergkamp was flying – only metaphorically, of course. The movement and freedom of expression Wenger had encouraged and cultivated at Highbury meant an array of willing runners and passing options now orbited the Dutch creator, bringing to bear the total realization of his vision, execution and creativity. What had been unlocked within him by his switch to becoming a number 10 in his early twenties was now being unleashed at full force on the Premier League. For the 1997 edition of *The Independent*'s list, Bergkamp was number one, the best player in the country.

'As a defender and a back-four member, you're concentrating on your own game, who you're up against, what your opposition is defensively, how you're going to keep the ball out of the net collectively,' Dixon says. 'But at the back of your mind, you've got this comfort-blanket feeling that you've got Dennis in the team. I didn't worry, but I'd be concerned about playing against Ryan Giggs or David Ginola or whoever it was – my job was to stop them and I'd be concentrating on that. But in the back of my mind I'm getting a little massage on my shoulders and neck because I know that Dennis is in the team. I know that at any moment he's just going to do something brilliant. So, for God's sake, just do your job, keep the ball out of the net, and then we'll win. He's an amazing man to have in your side.'

'He was very important for me,' says Marc Overmars. 'He helped me settle in England. When you see the goals, many goals came from an assist from him to me. It often started with Dennis.

'Dennis was the rehabilitation of Arsenal, when they started to create a new vision of Arsenal, instead of "boring Arsenal". Dennis was one of the fathers of that.'

# 12

# Just Done It

It was a fine goal to mark an incredible achievement. Slid clear of the Bolton Wanderers defence by a pinpoint Dennis Bergkamp through-ball, Ian Wright fired across goalkeeper Keith Branagan and into the bottom-left corner of the goal – a typically unerring finish from the man who was now, officially, the most lethal scorer in Arsenal's history. Smile beaming in jubilant celebration, he removed his shirt to reveal a white vest emblazoned in bright red with the slogan '179 JUST DONE IT'.

Except he hadn't.

Wright had begun the 1997–98 season needing five goals to eclipse Cliff Bastin's 50-year-old record and become the club's all-time leading scorer. His precise finish in the twentieth minute against Bolton at Highbury, drawing the Gunners level after falling behind to Alan Thompson's early strike, was his fourth of the campaign. He'd drawn level with Bastin on 178 goals in the famous red shirt with white sleeves.

As he began to close in on the record tally at the beginning of the season, with a goal against Leeds on the opening weekend and a brace versus Coventry two days later, Wright came up with the idea of marking his eventual history-making strike with a bespoke undershirt. The striker decided a modification of the 'Just do it' tagline of his boot sponsor, Nike, worked perfectly.

'I remember saying "Just done it" because there was a massive thing around their slogan being "Just do it". I said to Nike, "Why don't we do

"Just done it"? There was a load of red tape to go through, because that's their strapline. They said, "Well, you can put it on a T-shirt." But they weren't happy about putting the swoosh under it. In the end, you can see what it did for them. If I'm going to do this, it has to say "Just done it", because I've literally just done it. In the end, they said, "Yeah, we'll do it."

'I had it on for about five games. I wanted to break the record against Tottenham two weeks earlier. I missed two good chances. I wanted to do it against Tottenham because that would have been unbelievable. To get the hat-trick against Bolton, on the day, felt different, especially when I scored the first goal. I felt like I was on a roll. I knew that something was happening today.'

Kit man Vic Akers tipped off club photographer Stuart MacFarlane about the celebratory vest.

'I'd been briefed and told to watch out for it,' MacFarlane says. 'But it was a long time coming. We were all just so relieved. I remember hanging around after the game pitch-side for Wrighty to come out of the tunnel. He was so funny. He was shouting, "Where was George Graham? He was playing golf when they signed me." It was so funny. It is one of those days when I felt lucky to be in the stadium to witness that. As he took his T-shirt off, he ran straight towards me. I was thinking, "Wrighty, you haven't done it yet."'

'We talked about it before the game, because obviously he had that T-shirt on,' says Lee Dixon. He did a knee slide next to me and I'm kneeling down, pointing to the number on his shirt as he pulled it up. There's a brilliant photo of me and him. Me and Wrighty are really big mates and we're still mates now. For some reason, he always ran down my side when he was celebrating, so I bumped into him quite a lot and I got in a load of photos and I wasn't involved in any of the goals, which was great. He was a goal machine.

'Immediately after that photo was taken, we realized he hadn't broken it, he'd only equalled it. I went, "You nugget. You've got another one to go." He went, "Have I?" I said, "Yeah. You've only equalled it." He went, "Oh, shit!" We went back and obviously he got it with probably the easiest goal he's ever fucking scored in his life.'

That goal, and the outright record, arrived just five minutes later. Profiting from some calamitous defending after Bergkamp's initial shot had been parried, Wright strolled into the 6-yard box to tap the ball into an unguarded net. History.

'I think the anticipation was too much,' he says. 'I wanted to get it over and done. Then you can hear the murmuring in the crowd, them working it out – "He's equalled it; he's not broken it." Then when I scored the second one, I didn't even realize what I'd done. When we went inside, the reporters are asking, "How did it feel to take your shirt off when you didn't realize?" That's when it hit me. I was caught up in the whole moment.'

Understandably so. It was a landmark moment in the unlikeliest top-level football career. Wright had grown up in Brockley, South-east London, the youngest of three brothers, raised by his mother and an abusive stepfather. He showed a talent for football at a young age and was tutored in the art of goal scoring by one of his school teachers, Sydney Pigden. Wright has called Pigden the 'first positive male figure' in his life. The teacher clearly saw potential in the young Wright and would speak with him about how legendary Tottenham striker Jimmy Greaves would score goals by 'passing the ball into the net'.

As a teen, Wright went on trial with Millwall, Southend United and Brighton. All proved unsuccessful. He was childhood friends with Arsenal midfielder David Rocastle, and 'Rocky', a couple of years Wright's junior, had encouraged the striker to persevere with football in the wake of these knockbacks. He'd all but given up on a professional career in the game by his late teens, though, and instead played at non-league level while working as a labourer. Straddling the poverty line, he spent 18 days in Chelmsford Prison at age 19 for failing to pay fines relating to driving offences.

That was Wright at his lowest ebb, but redemption was around the corner. In 1985, when he was 21 years old and playing for Greenwich Borough, he was scouted by Second Division side Crystal Palace and invited for a three-day trial.

'He was hungry, desperate to be successful; desperate to show people how good a footballer he was,' then Palace manager Steve Coppell says. 'Within three days, we offered him a three-month contract. When I spoke to Ron Noades, my boss, about Ian Wright, I said, "This is going to sound stupid, but this kid has got the talent to play for England."'

Three months became six years, as Wright established himself as a cult hero at Selhurst Park, forming a sympatico partnership in attack with Mark Bright. His goals made him the most feared striker in the second tier and would eventually fire Palace to promotion in 1989 and an FA Cup final a year later. And Coppell's prophecy was proven correct in 1991, when Wright earned the first of 33 senior England caps.

All the while, Wright had been learning on the job. His circuitous route to the game's upper echelons meant he hadn't been exposed to high-quality coaching from a young age the way many of his peers had been. He entered professional football belatedly and as something of a rough diamond. His refinement into one of the deadliest strikers in the country came gradually as a result of examples set by teammates and his own thirst for improvement.

'When I played Sunday-morning football, movement wasn't

something that I needed to worry about, because I was so quick,' Wright says. 'I didn't realize that I could wait for the midfielder to get the ball, look up, and then I'd make the run; they'd just put it over the top, and I'd run over there. What happened was, once I got to Palace, my movement wasn't great. I didn't know that when the ball goes from the centre half into midfield, you've got to be doing something so the defender is thinking, "What's he going to do?" You can't do that unless, by the time it gets to the midfielder and he takes that touch to look up, you've already made a move for the defender – whether it's to come towards the ball or not – so that when the defender looks up, he either sees you going the other way or coming towards him.

'When I got into England, I watched Gary Lineker. I saw him roast Des Walker once – and Des Walker was the best – by bringing him towards the ball then just spinning him. The way he did it, he was like a possum; he sucks you in like he's not interested, running towards the midfield, then bang! He's obviously already spoken to the midfielder and said, "If you see me coming towards you and there's space behind me, that's where I want it." I'm the same: I don't want the ball to my feet, coming into play; I want it into space.

'I got into the England team and we played against Russia. This fella marked me so tight. I don't know whether he didn't have a shower on purpose, but he hummed. He did not give me half a yard in the whole game. He wasn't even looking at the ball. If I got away, he just fouled me. I remember watching that game intently, thinking "Why am I letting him so tight to me?" What I learned from that was, if he wanted to get tight to me, don't let him – keep moving. Once I watched that game, I thought, "Right, OK, I get it now." Then you've got to work on your touch, just in case it does come into your feet.'

Wright worked relentlessly. From his earliest training sessions with

Palace, he made a habit of staying behind once his teammates had gone home, taking a bagful of balls and perfecting his finishing, touch and turns through relentless repetition. It paid off to the tune of 118 goals in 277 games for the Eagles. He was named the club's Player of the Year for their promotion season of 1988–89 and, in 2006, Palace fans voted him their Player of the Century.

In the early weeks of the 1991–92 season, Arsenal paid a club-record £2.5 million to sign him. On his way from Selhurst Park to London Colney to undergo a medical before signing for Arsenal, Wright called Rocastle to tell him they were about to become teammates. After the routine tests, he met Rocastle at his house near the training ground and the pair chatted excitedly through the night about their club.

Wright claimed the First Division Golden Boot in his maiden campaign as a Gunner, scoring 23 league goals and 30 in all competitions. He was also named Arsenal's Player of the Season after each of his first two terms at Highbury and would finish as the club's highest scorer for six consecutive seasons, his goals powering the FA Cup and Cup Winners' Cup triumphs under George Graham. It's a testament to the consistency and relentlessness of Wright's goal scoring that the three games in which he had not scored prior to the Bolton match in September 1997 constituted a worrisome drought for the 33-year-old.

An international break early that month proved timely as Wright found his scoring touch with two goals against Moldova at Wembley in a World Cup qualifier. Three days later, the drought was over; the record was his. As his heart swelled with pride, his mind raced back in time. He waved up to his older brother Morris, who was sitting in a director's box above the East Stand. His mother, Nesta, was there, too, the only time she'd ever gone to watch him play. He thought of

Rocastle, who was playing for Chelsea at this stage. It was three and a half years before Rocky would die tragically from non-Hodgkin's lymphoma at the age of 33. Wright thought back to how Rocastle had encouraged him to keep pursuing his football dream. He reflected, also, on his remarkable, unorthodox journey.

'People have to remember that I got to Arsenal at 28 years old,' Wright says. 'It was a dream come true. To be playing there with David Rocastle, with us coming from where we came from, was a dream in itself. I remember watching the news at six when I signed for Arsenal. They went on the roads around Highbury and Islington doing vox pops with people. They were saying, "We don't know what we've bought him for. We don't need him. We don't need a striker. We've got players who are scoring." They had been champions two out of the last three years, I was nervous enough as it was. Hearing the fans say "we don't really need him" kind of made me feel, "Oh, my God. I've got to do something extra special for these fans, because they don't even really want me here."

'I went from thinking, "Am I ever going to get a shirt? Am I going to start?" to going on to score the goals, getting to break the record, winning FA Cups, winning the European Cup Winners' Cup. I only now look back on that and think it was amazing. It was euphoric. It was unbelievable. I'd broken the scoring record, and it was *Arsenal*. I genuinely thought that 179 goals was nowhere near enough goals for a club of Arsenal's stature. My idea, when I did break it, was to take that to two hundred. I believed that a club of that stature should have a goal scorer in the 200s, 250s.

'When you're at Crystal Palace, if you lose, it's fine; if you win, it's brilliant. When you're at Arsenal, if you lose, there's nothing good about that. And if you win, you're expected to. I was so focused on doing that, it was only when I got up to about 150 that I started thinking about the record. To keep getting the goals, to get closer and closer and closer, and then to finally do it and to know that every goal after the 179 was a historic goal – it's *the* goal that's taken the record further – that was really quite hard to comprehend. It's not just a goal now. Every goal I score from 179 is historic. It was quite something. It was a really strange time, simply because of those feelings. It was almost a feeling of, "Well, I've done it." You can almost get into a false sense of security, thinking, "I've done it. It's done." It was a very strange time. But I can't explain how pleased and proud I was to be top goal scorer of that club. Even now, to be second to Thierry Henry, it's not bad. The time I held that record, it was the greatest time in my life, in respect of achievement. It's the greatest achievement of my life to do that.'

Wright ultimately notched a hat-trick against Bolton, securing a 4-1 victory and extending the top-scoring mark to 180 with a scuffed shot from the edge of the penalty area in the second half. Speaking post-match, Wenger shared Wright's belief that the striker was far from finished.

'It's a big moment for the club because Bastin's record has stood for such a long time and they have had some great strikers here since he set it,' he said. 'Maybe we'll have to wait another hundred years for Ian's record to be broken.

'I think now he will want to go for two hundred goals, or two hundred and ten. That's the way champions like him are.'

Wenger had substituted Wright eight minutes before the final whistle, allowing the striker to leave the pitch to a unanimous standing ovation from Highbury's home supporters. But if there was sentiment in the substitution, there was symbolism in it, too: on to take Wright's place in the Arsenal attack came Nicolas Anelka.

# 13

# A Wonderful Time

Arsène Wenger had first been alerted to a prodigious striker rising within Paris Saint-Germain's youth ranks while he was still in charge of Grampus Eight. Nicolas Anelka had made his senior debut at the Parc des Princes as a 16-year-old in February 1996 against Wenger's former club Monaco.

Despite being so young, the striker possessed unshakable belief that manifested as impatience. By the midway point of the 1996–97 season, he'd made 12 first-team appearances for PSG and was representing France at under-21 level, but he wanted more. He grew disgruntled at a perceived lack of opportunity under manager Ricardo Gomes, who'd replaced the man who'd given Anelka his debut the prior term, Luis Fernandez.

'Allegedly, the reason I wasn't playing was because I was a kid,' Anelka later said. "That was nonsense. So I went to see Ricardo and told him, "Coach, I want to play. Trust me." I wasn't asking to be the player the team had to be built around or anything. I just wanted to get a chance to prove my worth. Ricardo replied that I should wait a little, that I should be patient. This went on for three months, and still nothing happened. I couldn't take it any more.'

Wenger was in France attempting to close a deal for a young Auxerre player when he first met Anelka. Now in charge of Arsenal, an agent had made him aware of the striker's unhappiness in Paris.

Wenger travelled to PSG's training ground to speak with the wantaway player.

'He was a shy seventeen-year-old, but he seemed determined to leave and he told me he wanted to come to Arsenal,' Wenger wrote in his autobiography (*My Life in Red and White*, 2020). 'I returned to England and waited; I had the feeling he might change his mind and want to stay at PSG. But two months later, he was still totally determined. I came to an agreement with PSG and we bought him. He arrived in February 1997.'

Of course, it wasn't quite as simple as that. Arsenal exploited a loophole in the French football administration system to sign Anelka. The rules of the time dictated that young players could only sign their first professional contract with the club with whom they had been registered at youth level. It was a measure aimed to protect French clubs against having their top talents poached. In this instance, it backfired. Once Anelka refused to come to terms with PSG, he was prohibited from signing for another French club. But the advent of the Bosman ruling in 1995 – which granted freedom of movement for out-of-contract players – meant that there was nothing to prevent a foreign team from swooping. Arsenal snapped up Anelka and PSG raged. The Gunners were eventually forced to compensate the Parisians. A modest sum of £500,000* was settled upon, which amounted to just a tenth of the fee they'd received from West Ham for

---

* Anelka's £22.3 million sale to Real Madrid in 1999 not only represented a tremendous profit for Arsenal but it also covered the cost of the £12 million training ground, designed according to Wenger's specifications, that the club opened months later. Paris Saint-Germain would pay £20 million to re-sign Anelka a year later after his dismal single season at the Bernabéu yielded just two La Liga goals.

John Hartson the same month. The 17-year-old signed a six-year-deal at Highbury.

Wenger had teased the possibility of signing a new striker in the wake of Hartson's departure. AC Milan's Marco Simone was reportedly a target, likewise Ronald de Boer of Ajax. 'We will sign somebody for sure before the transfer deadline,' he said, 'and it could be a surprise name.' It was a surprise indeed when, rather than a proven scorer with European experience like those rumoured to be on the Gunners' wish list, it was an unknown teenager from the Parisian suburbs who arrived.

Although supremely confident in his ability as a footballer, Anelka was a deeply introverted character. He would later be nicknamed 'Le Sulk' by the British press for his constantly downcast demeanour and propensity to air grievances. When he first arrived in North London, he was shy to the point of being withdrawn. He knew little English and was entering an environment replete with grizzled veterans and long-time teammates. It could be an intimidating atmosphere for any newcomer, let alone one so young.

Anelka had no trouble expressing himself out on the training pitch, however. After an early session with the first team, Paul Merson remarked to teammates of how the new French kid reminded him of Ronaldo, the Brazilian reigning World Player of the Year who was starring for Barcelona at the time. And while Anelka's introduction into the first team would be gradual, he made an instant impact with the club's reserves.

'I played in Anelka's first game for the reserves,' remembers Adrian Clarke. 'He turned up in jeans and casual clothes for the game. No one knew who he was. He didn't speak a word of English. Geordie Armstrong, the reserve-team manager, introduced him to everyone.

He said, "This is Nico. He'll be joining us. He's on the bench today. He'll be coming on later in the game."

'He came off the bench at half time in this reserve game and exploded. His pace was on a different level to pretty much anything I'd seen growing up as a player. He was just so rapid. I think he won a penalty that day by getting to a ball he had no right to get to. You could tell right away that he was too good for the reserves. With him coming in after Patrick [Vieira], who was outstanding, both of whom nobody had known previously, it was like, "Wow, the bar has been set really high here." It set a benchmark for what the manager was looking for going forward. I don't mind admitting it made me doubt myself. Until that point, I'd always been wanted by Arsenal and one of the better young players. Then these two came along, who were a bit younger than me, and they were both better than me. It made me doubt whether I was going to be good enough to play for this team. Absolute game-changer, those two signings.'

Prior to the 1997–98 season, Arsenal's squad was small and ageing. Thirteen players had started fifteen or more Premier League games the previous term. Nine of those were aged thirty or older. Summer signings such as Matthew Upson, Luís Boa Morte and Alex Manninger sought to remedy this age issue by retooling the squad for the long term. With his speed when released behind opposition defences and his unerring finishing in front of goal, Anelka was the obvious heir to Ian Wright. The fact he was handed the number 9 jersey after Merson's departure suggests the confidence Wenger had in the youngster's readiness to star at the point of the Gunners' attack. But Anelka claims he always viewed himself as more of a Bergkamp type – a number 10 – preferring to receive the ball to feet and provide for others. It is interesting to note, then, that the French teenager's emergence in the Arsenal first team came as a stand-in for the Dutchman, playing alongside Wright in attack.

After four appearances off the bench in the final months of the previous season, Anelka's first start for the Gunners came on 16 September 1997, a UEFA Cup first-round fixture away to PAOK Salonika. Bergkamp's refusal to fly meant he was unavailable for the match in Greece, so Anelka was thrust into the line-up. Arsenal were beaten 1-0. Bergkamp returned to the team for the second leg at Highbury and scored the game's opening goal, but an eighty-seventh-minute equalizer from Zisis Vryzas meant the Gunners crashed out of Europe.

Wenger had planned to hand Anelka his first start sooner. Arsenal played Derby on the final weekend of the 1996–97 season. After the young striker had scored in three successive reserve outings the previous month, the manager was ready to promote him to the first-team line-up. But, on the eve of the campaign-closing fixture at the Baseball Ground, the Arsenal squad boarded the team bus to travel to the East Midlands and Wenger noticed Anelka was not among their number. He found the teenager in his room, packing his bags and preparing to return to France, frustrated at not having already been thrust into the first team.

'We had a long conversation that was to change everything,' Wenger said. 'I asked him not to give up yet. I told him he needed to carve out a place for himself with his playing skills, not with sudden bursts of brilliance, and not to run away at the first sign of difficulty. And I convinced him to stay. The next day, Paul Merson was injured ten minutes into the match. I brought Anelka on, and he became one of the men of the match. In the dressing room after our victory, I found him with a huge celebratory smile on his face. I told him never to forget what had just happened in only twenty-four hours.'

'Nico always had great belief in his ability,' says David Platt. 'When he came in as a youngster, a lot of it was, "Why am I not playing? I'm better than anybody here?" Many would term that as arrogance, and there was an aspect of arrogance in there, but it wasn't misplaced arrogance. Nico backed this up on the training pitch. And the person he had to displace [Ian Wright] was a bloody good goal scorer who wasn't doing anything wrong on the football pitch. So when you looked at Nic's ability, his speed and how he would frighten people, I think Nic came in and thought, "I should be playing, because I'm better than them, from my technical ability and my speed." Well that's fine, but the boy who's in your place at this time is scoring goals left, right and centre and doesn't deserve leaving out.

'Nico was a little bit sulky in that period. But his ability was never in question and the boys knew that. What you also had was a dressing room that was strong enough to accept that if somebody wants to be arrogant but can back it up, that's fine. That's more than fine. You be as arrogant as you want and back it up. That was a strong dressing room. Everybody had their own arrogance and none of it was misplaced. Arrogance can be a word that conjures up negatives. I'm not using it as a negative at all. It actually aided the dressing room massively that there was this sheer belief and total belief in itself as individuals and in its teammates.'

A second start arrived for Anelka on 1 November 1997, with the young striker this time deputizing for Bergkamp domestically for a trip to take on Derby County at their new Pride Park Stadium while the Dutchman began a three-match suspension. Arsenal were thrashed

3-0, ending what had been an unbeaten start to the Premier League season.

It had been an inauspicious start to Anelka's major first-team involvement. Yet Wenger elected to stick with the faltering Frenchman for the potentially pivotal visit of Manchester United eight days later. It was a bold decision, considering the Gunners had drawn a blank in their last three league outings, with goalless draws against Crystal Palace and Aston Villa prior to the Derby reverse. Critics had begun to question Wenger's wisdom in allowing John Hartson and Paul Merson to leave the club.

Ian Wright's record-breaking afternoon against Bolton had been followed by a pulsating 3-2 win over Chelsea at Stamford Bridge, with Nigel Winterburn netting a spectacular, match-winning 30-yard strike from the left in the eighty-ninth minute. 'I probably scored five or six like that every training session,' the full back laughs. 'Most people will know that I was probably one goal a season. On that day, it just fell into place. The ball came across to me. Dennis Wise slipped over and it just opened up. I decided to take it forward and I wasn't closed down. To be honest, I didn't realize it was so late into the game. It just sat up nicely when I was moving forward and I decided to hit it. I knew pretty quickly that it was going in. It was nice to get that goal so late in a London derby game. For me, not getting many goals, it was a great way to finish that game.'

A 2-2 draw away to Everton was then followed by a 5-0 demolition of plucky promoted side Barnsley at Highbury as Arsenal topped the table after ten games. United were second and something of a wounded animal, thanks to the shock retirement of their talismanic French forward Eric Cantona at the end of the previous campaign and the season-ending knee injury Roy Keane sustained in an October loss at

Leeds. The Gunners were briefly installed as title favourites with the bookmakers.

But Arsenal's dip in form prior to United's arrival at Highbury in November allowed the champions to regain top spot. The Red Devils had won three of their four league games since the start of October and had scored thirteen goals in their last two, with a 7-0 battering of Barnsley – poor Barnsley! – and a 6-1 drubbing of Sheffield Wednesday. Even at this early juncture, the title race was beginning to take on a familiar feeling of inevitability. A win in North London would put Alex Ferguson's side seven points clear.

'Even without Bergkamp we are capable of beating them,' Wenger insisted, 'and it would be a wonderful time to do so.'

It took Anelka less than seven minutes to make his mark. Collecting a loose ball on the left edge of the United penalty area, he shifted the ball on to his right foot, creating a yard of separation between himself and his nearest defender, Gary Neville, before rifling a low shot beyond Peter Schmeichel's dive and into the near corner of the goal. It was explosiveness and precision, attributes that would hallmark his game. Anelka had arrived.

'He tore Gary Neville to pieces, which was perfect from my point of view, because he was the enemy right back,' Dixon says of Anelka's instant impact against United. 'It's so much better on a match day when he's not playing against me and he's running against Gary. He was sensational. And it didn't matter that he wasn't the life and soul of the party and joining in with everyone.'

Anelka wasn't allowing the United backline to settle and he could have extended Arsenal's lead a couple of times in the first half. Perhaps exposing his inexperience, he scuffed a 20-yard shot after racing clear of Gary Pallister and then blazed a left-footed shot over the bar from 8 yards when picked out by David Platt.

It was Arsenal's other young Frenchman who put them 2-0 up in the twenty-seventh minute. When a corner kick was half-cleared towards the right corner of the United box, Vieira raced to meet it. With a swing of his telescopic right leg, he whipped a flat, swerving shot at goal that evaded Schmeichel's desperate swipe as it crashed into the net.

That, though, would be Vieira's last meaningful involvement in the game – in fact, of the next month of games.

'When Patrick scored, he did that ridiculous knee slide and actually banged his knee into my foot and did his knee ligaments,' Dixon says. 'I thought he was going to jump up and jump on to me. But he did this slide and his knee hit my foot. He went "Ugh!" And I went, "Are you all right?" He said, "I think I've just done my knee on your foot." I put him out for weeks.'

Vieira persevered until half time when he was replaced by Steve Bould. By then, United had drawn level. The architect of the away side's comeback was a familiar foe.

There was a sense of underwhelm among United fans when 31-year-old England striker Teddy Sheringham was signed in a £3.5 million deal from Tottenham to replace Cantona. The enigmatic Frenchman had been central to four Premier League title triumphs in his five years at Old Trafford. He had become an iconic figure at the club and the perception that United had attempted to replace him on the cheap only made his surprise retirement at the age of 31 all the more difficult to stomach. But Sheringham insists he felt no additional pressure in filling the Cantona-shaped void in United's attack. Filling big boots was nothing new.

'I'd followed Gary Lineker at Tottenham, Peter Beardsley for

England and Cantona at United,' he says. 'If these managers want you to play football for them, you've got to take the positive out of it and say, "Wow, I'm playing for a fantastic club and the manager wants me to play for them. Let's go and play."'

Just one goal from his first eight appearances for his new club did little to dispel the doubts. But by the time United, decked out in their blue third kit, turned up to Highbury in November, he had scored five goals in his last six games. In five years with Spurs, he'd managed just two goals against Arsenal. He matched that tally for his new club in 41 minutes.

His first goal came just six minutes after Vieira's. He escaped the attention of Gilles Grimandi and Dixon to nod a simple, 6-yard header beyond David Seaman from a Gary Neville cross. His second came with a greater degree of difficulty. When Ryan Giggs found him on the edge of the penalty area with a back-heel flick, Sheringham pivoted on his standing right leg and swept an instant, first-time finish across Seaman and into the bottom-right corner with his weaker left foot. The former Tottenham man had single-handedly extinguished Arsenal's lead by half time.

The United fixture offered what was to become a rare start for Platt. The summer arrival of Emmanuel Petit – who, like Bergkamp, was suspended for the United game – coupled with the tactical switch to 4-4-2 meant the former England captain was squeezed out of the Gunners' full-strength line-up. The previous season, he'd started twenty-seven times in the Premier League, coming off the bench just once. In 1997–98, he'd accumulate just 11 starts, supplemented by 20 substitute's appearances. It marked a new phase in the career of a veteran midfielder who, at 32, was already being linked with various managerial vacancies.

'It wasn't discussed with me,' Platt says of his changing role. 'That's Arsène. It didn't need discussing. It was pretty obvious. I knew that I wasn't the player I'd been, in terms of being able to get around the pitch. When I joined Arsenal, I had a knee injury after a few games. It was a minor knee injury that didn't go well in terms of my rehab and I finished up having a second operation on it. My knee was never the same again. It's never been the same since. My game was built a great deal on physicality. It was built a great deal on an abundance of energy, getting forward, being fitter than my rivals. And that, in many ways, had been taken away from me, so my game had to change.

'Because of my four years in Italy, I'd become much more tactically astute than I was when I left England. I wasn't the David Platt who was going to get you 15, 20 goals a season. That wasn't going to happen. If I got an opportunity, I'd score a goal, but it was more about coming on for the last 20, 25 minutes and making sure that the game was over. I guess that that's how Wenger saw me. I guess that he saw that he had somebody on the substitutes' bench who could go on and change the way the football match was going, in both a positive way and a destructive way – go and fill those holes. "We need a goal, David. Go on and maraud upfield." And I was able to seamlessly fit into the role.

'I had a knack – and I'd had it all my career – of understanding where a ball was likely to go. And not only that, I had an ability to have pictures in my mind and be able to execute those pictures of what's the best way to score.'

It was a knack that proved invaluable that Sunday afternoon at Highbury. The frantic, frenetic, four-goal first half gave way to a scrappy second period of few chances. The match lumbered towards a draw that both sides could have framed positively.

Then, in the eighty-third minute, Arsenal won a corner after

Schmeichel parried substitute Christopher Wreh's deflected effort. Nigel Winterburn jogged forward to take the set piece. Platt saw a picture.

Winterburn's left-footed delivery swung towards the penalty spot. Platt was already in motion. He reached the ball before his marker, David Beckham, glancing a header across Schmeichel and in at the far post. Wreh ought to have put the result beyond doubt in stoppage time, but the Liberian screwed wide from 6 yards after some excellent set-up play from Wright.

In the end, the game had been won by a midfielder who hailed from the Greater Manchester area and had been released by United as a teenager. With that flick of Platt's forehead, Arsenal recorded just their second victory over his former club in the Premier League era. They moved to within one point of the champions while eroding any semblance of an inferiority complex that might have taken hold over the past half a decade.

What's more, Arsenal's emergence as a serious contender in the Premier League reflected a cultural shift taking place in the nation in 1997. The 'Madchester' scene that had arisen in Manchester in the late 1980s, fuelled by indie-dance music and Ecstasy, had begun to decline by the mid-1990s. The Haçienda, the nightclub that served as the mecca of Madchester, closed in June of '97. The critical cachet of Oasis, the city's Britpop superstars, had dwindled when their third album, *Be Here Now*, was released in August to unflattering reviews. Just as the epicentre of 'Cool Britannia' had migrated south, Arsenal were the attractive coming force of English football.

'The film *Fever Pitch* came out in 1997,' says author and Arsenal fan Jon Spurling. 'It was a time when football was becoming cool to the middle class, and here you had Colin Firth – Mr Darcy – in a retro

Arsenal shirt. I remember walking to Highbury for the first game of the season and in one of the newsagents I saw the front cover of *Cosmopolitan*. There was something about Arsenal, so I opened it up. There was an article about the top ten coolest footballers in Britain. As I was growing up, Arsenal were certainly not cool. But now you had Petit with his ponytail. You had this manager who was faintly glamorous for the fact he'd managed abroad. You had Bergkamp, with all his Nordic blond cool. Arsenal were suddenly the in thing.

'But also at that time Islington was becoming cool. House prices were rocketing anyway. When Tony Blair became prime minister in '97, he flogged his house in Islington for an absolute packet. Suddenly Islington was the place to be and to go.'

And Arsenal were the club to watch. They were the best hope non-United football fans had of seeing the dominant goliath of the Premier League challenged and toppled. And they were doing so with an exciting, fast-paced and free-flowing style of play. Where once rival supporters derided 'Boring, boring Arsenal', neutrals were now bustling aboard the Wenger bus.*

The rising antipathy between the two clubs was evidenced at Highbury when both Schmeichel and Winterburn were struck by projectiles from the crowd. After the match, Ferguson conceded with a humble brag – that, while he was disappointed with the result, Arsenal's victory was good for the Premier League. 'It's unhealthy to keep reading in the papers that it's a one-horse race,' he said. The winning post was not yet in sight, but Arsenal had kept themselves within a head of the league leaders, just one point back. Wenger was right. It was, indeed, a wonderful time to beat them.

---

* Sorry.

'The way the game was set out – we scored first, then they got back into it – it was a real ding-dong battle,' Dixon says. 'To get one over on them in that type of way made us think, "Do you know what, we're on the level with them." It gave us probably that little bit of a gee-up that we needed from a belief point of view. In professional sport at that level, that can be the making or breaking of you. It doesn't matter how much talent you've got; you just need to believe that it's going to be OK and that what you've got going is good enough to beat the best, and they were the best. We were competing with them for a period of years. To put us on the same level as them, I think it really validated what Wenger was doing. And it was such a brilliant game, a classic; it had everything.'

'At the time, I don't think it felt like a significant result in terms of who would win the league, because there was still a lot of games to play,' adds Platt. 'I think what it probably did was say to the team, "Actually, we can compete against these."'

'When you beat one of the best teams, it gives you a massive boost,' Winterburn concludes. 'It was a big, big win for us.'

# 14

# A Winter of Discontent

Chris Birkett could scarcely believe what he was seeing. Ian Wright, stripped to his underpants, hanging out of the window to Highbury's first-team dressing room, berating a fan on the street below.

'It looked like he was shouting back at somebody who was shouting at him,' remembers Birkett, who was a journalist working as a producer for the newly launched BBC News 24 channel at the time but, as a lifelong Arsenal supporter, had attended the game in the capacity only of a fan. 'Rather than it being general abuse to everybody, it looked like he was going at one guy who was pointing back at him.

'I stopped to watch. I was standing next to two policemen. They looked at each other, then one got on his radio and said something about needing to go up to talk to Wright about what was going on, so one of the coppers went up into the Marble Halls. I stood there for a few minutes and Wright went back in. It only lasted a couple of minutes.'

It was a quirk of Highbury's quaint architecture that the red-rimmed swing windows of the dressing room opened out on to the post-match bustle of Avenell Road. More modern stadiums keep the players safely secluded from the public. Not Arsenal's old ground. Fans knew that they could be heard whenever those windows were open. Sometimes players would throw down scarves or socks as mementos after wins; on other occasions that spot on the street would serve as a prime location for a vociferous protest.

On this afternoon, it was the latter. It was 13 December and Arsenal had just been emphatically beaten 3-1 by Blackburn Rovers. Marc Overmars had given the Gunners a first-half lead, clipping the ball past Tim Flowers after Emmanuel Petit's low pass had torn asunder the visitors' backline. It was all downhill from there. The villain of the last Highbury meeting between the two sides, Chris Sutton, was booed throughout, but the England striker had his revenge, helping to create two goals for his team. By the final whistle, many Arsenal fans directed their boos towards the home team instead.

Sutton is more complimentary of Arsenal's efforts that afternoon. Buoyed by having pulled to within a point of league leaders Manchester United, he remembers reflecting on a hard-fought win over a top opponent ahead of the festive period.

'We were going well,' he says. 'Roy Hodgson had come in as manager and we went to Highbury and beat them 3-1. They had a hell of a team. That felt like a good victory against them because they were such a good team. They were a team who could compete physically, then they had the pace of Overmars, the brilliance of Dennis Bergkamp and Wright's finishing ability. We were flying at the time and thought we could go on and challenge. But when you look at that Arsenal team compared to us, they had much better balance. We had our Christmas party after that game; we stayed down in London. I can remember sitting in the dressing room afterwards and thinking, "Blimey, they're a proper team."'

Except Arsenal hadn't been playing like a proper team, a serious contender. They had not been able to build any momentum off the back of beating Manchester United at Highbury in November. The Blackburn defeat meant they'd won just two of their last eight Premier League matches. During that run, they were hampered by suspensions for

Bergkamp, Steve Bould and Emmanuel Petit, as well as injuries to Vieira and Overmars. But such absences could not excuse the drastic slip in the team's performance levels. Prior to the United win, they'd suffered a 3-0 battering away to Derby County in which Wenger's side were ripped to shreds by Dean Sturridge and Paulo Wanchope after Wright had crashed a first-half penalty against the crossbar. Then there was a 2-0 loss to Sheffield Wednesday – 'If you want to be a big team, you cannot give away goals like that,' Wenger said after Gilles Grimandi's sloppy pass gifted Andy Booth an opener at Hillsborough – followed by a 1-0 reverse against Liverpool at Highbury to close out November.

'As far as we are concerned the title is now just a dream,' said a downcast Wenger. 'Yes, it's possible for United to be caught, but I don't know who can catch them.'

Arsenal began December with a 1-0 win over Newcastle, with Wright scoring for the first time in two months, but that was followed by the nadir of the Blackburn defeat. And so the boos rained forth from the Highbury stands.

'It just felt like something was off with the team,' says the writer Tim Stillman, offering a fan's perspective. 'We'd won away at Newcastle the week before, so we were thinking, "OK, we've got the players back now, Ian Wright is back. Here we go." Then that Blackburn game was a real slap in the face. There was a lot of disgruntlement. We were sixth after that. Absolutely nobody was expecting a title challenge. It felt like we were back to where we were under Bruce Rioch.'

'It was one of those days where everything was going wrong,' adds another writer, Josh James, who was at Highbury that day. 'You started to think, "Maybe this isn't going to be our season." The atmosphere was one of frustration. We were well beaten and it felt like a low point.'

'I can't remember a previous game where the Wenger revolution had been booed,' adds Birkett. 'It was very discontented. We'd come off some pretty bad results, including a terrible result at Derby. Blackburn in those days were a contender, but in the second half we were just awful. I remember the booing at the end. A couple of scarves were lobbed off the East Stand on to the pitch. It was frustration.

'In the run-up to it, the game that really raised questions about Wenger in the minds of the fans had been going out of the UEFA Cup to PAOK Salonika in September. I date it back to that. I remember never having heard of this Greek team and they got a draw at Highbury. The atmosphere wasn't toxic, but there was rumbling discontent.'

After Wright had climbed back inside the dressing room to receive a dressing-down from the attendant police officers, Birkett turned and headed to the Highbury Barn for a post-match pint. He was halfway up the hill to the pub when his journalistic instincts kicked in.

'I thought, "Oh, actually, I think this is a story,"' he says. 'I rang up the news desk and said, "I've just seen Ian Wright have a row with a fan and I think the police have gone up to speak with him."'

The story circulated and the police warned Wright about his future conduct. The biggest news inside the dressing room, though, was that Arsenal were now ten points behind United. The fans were turning and doubts began to fester within the squad.

In the days after the game, Tony Adams met with Wenger at Sopwell House. The pair shared a typically frank conversation over cappuccinos.

'I invited my friends over to see you play,' Wenger said. 'And I think they were surprised because I had told them so much about you. They have not seen the best of Tony Adams and neither have I.'

The disconsolate captain was so unhappy with his performance against Blackburn, so distraught with his inability to match Sutton and co. physically due to a persistent ankle complaint, that he offered to quit the club.

Wenger rejected the idea and instead authorized some time off for the skipper. He'd fly to the Côte d'Azur in the new year for a change of scenery and some fitness work with Tiburce Darou, a French trainer recommended by Wenger. Meanwhile, Adams consulted with Wenger's go-to osteopath, Philippe Boixel, and even sought the counsel of Eileen Drewery, the 'faith healer' favoured by England manager Glenn Hoddle, in an effort to fix his troublesome ankle.

'Tony Adams didn't play again for a few weeks,' Ray Parlour remembers. 'Tony was struggling a little bit at that time, playing with a bit of an injury. That was the last straw. He said, "I can't play any more." But at Arsenal, November was always a bad month for us. I don't know why. November was a dodgy month.'

Not all of Arsenal's players were able to write off their period of poor form as easily as Parlour, though. Some were shaken by the fans' angry reaction at Highbury. 'That did hurt the players,' says Gary Lewin. 'That's where Arsène was good. He'd individually go round and talk to the players and say, "Look, how you win them over is performing. We will turn this around. We will perform."'

At 9am most mornings, Wenger would place a call to his confidant and France-based scout Damien Comolli. The two might chat about a prospect they had their eye on or break down the previous weekend's match. When Wenger phoned the Monday after Arsenal's shattering loss to Blackburn, Comolli feared the manager was calling to say he'd been sacked.

'But he was so calm,' Comolli says. 'Typical Arsène: the more difficult a situation is, the calmer he is.

'You know he's going to find a solution.'

# 15

# Song of Himself

*Do I contradict myself?*
*Very well then I contradict myself,*
*(I am large, I contain multitudes.)*

Walt Whitman's 1855 poem 'Song of Myself' is a sprawling celebration of individuality, exploring themes of democracy, sexuality, spirituality and nature. It is regarded as one of the most influential works of American poetry ever written and has served as an enduring cultural reference point ever since its publication. And in that verse from the penultimate section of the 1,300-line epic, Ian Wright might have recognized a slice of himself in the winter of 1997.

He was large. He contained multitudes.

One of those multitudes – perhaps the most prevalent – was his humour. His booming cackle and gleaming smile illuminated the Arsenal squad's shared spaces. He could make monotonous coach journeys a riot, training sessions a joy and tense match days a laugh-filled delight.

His pranks and jokes were numerous and are best recounted by his teammates and by Wright himself.

**Ian Selley:** 'We used to get the Arsenal bus – it was like a half-size coach – at Sopwell House. We'd have breakfast there, then go across to training. Arsène hadn't been there very long at the time. One of the kit managers was the bus driver. The players were waiting on the bus while the driver loaded the kit. We were pushed for time to get to the training ground. I remember looking across and David Seaman was sitting there, going through his phone. Then Wrighty started shouting and hollering – 'Let's get a move on!' The kit man was farting around, moving stuff around. Wrighty got into the driver's seat of the coach and started up the bus. He was trying to jam the gear stick into first gear. Sopwell House is on a tight country road, with a golf course and fence on one side and a big hedge on the other. When cars came the other way, you had to pull over. Wrighty jammed it into first gear and started belting down the country lane. I remember standing up and looking behind the coach and the kit box had come out the back. The kit man was running behind the bus. I looked across to David Seaman and he was crouching beneath two seats, trying to stay low. We were tearing down this road. We didn't get very far before a car came the other way and he panicked. He started to stall the bus and basically ripped all the fence panels from the golf course for about 200 yards. He destroyed the bus, but I don't think Arsène found out. The kit man took the blame and Wrighty paid for the damage.'

**Ian Wright**: 'Crashing the bus, it was so funny. We used to go from St Albans to Colney, because the training ground burned down. We were waiting for the driver. Everybody was on the bus. I remember just jumping in and just turning it on. Everyone was saying, "No, Wrighty, no!" I just started driving around like crazy. Bam! Smashed it. It was so funny.'

**Adrian Clarke**: 'He was a real mickey taker. He used to grab my phone and talk to my girlfriend. Or if I was on the phone to my parents, he'd be making noises in the background. He used to make up nicknames for people. I was quite clean-cut. I used to do extra studies and things. He said, 'You're like a reverend.' And it stuck – "Hey, Rev, Rev!"'

**Lee Dixon**: 'He always used to try and get at the opposition. We were playing a lower-league team in the FA Cup at Highbury one year. I always used to go out third – the captain, Tony Adams, Dave Seaman and then me in the tunnel. Wrighty always used to go behind me. It was a bit of a ritual. The Highbury tunnel is really narrow. Before the game, the team sheet goes up. We didn't know any of the other team's players. We were elitist – "We don't look at *them*." Pat Rice was saying, "There's a kid making his debut." I think he was 18 years of age. Wrighty went, "What's his name?" And I knew exactly what he was doing. Pat said his name. Wrighty said, "What number is he?" Pat said, "Number 11." Wrighty goes, "Oh, right . . ." I shouted across, "Wrighty, leave him alone." He said, "No, it's my job." I said, "It's the FA Cup third round. It's a big day for him. He's playing at Highbury. Just leave the kid. Give him five minutes, yeah?"

'I knew this lad was a left winger, so he was playing against me. We're lining up in the tunnel and as the other team came and stood next to us, lo and behold, this bloke was fourth in line, next to me and Wrighty. He's standing there, he's 18 and he's absolutely shitting himself; he's shivering. Wrighty's standing next to him. The kid's looking around, and Wrighty looks at him. I went, "Wrighty, leave him." He said, "I'll just have a little go." So he goes, "All right?" The lad looks at Ian and Ian goes, "Oh, my God. Just look at you." So the lad looks down at his kit. His shorts are too big and his shirt is hanging over his hands, he's got dirty boots on. He went, "Just take a look at yourself. Look yourself up and down." Then Wrighty does this pose. He's got oil all on his legs and he's pulled his shorts up high so his legs look bigger. He looks at this kid and he goes, "Just look at you and now look at me. What chance have you got when we get out there if you look like that and I look like this?" And this kid melted in front of our eyes. We went out and I think the kid went off after about 20 minutes, got subbed. I looked over at Wrighty and said, "You did that." He just said, "It's my job, Dicko. I want to win the game." It was cruel to the limit.'

**Selley**: 'He would never shut up, basically. He'd be on the go all the time. I remember one preseason in Norway. George Graham had gone to meet some sponsors or something, so Stewart Houston was in charge of the squad while we went on a boat trip. It was a night out for us. We went down to the harbour and there was a bungee jump at the harbour. Wrighty was trying to get up on it and Stewart was trying to hold him back. He got up there and got on it, and when he jumped down he pulled his groin. He ended up missing a couple of games over there. He would do whatever he wanted to do.'

**David Platt**: 'I'd been in an England dressing room with Wrighty, so I knew his humour, I knew what he wanted to do, how he wanted to play. I remember him scoring a goal early in the 1995–96 season at Everton. I'd scored as well. I remember shouting in his ear as he went down, deliberately screaming in his ear. But unfortunately I scored again the week after and he remembered it and did the same to me.'

**Alex Manninger**: 'He was the DJ before the games. On a long trip, being demotivated, tired, he was the first to say, "Come on, lads, it's a game of football; let's have fun." He was the guy who motivated everyone. He was the second motivator, after Arsène Wenger. Ian Wright was the one before the game with the stereo, making some noise.'

**Wright**: 'I was just being myself. I just did stuff. It was never a problem for me, because when I put my boots on, when we got going, there's no one more serious. I do believe that we were very fortunate to be footballers, being in that kind of environment. But it doesn't mean that it has to be that regimented all the time. I had fun. I went through a phase of just frightening people, for example. Jumping out on people. Everybody was petrified of who is going to get frightened next. It's just that kind of thing to lighten the mood. I was always like that. It wasn't a conscious thing. I was just that kind of rogue. But they knew that when I played, there were no prisoners. I suppose that's why I was accepted, because they knew that when I played, there was no joking.'

**Selley**: 'I remember one time seeing him rollerblading through the car park at Highbury and into the Marble Halls. It was a European game and he was coming down on these rollerblades, smashing into walls. That's just how he was. It was part of his character.'

**Wright**: 'The rollerblading thing came about because I'd bought some really cool rollerblades. You'd have thought that the one place you don't do it is the club, simply because of the stipulations in our contracts that prevented us doing dangerous things and risking injury. When you read the contract, they're just happy with you driving, just so you can get to training. You're not meant to do anything else apart from that. You're not meant to even *run* outside of Arsenal's time. I thought, "I don't want no one seeing me doing this, so I'm going to do it on the car park at Arsenal," because it was amazing down there, very smooth, really nice. I thought, "Yeah, that's the place to do it." I'd go there an hour before everyone normally arrived for the game, do some rollerblading.

'I remember thinking to myself, "I wouldn't mind just rollerblading through the Marble Halls." That's never been done before and it will never be done again. But I have done it. I have rollerbladed in the Marble Halls. I was going to do it, then I was going to take them off, give them to Vic Akers and get them after the game and go home. The one person you don't want to be in the Marble Halls at that time is

Arsène Wenger, and he was there. He said, "It's not acceptable." I had to apologize and that sort of stuff. That might have been the last straw for him. For where Arsène Wenger was going, he was getting ready to take the guys into a mindset, and the way he wanted it to be was a lot more serious than maybe I was.'

Wright's playfulness might have been a contributing factor in Wenger looking ahead to a near future without the club's record scorer as a key figure, but it was not the only one. In his post-playing career as a television pundit, Wright is regarded warmly for his sage and honest insights on the game, for his gushing joviality and for the firm stances he has taken in support of social justice causes. Throughout the 1990s, though, the public sentiment towards Wright was more complex and, often, adversarial.

His smile was infectious and his sense of mischief was endearing, but he was also hot-tempered and volatile. His rap sheet of indiscretions and FA charges reads almost as long as the episodes of his escapades.

**November 1991**: Fined £1,500 for spitting and making obscene gestures at Oldham fans.

**December 1992**: Hit with a three-match ban after TV replays catch him punching Tottenham's David Howells.

**July 1993**: Fined £5,000 for making an obscene gesture at assistant referee Brian Wigginton during the FA Cup final two months earlier.

**October 1993**: Apologized to assistant referee Richard Saunders, a thalidomide victim, after comments directed towards the official during a match against Norwich.

**September 1994**: Fined £1,000 for calling referee Robbie
    Hart a 'muppet' and £750 for spitting at a female steward at
    Queens Park Rangers.

**December 1995**: Apologized to the FA after calling referees
    'incompetent little Hitlers'.

**January 1996**: Sheffield United player Roger Nilsen accused
    Wright of spitting in his face.

**October 1996**: Charged with misconduct by the FA after
    calling David Pleat, the Sheffield Wednesday manager, a
    'pervert'.

**July 1997**: Fined £15,000 by the FA for recurring misconduct,
    relating to remarks made against a referee in a game versus
    Blackburn and gestures towards opposition fans during a
    match against Coventry.

**August 1997**: Reported to the FA for his involvement in a
    fracas during a 3-3 draw with Leicester.

**December 1997**: Spoken to by the police after a row with
    Arsenal fans outside Highbury following a 3-1 defeat to
    Blackburn.

That most recent indiscretion – and perhaps one or two of the others – could be attributed in no small part to another prominent facet of Wright's personality: his sensitivity.

'My feelings are always close to the surface,' he says. 'Even when I was at my pomp, when I was at my peak, when I started, my feelings are always close to the edge. Always. I'm going to let people know what I'm feeling.'

'I can't tell you what a great bloke Ian was,' says Clare Tomlinson, the club's press officer at the time. 'There wouldn't be an autograph unsigned. In fact, there were a couple of members of the squad who would wait until Ian was out there signing autographs and then run behind him to get on the bus, so they didn't have to do any.

'That's why he took it so personally when the fans turned, because he gave so much. He was volatile, sensitive and he got upset very easily by things, but that was just his personality. He was also generous and kind and just loved football and appreciated it because he'd started so late.'

'Wrighty is either bubbly, happy or he's the opposite,' Dixon says. 'There's no in between with Ian. He's very hyper and very upbeat most of the time, but when he has his lows, he has big lows.

'There were times in that season where he dipped. It must have been difficult.'

The Blackburn game – individually and collectively – was certainly a low. And one made all the more stark for the fact it followed swiftly after two of the most fulfilling moments of Wright's career.

After the elation of breaking Arsenal's all-time scoring record in September, the following month brought his finest moment in an England shirt. With Glenn Hoddle's men needing only a draw away to Italy to secure qualification for the 1998 World Cup and with star striker Alan Shearer injured for the trip to Rome, Wright, less than a month shy of his thirty-fourth birthday, was to make his fifteenth international start. He led the line valiantly, harrying and tiring out a star-studded Italian defence that included Fabio Cannavaro, Alessandro Nesta and Paolo Maldini. He almost scored late on, too, striking the post after dribbling around goalkeeper Angelo Peruzzi. The game finished goalless. Although he had not added to his tally of nine England goals, he'd played a crucial role in earning the pivotal point and sending the Three Lions through to France 98.

'That is the greatest football match I've ever played,' Wright says.

'I remember Alan Shearer was injured. I remember joining up with the squad and we were playing little eight-a-side games. I kept flicking it first time and Glenn Hoddle went mad. He slaughtered me in front of everyone, saying, "Stop flicking it. Hold it. We need to keep the ball." That is when I knew I was playing. Glenn Hoddle pulled me and said, "It's not the strength of your game but you can do it. You'll frighten them in behind but you're going to have to keep the ball. I want you to move them all over the place." I almost scored at the end. That would have rounded it off as the best game I ever played in. It was my best-ever 90 minutes.'

Wright returned to club duty and slumped into a six-game scoring drought. Then came the devastating Blackburn loss. In the days after the match, Everton, Middlesbrough and Benfica – who were managed by former Liverpool midfielder Graeme Souness at the time – lodged bids for the Gunners' number 8. 'It took Arsenal 40 years to find a goalscorer like him,' Wenger said in dismissal of the exit rumours, 'and maybe there will never be a true replacement.' Yet Wright could see not only his shrinking future as an Arsenal player but also his footballing mortality.

What cut Wright deepest about the fans' reaction after the Blackburn game was that it reflected his fears back at him. His body was beginning to break down. Knee and hamstring injuries would severely limit his opportunities in the second half of the season. He had already begun to think ahead to life after football, laying the groundwork for a career in television with a guest appearance as host of the BBC's iconic music show *Top of the Pops** and as an interviewee on the chat

---

\* The episode Wright presented, on 28 February 1997, saw him introducing live performances by the Bee Gees, Prince and the Spice Girls.

show *Clive Anderson All Talk*. The memory of walking off the pitch to a standing ovation after breaking the club's all-time scoring record just two months earlier suddenly felt distant. And in the young man who took his place that afternoon, Wright saw a bright Arsenal future that did not include him.

'When Nicolas Anelka came in, obviously being 17, you're not instantly worried, simply because he's 17,' he says. 'You think maybe he's going to take a couple of years, so you're fine. And then when I saw Nicolas play, I knew time was short. You can't hold back that kind of talent, that kind of ability. I didn't know much about him from France, but when you know what you know about him now, he was "Le Prodigy". He was in the same place as Thierry Henry and David Trezeguet, all of those unbelievable players. He was the one that they thought was going to be the most successful one.

'I remember Paul Merson saying to me, after he'd played with him in the reserves, that Anelka was the closest thing to the Brazilian Ronaldo that he'd ever seen. It made me realize that I've got to maintain a standard, because I'm not going to be able to hold this guy off for much longer. In the end it came to be. I got injured in that season. Nicolas was just phenomenal. When I saw him, my first impressions were, "The end is nigh." And it wasn't, "Oh, my God, I'm gutted." It was, "Oh, my God, Arsenal fans don't realize what they've got." When Nicolas came in, I'm thinking, "This guy is going to be the one. He'll break this scoring record, no problem."

'I was confident we could get the fans back on side, because what you find is that when you're doing well, they'll be fine again. George Graham used to say, "Don't worry about the fans. They'll always come back on side when you're doing well. Don't worry about that." But what you want from the fans, and what I was angry about and showed my dislike for what they were doing, was when you're in moments like that, you need them more. I think the reason why they were being like that, especially with me, is because they knew Anelka was there. That's one of the reasons why I was upset, more than anything else. Some of the things that they would shout, you could hear that they'd had enough of my antics. They were starting to lose patience. And the reason they were losing patience is because they saw that there was somebody in the wings that could probably come through and do the business. That was my relationship for the whole of that season with them.'

> *Who has done his day's work? who will soonest be through with*
>     *his supper?*
> *Who wishes to walk with me?*
>
> *Will you speak before I am gone? will you prove already too late?\**

---

\* 'Song of Myself', Walt Whitman (1892).

# 16

# Blackout

Precisely 13 seconds of the second half had elapsed when the Selhurst Park floodlights went out. The Wimbledon and Arsenal players were ushered from the pitch as engineers struggled to resolve the issue.

Back in the away dressing room, Arsène Wenger had stayed behind when his players trotted out for the second period while he used the toilet. After exiting the bathroom, he was puzzled to see his squad returning.

When the perplexed manager asked what was happening, Ray Parlour couldn't resist the opportunity to play an impertinent prank on the man he'd nicknamed 'Clouseau' after the clumsy detective from the *Pink Panther* movies.

'Zehr is a berm in ze stand,' he blurted, summoning his best impersonation of Peter Sellers as the inept French police inspector.

'What did you say, Ray?' Wenger said, startled.

'Erm, we should be winning this game,' the midfielder improvised.

'We'd just watched that film on the coach,' Parlour says. 'We were watching it on the way to the game. All the French lads at the front of the coach were going, "What's this rubbish? We don't want to watch this." All the English guys at the back were laughing.

'The lights went out that night, we came into the changing room. Arsène Wenger was in the toilet. It was behind a big post at Selhurst Park. Tony Adams was sitting next to me. Wenger said, "What is this?"

I don't know why I said it, but I just said it. I could see Tony Adams going, "You idiot." All the other staff were holding it in, going, "Please don't laugh."'

The level of their performance against Blackburn, and the fans' reaction to it, had shaken Arsenal's players. On the Monday morning after the match, they decided to call a meeting at Sopwell House to clear the air and find a way forward. Their season had reached an obvious crossroads. A campaign that had begun so positively had rapidly descended. If anything was to be salvaged from it, the Blackburn defeat had to serve as a wake-up call.

When the players gathered at the hotel, a frank exchange of views proceeded. Fingers were pointed, blame thrown and one or two harsh home truths expressed. The key bone of contention was aired by the members of the backline – David Seaman, Tony Adams, Martin Keown, Steve Bould, Lee Dixon and Nigel Winterburn. The veteran defenders felt they were not being adequately shielded, that the central midfield pairing of Patrick Vieira and Emmanuel Petit was too often leaving them exposed and overstretched. 'You haven't got a clue what your job is,' the French duo were told. 'We need some protection. We're not getting any cover from you.'

'I remember us losing the game and it being almost like a crisis meeting after the game – "That's not acceptable. We've dropped our standards,"' Lee Dixon says. 'It was the culmination of a bit of poor form and us realizing we needed to do something about it. That was another plus of that season, that you've got enough about you as a team to do something about it. There's loads of times playing in a side where you might say, "We need to do this, we need to do that," but we're not really capable; we haven't got the quality, we haven't got the mindset. So I think we knew, from what had gone before that period, that we did have the capability, but you have to sort of shake yourself out of it and go, "All right, let's go again." We were so far behind United and we needed to go on a run to catch them up. That was testament to the mentality of the team.'

'We were well behind Man United,' Parlour says. 'Man United, with the team they had, you're thinking, "They can't throw it away now." We still had to win our games as well. At one stage it looked impossible. I'm sure the bookmakers would have had Man United massive odds-on favourites to win the league. But there was a lot of belief in the team, a lot of winners in the team from the famous back six, as I call them. They'd been there and won championships before. Lee Dixon, Winterburn, Bouldy – all them guys had won trophies. So we knew you never give up, but it was always going to be a daunting task to get back into the title race.'

Arsenal's next match, and their first opportunity to right the ship and banish their barren winter form, was away to Wimbledon on 22 December. The game was scoreless when the floodlights failed early in the second half. Engineers worked to restart them and, 12 minutes later, the players were back out on the pitch, going through a swift warm-up routine before the fixture could resume. But then the lights went out again and did not come back on. The match was postponed and rescheduled for later in the season.

The 22,832 paying fans inside Selhurst Park trudged home disappointed. Some 6,500 miles away in Malaysia, members of an illicit betting syndicate celebrated a reported six-figure pay-out. This was the third Premier League fixture of the 1997–98 season to be scuppered by faulty floodlights. The elaborate scam run by Fast East betting fixers was scuppered two months later when the technician who had been bribed to ensure another blackout, this time in a match between Charlton and Liverpool, confessed the plan to a colleague who then informed the police. Four people – two Malaysians, a Chinese man and Roger Firth, the Charlton security supervisor – were jailed for between 18 months and 4 years.

The scandal had robbed Arsenal of the season-turning reset they'd hoped to spark in the aftermath of the Blackburn game. In the event, it was likely a blessing in disguise for the Gunners.

'I was at that game,' says Arsenal fan and writer Tim Stillman. 'The first half of that game was played and Arsenal were terrible. You got the sense this was going to be a nil-nil or a one-all draw. I think any team that want to challenge for the league needs these little moments of luck along the way. People don't quite realize how important this moment was.'

Two days later, at the Café de Paris in London, Arsenal held their team Christmas night out. Thanks to Adams's newfound sobriety, it was a less raucous affair than it might have been in years past. In lieu of sinking several pints of Guinness, the skipper reiterated the grievances aired at the Sopwell House showdown the previous week, this time going directly to Wenger to spew his disgruntlement at the protection he felt the midfield owed the backline.

'He listened to me,' Adams later said. 'Obviously, he made his own decisions after I'd said my piece, but he was very sympathetic to his players' point of view. He was very approachable; much more so than Bruce Rioch before him. That day, he took all of our opinions into consideration. I told him what I thought, and that helped us build a more honest relationship.'

Arsenal's fight to save their season began on Boxing Day. Leicester

City were the visitors to Highbury. The home side's display was still some stretch short of their early-season best, and an Emile Heskey header against the post at 0-0 and later a David Seaman mistake to allow Neil Lennon to score with 13 minutes to play betrayed a nervous tension among the Arsenal ranks. But David Platt's glanced header from a Dennis Bergkamp free kick and an own goal from Leicester captain Steve Walsh were enough to endure through the drama of the Foxes' late rally.

Arsenal then closed out the year against Tottenham at White Hart Lane. With Wright suspended after collecting his fifth yellow card of the season against Blackburn, Anelka started and hit the post after half an hour. The Gunners had to settle for a 1-1 draw, though, with Parlour's deflected strike equalizing in the second half after Allan Nielsen had given Spurs a lead in the first period. Any disappointment at not extracting full bragging rights from the North London derby was mitigated by the fact the result, coupled with a win for struggling Everton, meant Tottenham slipped to nineteenth in the table. Hoping to emulate Arsenal's success with a foreign coach, Spurs had appointed the Swiss Christian Gross in November. He would last less than a year in the role.

So Arsenal began 1998 still in sixth place and 12 points (albeit with a game in hand) behind Manchester United. But their slowly improving form meant the new year brought renewed hope.

'You're always trying to believe that the next result is the most important,' says Nigel Winterburn. 'I think we had a few injuries in that period. For me, I'm always trying to focus on the next game. Form is temporary. The next game is the most important. If you win it, it's only one game but you're on a winning run. We were struggling to get anything going. You would've thought that the Manchester United game in November was the springboard forward, but it wasn't. Then you've got to hope that you can turn things around quickly.

'I think ours started because we had the game called off against Wimbledon because of the floodlights. We got back to our early-season form. I was hoping that that middle section of five or six games was a bit of a blip.

'Once we got back on a winning run, we were pretty much unstoppable.'

# 17

# With Blinded Eyes

Emmanuel Petit was a couple of months shy of his twenty-seventh birthday when he signed for Arsenal, an established international for France and entering the peak of his football career. Playing in England was the fulfilment of an ambition he'd held since childhood. Growing up in Dieppe, a small fishing town on France's north coast, dreams of a life of fame and glory just the other side of the Channel were inspired by fiction.

'I read a comic book,' he explains. 'The hero was a skinny kid who lived on the streets, but he was so talented that he became a star in English football.'

Although he shared the ambition of the story's protagonist, Petit couldn't relate to the hardship of the main character as he devoured the pages of the comic. As a small child, he'd spend weekend afternoons watching his father, an accomplished amateur footballer, play on the local pitches. At home, he'd kick around with his two older brothers, perfecting the skills that were to fuel his football dream – and drive his mother mad as he crashed into furniture at the same time. He signed for Monaco's academy in his mid-teens. He was tall, blond, handsome and had the world at his feet.

Until his world crashed down.

Petit was 18, weeks away from penning his first professional contract, and playing for Monaco's youth team when his father received an earth-shattering phone call. Petit's eldest brother, Olivier, just 21 at the time, had suffered an aneurysm during a football match in Dieppe. Petit's parents were visiting him in Monaco, but the middle brother, David, had been playing in the same game back home. Olivier was rushed to hospital, but he died shortly after.

Following Olivier's death, Petit admits he 'hated everything to do with football' and 'lived a life of debauchery'. He came close to quitting the game. Football held too much associative pain, a feeling he expressed poetically in his 2015 autobiography *Franc-Tireur*: 'The theatre of our joys then became the symbol of our mourning.'

He persisted, even breaking into the Monaco first team shortly after his family tragedy. But Petit believes it took him three years to rediscover his love for the game and his motivation to manifest his long-held dream. That was when, aged just 20, he overheard a group of Monaco fans calling him a 'has-been'. Rather than shrink in the face of the criticism, he redoubled his commitment to the game. He soon established himself as a fixture of the first team at the Stade Louis II and earned a first call-up to the national team.

By the time he arrived in England in the summer of 1997, he'd faced, fought and overcome harsh adversity. He was hardened and ready to test himself anew.

Yet, while he settled quickly in London in respect of his personal life and living arrangements, Petit admits he endured a trickier assimilation to the bustle of Premier League play than he'd anticipated.

'I needed to improve my English,' he says of his early months as an Arsenal player. 'I only knew the basic, school English – "How are you? It's raining today." Tourist things. After a couple of months, I realized that I could have a conversation with the English players, and that it was more easy for me in terms of communications. I really loved my time in England, I really loved living in London; it's a city I always love to come back to. I had no trouble at all setting up myself with my family, with all the traditions, the culture. That was not a problem at all.

'It was more on the pitch I had some trouble in the beginning. I remember a game away at Southampton. I remember at half time. I'd received a big kick on the knee and I was bleeding. I remember saying to Arsène after the game that I was a little bit down. I said, "Sometimes I have the feeling that we don't play football here; it's only a battle on the pitch. The fans love it, most of the players love it, but I want to put the ball on the ground. I want to play proper football. With our mental strength and the physical strength we have in the team, I think if we put the ball on the ground we can play differently, because most of the players up front and in midfield are foreigners. We have the back four of typical English guys. This is our strength. But we need to play proper football on the ground. I'm tired and fed up of seeing the ball in the air all the time."'

Petit's frustration peaked on 26 October when, seven minutes from the end of a 0-0 draw with Aston Villa at Highbury, he placed his hands on referee Paul Durkin. The Frenchman was sent off, incurring a three-match suspension. Wenger protested that Petit had not intended to push the official, but the manager's complaints fell on deaf ears. The midfielder's ban was later extended by a further match, with the FA deeming his actions to constitute misconduct.

His return from suspension coincided with the Gunners' worst form of the season, with the ponytailed playmaker present for December's home defeats to Liverpool and Blackburn.

Then came the turning point. After listening to the concerns and criticisms of his colleagues during the team's showdown talks at Sopwell House, Petit rose to the challenge.

The Gunners grew slowly into the new year at first. After a shock 0-0 draw in the FA Cup third round at home to First Division strugglers Port Vale, who were in the midst of an eight-game losing streak prior to their Highbury visit, Wenger admitted he had expected more from Nicolas Anelka. The teenage striker deputized for Ian Wright in attack but had not scored since his maiden Arsenal goal against Manchester United in November. 'It is not just Anelka's fault that we did not score,' the manager said, 'but he has not produced as much as I hoped he would.'

Wenger's side required a penalty shoot-out to overcome Port Vale in the replay, a midweek fixture that was sandwiched between a narrow 2-1 victory over Leeds United at Highbury, in which Marc Overmars scored both of Arsenal's goals, and a 2-2 draw away to Coventry. In the latter match, Patrick Vieira was sent off after his 'foul and abusive language' earned him a second booking. The lanky midfielder had just conceded a costly second-half penalty, which Dion Dublin duly converted, when referee Steve Lodge deemed his vociferous – and presumably expletive-laden – protest intolerable. It was Vieira's eighth yellow card of the season and the ninth red of Wenger's 16 months in charge. Arsenal's shabby disciplinary record had begun to garner criticism in the press. In an effort to foster an improvement in this area, Wenger levied Vieira with a fine of one week's wages, costing the player around £10,000. The efficacy of the fine was made questionable by Vieira's second sending-off of the season a month later, as Arsenal were eliminated from the League Cup by Chelsea at the semi-final stage.

By then, though, their Premier League form had been restored. An unbeaten start to 1998 in league action extended right through February. They hammered Southampton 3-0 at Highbury on

31 January, with Anelka emphatically ending his goal drought by scoring for the second successive game. It was a goal laid on a platter for the Frenchman by Dennis Bergkamp, who himself had rediscovered his best fettle following a middling mid-season. After going eight games without a goal, the former Inter and Ajax star embarked on a run of six strikes in ten games. Hamstring trouble afflicted Ian Wright, but Arsenal did not miss their greatest goal getter. Anelka and Bergkamp formed a tandem that was beginning to look even more deadly than Wright's relationship with the Dutchman had been.

'As a strike partner, Nicolas was probably the best I've had at Highbury in terms of understanding,' Bergkamp said in 2002. 'That's quite a plaudit when you understand all the partners I've had here, from Ian Wright and John Hartson through to Thierry Henry and even Francis Jeffers.

'The way Nicolas played suited me perfectly because he was always looking to run forward on goal. That made it easy for me to predict what he wanted and to know instinctively where he would be on the pitch. That directness was just right. Nicolas was focused on heading for goal and scoring. He loved having the ball played for him to run on to and going one on one with the keeper. That made for a successful and enjoyable partnership which I think is reflected in the statistics.'

The pair were showing they could create for others, too. As the Arsenal players were boarding the team coach to head north for an FA Cup encounter with Middlesbrough at the Riverside Stadium that reunited the club with former Highbury hero Paul Merson, Tony Adams, preparing for his first game back after his mid-season sabbatical, paused next to Bergkamp before he continued on his way to the back seats.

'You've been over here two and a half years, Dennis,' the captain said. 'Isn't it about time you won something? It would be a shame not to with your ability.'

Perhaps inspired by the skipper's words come kick-off, Bergkamp combined with Anelka in midfield to release Overmars to score after less than two minutes. Anelka then provided another early goal, this time for Parlour, before Merson reminded the Gunners of his gifts with a goal in the second period that he celebrated vigorously, even though it was not enough to prevent Arsenal's passage to the fifth round. At that stage, Crystal Palace were the opponents and, after a scoreless first leg, Anelka and Bergkamp shared the goals once more for a 2-1 victory in the replay at Selhurst Park.

In the league, Chelsea were vanquished by a brace from the young midfielder Stephen Hughes before Gilles Grimandi's first goal for the club – a delightful, looping volley – was enough to score another win over Palace. The latter result took Arsenal up to third in the table. They were still 12 points adrift of Manchester United, but they had three games in hand over the champions and momentum behind them.

There was minor disappointment to begin March as, with Arsenal in such form, a 0-0 draw away to West Ham felt like two points dropped rather than one gained. Next up, on 11 March, was a trip to Selhurst Park to take on Wimbledon, the rescheduled fixture after December's floodlight failure. The Dons were this time confronted with a different, more confident Arsenal.

'The first game that was postponed due to the floodlight failure in December, that was probably the right time to play them,' says Wimbledon striker Marcus Gayle. 'The fixture was rearranged for March and once a team gets its head of steam, especially with the talent they had in that squad, there was only going to be one outcome.'

The outcome: one-nil to the Arsenal, this time with Christopher

Wreh notching his first goal of the season. The diminutive relative of George Weah providing the decisive strike was a theme that would recur as the season progressed. Another clean sheet meant the Gunners had not conceded a single goal in their last five Premier League fixtures, a run encompassing four wins and a draw.

'You feel a buzz around the place,' physio Gary Lewin says of Arsenal's relentless new year form. 'You get this momentum going. You can't wait for the next game. You're looking forward to the next game all the time. You don't want the games to stop. When you get injuries to key players and things like that, if you're not on a good run it affects everybody; when you're on a good run, it's, "Oh, don't worry. We're going to win this game anyway."'

If there was a sense of inevitability towards upcoming matches within the Arsenal camp as the Gunners hit their stride, it was a feeling of futility with which their opponents were often struck. In stark contrast to their pre-Christmas form, Wenger's side were now exhibiting few weaknesses. They had invention, endeavour and creativity in spades, but even when their attacking stars experienced an increasingly rare afternoon of frustration, they could lean on their renewed defensive stubbornness. They were at once the immovable object *and* the irresistible force.

'When you're playing against a team that's playing at that level, as Arsenal did and United did at that time, there are some common components,' says Chelsea defender Graeme Le Saux. 'With Arsenal, they had the physical ability to make life so difficult for you as a team and then also the technical ability to control the game. I always felt that I was one of the big outlets for the team when we played against Arsenal. When I played either as a left back or as a left midfielder up against Lee Dixon, I always felt I could create chances down my side.

I went into the game against them that February really positively, but then I ended up disappointed because we lost. I ended up with a terrible record for Chelsea against Arsenal.

'They didn't have many weaknesses, that was the problem. That defensive unit was so difficult to break down. Their wide men worked so hard for the team. People overlook Ray Parlour's ability. He always gave you a tough physical contest and he made good decisions with the ball. The beauty of that Arsenal team was that the Winterburns, Dixons, Parlours all knew what their job was. They would do their job and then – and Lee has said this himself down the years – give the ball to Dennis Bergkamp. They had that amazing balance, with the creativity of Overmars, Anelka, Vieira. Petit was a superb passer as well. They had the physicality of a really tough team and the grace and technicality to go with it. That combination was impossible to break down.

'Lee and I often reminisce about old games between Chelsea and Arsenal. He says that he and Ray Parlour's approach to defending me was that they knew they could get away with kicking me once each, and then the second time would be a yellow card, so they'd effectively have four kicks at me. He says it half joking, but it shows the physicality of that side, and it was never more prominent than during this period. Lee could give a kick, but he read the game brilliantly and had tremendous discipline. And Ray would sacrifice his whole game to double up defensively on that wing. They'd outwork you and then they'd outplay you. They were a team that I always felt had lots of different ways in which they could win a game, and they could do it from minute one to minute ninety.'

Nobody better exemplified this combination of physicality and technicality than Petit and Vieira.

Arsenal's unimpeachable defensive record through this period stands testament to the improved solidity and stability provided by the Frenchmen after the club's veteran defenders had pleaded for more protection from the midfielders at Sopwell House in December. They had begun to sit deeper to shield the ageing backline and Petit had grown accustomed to the league's physicality. They offered so much more than defensive cover, too. With Petit's crisp and ambitious passing and Vieira's indefatigable drive through the middle third of the pitch, they were quickly becoming as complete and dominant a midfield pairing as the Premier League had seen.

'We used to be opponents,' Petit says of his former midfield partner. 'He was in Cannes, in the south of France; I was in Monaco, not far from him, 50 kilometres. I remember that when we used to play against him in the French championship, we used to beat them all the time, Monaco against Cannes. And I remembered this tall Black guy in the centre of defence. He was monumental. He was so young. I think he was 18, 19, and he was playing in central defence like a big, macho guy, with all the leadership he needed. He was controlling all the players on the pitch all the time. He was brilliant in terms of his display. I was thinking, "Whoa this guy at the back, he won't stay at Cannes for ever." And he went to Italy straight away.

'A good partnership is based, of course, on qualities, but I think it is also based on personality and honesty. We were – and we are still – very honest with each other. We love each other. Patrick is like a brother, and I suppose I am like a brother to him. We were very complementary together. He was right-footed, I was left-footed. He used to run with the ball, I used to play long balls. And we were both warriors on the pitch, with fighting spirit. But we wanted to play quality football on top of it. The friendship developed on the pitch but also outside of it as well. The connection we had outside the pitch was brilliant – and is still brilliant. For me, I have nothing to say in a bad way to Patrick, because he always gave 100 per cent, in terms of on the pitch, but he also gave 100 per cent in his relationship with me, in terms of honesty.

'Every time I was on the pitch with him, I felt like I could play with blinded eyes, closed eyes, because it was based on trust.'

After edging out Wimbledon on 11 March, Arsenal were second in the table, nine points behind United but with three games in hand.

'I honestly think we can do it,' Wenger said of Arsenal's title hopes. 'But then perhaps I am a little bit crazy.'

Next stop: Old Trafford.

# 18

# This Is the One

Throughout Arsenal's preparation for their potentially title-deciding clash with Manchester United on 14 March, Arsène Wenger preached calm.

The French tactician wasn't one to bombard his players with instructions or in-depth insight into what he expected their opponents would do, rarely altering how his team would play in reaction to what he thought his opposite number had planned. He kept his focus on his own side, emphasizing the strengths of his own players and how, if they played to their fullest potential, it wouldn't matter what the other side did. Control the controllables. This match was no different.

And while the media hype machine cranked into overdrive in the build-up to a game that had the makings of being one of the most significant fork-in-the-road fixtures since the Premier League's formation, Wenger insisted it was just another match. There would be three points on offer – no more than in any other game they had played that season. He presented a front of stoicism. As the outside world piled on pressure, Arsenal's manager sought to alleviate it.

'That was another thing that Arsène was really good at and really strong about: making games very low-key, not building them up to be something special,' says Gary Lewin. 'For cup finals, we would do the same preparation we'd do for a league game. That was something he really believed in – if the players are relaxed, they'll perform.'

'I very rarely saw him hyping up a game,' adds Matthew Upson, a substitute at Old Trafford. 'That wasn't part of his preparation or his make-up. He trusted his players. He would give you that trust and belief and never want to apply pressure in that way. To him, every game had the same importance. Whether it was a friendly or a Premier League game, that was the mentality he had.'

Except no one was really falling for it. Not this time. This was a fixture of mammoth consequence – for the Premier League, for Manchester United, for Arsenal. And Wenger knew it.

In one of his regular telephone conversations in the week of the game with Damien Comolli, his France-based scout, Wenger revealed his true feelings about Arsenal's pivotal Old Trafford trip.

'If we win this game,' he said, 'we are going to win the league.'

In contrast to Arsenal, United had begun 1998 in stuttering form. They'd lost their last fixture of 1997, felled by relegation-battling Coventry 3-2 at Highfield Road. They then lost two of their three league appointments in January, beaten by Southampton and Leicester City. Three wins in four games in February appeared to right the ship. So much so that, with Alex Ferguson's side 12 points clear at the top of the table, Fred Done, a United-supporting bookmaker paid out on bets that they'd secure a fifth Premier League title in six years by the end of the season.

Their return to form in February proved to be a false dawn, though, as they closed the month with a shock FA Cup fifth-round replay loss to Barnsley – mighty Barnsley! A league defeat to Sheffield Wednesday on 7 March and a draw with West Ham four days later meant United went into their showdown with the Gunners having won just four of their last ten league games. A goalless draw in Monaco in the first leg of their Champions League quarter-final ensured United's focus was split ahead of the Arsenal game, too, with the return fixture against Wenger's former club coming just four days later.

Still reeling from the loss of captain Roy Keane to a season-ending cruciate knee ligament injury in October and the bombshell retirement of Eric Cantona the previous summer, their woes were further compounded by a hamstring injury to Ryan Giggs. The Welsh winger had been playing some of the best football of his career before going down in a 2-0 victory over Derby on 21 February, a game in which he'd scored. He would not play again until early April. United were wounded and, with Arsenal fast approaching, they were vulnerable. They remained nine points clear of Wenger's side, but Arsenal had played three fewer games.

'After the Boxing Day game, we had three or four games in hand,' says Emmanuel Petit. 'We knew if we won all of them, we could put pressure on Manchester United and the title would be decided at Old Trafford when we were away from home. We knew that and we tried to do everything to play game after game, not projecting ourselves to the Old Trafford game. Before that, we needed to go step by step. If you want to have the chance to contest the title at Old Trafford, it was simple, you had to win your games in hand. This is exactly what we did. If I was a Manchester United player, I would have felt, "Well guys, we are 12 points ahead. Of course they have games in hand, but even if they win them we're still in a position of control. We'll receive them at home for the crucial game." I would probably think that way. It's probably different when you think, in the space of two or three months, it had changed. When they saw us winning game after game, putting pressure on them, coming back on their neck, I'm pretty sure that they were feeling the fear – "What would happen if they come to Old Trafford and make a surprise, win the game? Then we are going to lose the title." This is exactly what happened. They were so confident after Boxing Day. In the space of two or three months, things changed radically and it became completely different for them psychologically.'

Unlike Wenger, Ferguson made no attempt to play down the significance of the match, nor the fact that he recognized Arsenal as a coming force to be reckoned with.

'He would always look to see if there was anything they were doing that we weren't doing,' says Dave Fevre, United's lead physiotherapist at the time. 'He would want to know how Vieira and Petit were as strong and dynamic as they were and how can we get like that.'

'They'd been pushing us close,' says United centre back Gary Pallister, who missed the crucial fixture through injury. 'We knew they'd been getting stronger. We knew how important they were. That was something that Sir Alex would talk to us about. Big games like Liverpool, or later on Blackburn and Chelsea in my time, you're aware of the importance of games like that. You're putting down a marker and you're letting them know, if you win the game, "We've got the wood over you."

'You get used to rivalries. It just puts a bit more spice on to that game and the manager is maybe a little bit more wound up before the game, as well as the players. Arsenal were certainly like that.'

Pallister's absence left a void at the heart of United's backline that required some uncomfortable reshuffling to plug. Defenders Ronny Johnsen and Phil Neville were required to make up the numbers in midfield, so right back Gary Neville was moved into the centre of defence. Nineteen-year-old John Curtis came in to make just the third league start of his career at right back, where his direct opponent would be the man quickly becoming the most feared winger in English football.

Marc Overmars had not scored in his last eight appearances before Arsenal's Old Trafford date, but he had already hit double figures in his first season with the Gunners. Today, wide players who play on the opposite side to their strong foot, allowing them to cut inside to create or score, are commonplace. In 1998, they were less so. As a right-footed left winger, Overmars fitted this mould and presented a conundrum for defenders used to channelling wingers on to their weaker side to prevent crosses. The Dutchman was a scorer first and foremost. His speed, low centre of gravity and surprising physical strength – owing in part to having worked on his grandfather's unmechanized farm as a child – made him a fearsome threat both in behind defences and when operating in tight spaces.

Like his compatriot Dennis Bergkamp, Overmars's outward seriousness belied a prankster's sense of mischief. At Christmas time, he'd disturbed the residents of St Albans after setting off an armoury of fireworks at London Colney. He'd settled well within the group, too. It was Overmars who gave Ray Parlour his nickname.

'Little Marc Overmars, he nicknamed me "the Romford Pelé" that season,' Parlour says, 'which was a bit of a nightmare. That was the season he nicknamed me it in the press conference. He said, "We will definitely beat Man United, we've got the Romford Pelé." I was like, "Oh, no, Marc, what have you done?" It was all laughed at. He was laughing about it. It was all in good spirits.'

Signed to help Wenger realize his 4-4-2 vision for Arsenal, Overmars's commitment to attack and determination to play on the shoulder of opposition defenders meant, in practice, the Gunners' shape was warped to resemble more of a 4-3-3. The former Ajax star was typically more advanced on the left than Ray Parlour was on the right, with the England midfielder acting as a counter-balance by tucking inside and providing a shuttling runner to aid both defence and attack on his side. This made Arsenal's tactical composition unconventional, despite their use of the English game's most common formation. But it worked, presenting a unique challenge to opponents while maximizing the strengths of their own most gifted players. By the time they travelled to take on United, Arsenal knew exactly how to exploit the advantages Overmars gave them.

'Marc Overmars was unbelievable to play with,' says Nigel Winterburn, who played behind the Dutchman on Arsenal's left side. 'I've always said he's probably the easiest winger I've ever played with. We did communicate, but we didn't really need to. I knew where he wanted it. Left foot, right foot, short or whether he wanted it in behind: he just used to look and set up his body position. I knew he'd drop his shoulder and go, and I'd just have to drop it over the top or around the corner. He was there and away. He was just a joy to play with, such a great player.'

While their list of absentees was not as extensive as their hosts', Arsenal were not at full strength at Old Trafford, either. A broken finger meant 22-year-old Austrian Alex Manninger would replace David Seaman in goal and Christopher Wreh was preferred to Nicolas Anelka as Dennis Bergkamp's partner in attack, with Ian Wright still injured. Yet the Arsenal players who'd line up at Old Trafford felt a total conviction in their ability to conquer the champions in hostile territory.

'I felt really confident that day,' Tony Adams wrote in his first autobiography (*Addicted*, 1998). 'There was no fear in me, just a calmness, and I knew we had the capability to win. In February, as part of the England squad for the match against Chile, I noticed how tired the United players looked and really began to think they might have shot their bolt in the Premiership by then after their pace-setting of autumn. Other things were also in our favour; they had been concentrating on a Champions League quarter-final against Monaco and they were also without Ryan Giggs, who was very important to them. They were the ones with the anxieties, the insecurities.'

'It was a game we couldn't afford to lose,' says Nigel Winterburn. 'We were on an unbelievable run. We had eight straight clean sheets through that period [from 31 January to 11 April]. That's what Arsène Wenger did very, very well: he focused on the players that were in the team at the time. Even if a key player was out of the team, he never really made reference to that. He always focused on the players that were in the team. They were the most important players. He made the players in the team feel that they were there for a reason. Even if you felt you were only in because someone was injured, he didn't make it feel like that at all.

'We all knew it was a big game, but a game that we all believed we could win because of the form that we were in. We went there with such a strong belief that we were going to win. That's what made those games so special. You had two teams that really did believe they could beat each other.'

'It was a huge game,' Petit says. 'I remember the atmosphere when we left the dressing room. I remember the looks some Manchester United players gave us, trying to intimidate us. And I remember the battle on the pitch as well. And I remember perfectly how confident we were before the game in the dressing room, because we were trying to do everything we could to get that game, to play for the title in that game. In the space of three months, we tried everything we could to put pressure on Manchester United. That was exactly what we'd done. For us, this game was the final. Not for Manchester United. I think it was different for them.'

Contrary to the calm within the Arsenal contingent, the game began at a frantic pace. The opening exchanges offered little quality but United could claim a slight edge. Playing through David Beckham on the right flank, they forced Manninger into action to deal with a dangerous cross and Sheringham sliced wide when set up by Andy Cole.

There was a heart-in-mouth moment for Arsenal fans after 22 minutes when Lee Dixon slipped while playing a routine pass infield. Cole intercepted the loose ball. Adams crashed in with a tackle but the ball rolled to Sheringham, giving the former Spurs man a clear sight of goal. Manninger rushed from his line to smother the United striker's attempt. The young keeper would be required to repeat the trick in stoppage time at the end of the first half to thwart a racing Cole.

Surviving Dixon's slip seemed to settle Arsenal's early nerves. Seconds later, Petit found Overmars and the winger was brought down inside the penalty area by a desperate challenge from Curtis. Arsenal appealed unsuccessfully for a penalty. Petit and Vieira then began to take hold of midfield and the Gunners put Overmars to work. The Dutchman had already flashed wide from a tight angle after rounding Peter Schmeichel, and as the first half wore on, he tortured United's inexperienced right back. He ought to have scored in the twenty-ninth minute after skilfully jinking between Curtis and Gary Neville only to fire wide at the near post. Ferguson switched Phil Neville to the right side of defence late in the first half in an effort to combat Overmars's threat. The teenage Curtis's afternoon ended early in the second half when he was replaced by the young winger Ben Thornley, but still

Overmars was rampant. Petit located him behind the United defence soon after. Schmeichel was quick to meet the diminutive wide man, forcing a rushed, lofted shot that dropped agonizingly wide.

Nicolas Anelka, celebrating his nineteenth birthday, replaced the ineffective Wreh after 66 minutes. He fizzed a shot just over the bar ten minutes later. Then, in the seventy-ninth minute, after Bergkamp had headed into the air after a hoofed Martin Keown long pass, Anelka nodded the ball on to release Overmars down the inside-left channel.

It was Gary Neville attempting to block the Dutchman's route to goal this time. Overmars knocked the bouncing ball forward with his forehead. Then he accelerated as only he could, racing past Neville and through on Schmeichel's goal. The United goalkeeper again rushed from his line to meet the bursting Arsenal attacker, but Overmars thudded a low, left-footed finish between the Dane's legs and into the net. Overmars stood before Old Trafford East Stand in still celebration, chin high like a meerkat surveying the savannah, before being mobbed first by Bergkamp and Anelka, then Vieira and Petit.

United tried to respond, but Arsenal continued to attack. Overmars was visibly growing tired but was still the fastest player on the pitch by a clear margin. He continued to test the shell-shocked and shattered United backline. Anelka almost wrapped up a victory when he raced clear to meet Bergkamp's clipped pass, but Schmeichel smothered his low effort.

Petit was outstanding in the final ten minutes, maintaining possession, playing through pressure and keeping Arsenal moving forward. United started to lump hopeful crosses into the box – food and drink for the towering Gunners defenders.

Schmeichel came forward for a late corner and the United goalkeeper pulled a hamstring when he had to race back to his own goal. The injury would keep him out of their midweek clash with Monaco, in which a 1-1 draw sent them crashing out of the Champions League on away goals. There was time for one more Manninger save from Cole, an uncharacteristically wayward Beckham free kick and a speculative 30-yard effort from Gary Neville that bounced off Sheringham and wide. Wenger celebrated with his staff; Ferguson threw his chewing gum to the ground and trudged out of view. Overmars's goal was enough to book Arsenal's first win at Old Trafford in the Premier League era.

'I remember I had some chances before and I was unlucky with finishing,' says the Gunners' match winner. 'When the pass came from Keown, I knew Anelka could jump fantastically, so I knew he would head it. I can feel the moment. I took the ball with my head because I needed to get an advantage on the defender. My defender was Gary Neville. He was a tough defender for me. We had big battles together. He was the same height as me, he was quick, he was strong. I didn't like to play against that kind of defender. I had to always be at 100 per cent to play well. I didn't like to play against him and he didn't like to play against me.

'United were the strongest team in that moment. They'd won the league a few times. The big change was at Old Trafford when we won 1-0. That's when we started to believe we could do it. That was a turning point for us. For me, and for many of the players, it was a boost to say, "Hey, we can go on and do it."'

Back in the United dressing room, Ferguson fumed. The United manager didn't dish out his infamous 'hairdryer' bollockings – so called for the ferocity and proximity of the Scot's expletive-laden rants at his players – nearly as often as football folklore would suggest. But he grasped the gravity of this defeat, United's seventh of the season in the league; they'd not lost more than six times in any of their previous four title triumphs. Irate at having lost control of a title race many – including the misguided bookie – thought they'd already won, he let rip.

'It was still a long way to go in the season, but that was a particularly dark moment,' the United winger Ben Thornley remembers. 'The manager went absolutely ballistic. I don't remember him having a go at me – and, trust me, if the manager has a go at you, you remember it. But there were three or four players he really laid into.'

The mood among the Arsenal contingent, of course, was the total opposite. Even those unable to make the trip to Manchester could feel how the momentum in the title race had shifted in their favour.

'The game that really sticks in my mind,' remembers David Platt. 'I was just watching on TV. There were two or three players that were injured while the boys went up to Old Trafford. I was one of the players that was injured and we were having treatment at Sopwell House as the game was going on. We were in one of the hotel rooms there watching the game. That win said to us that we can win this.'

'We had a couple of injuries and I was looking after them at the hotel,' says Colin Lewin, one of the club's physios. 'I was at Sopwell House treating the injured boys in a makeshift medical room. We were watching that game on TV. I was treating Ian Wright and I remember us both charging up the hotel corridor when we scored.'

There were no such exuberant celebrations inside Old Trafford's away dressing room, though. Arsenal's pre-game confidence had proven well placed, but the players were careful not to allow overconfidence to breed after the result.

'After the game we were still focused,' Petit says. 'We'd won the game, but the Premier League was not finished. In players' minds most of the time, they focus too much on the game; when they win the game, they forget that it is only the first step.'

'There was still a long way to go in the season,' says Parlour. 'It was a massive result for us, but we didn't celebrate like, "That's it, we've won the league now," because we'd still got quite a few games after that. We were happy, having a laugh. Fantastic, we've just beaten Manchester United at Old Trafford. But there was still a lot of work to do. I don't think it would have been like you've won the title or the FA Cup. If we'd have celebrated like that, we probably wouldn't have won it.'

'I don't think Arsène Wenger does celebrations,' adds Winterburn. 'We knew it was an unbelievable win, but we hadn't achieved anything. It was on to the next game, really. We knew that game was a massive advantage. That gave us real belief that we could go on and secure the title.'

In the dressing room and on the coach journey back to London, the Arsenal players discussed the significance of the result. 'That was the chat on the way back on the bus,' Upson says. 'It was, "We can do this. We can do it." There was absolutely no doubt that this was a key game, psychologically, in the title race.'

And while chatting post-match with Wenger, Tony Adams took it upon himself to impart a brief history lesson. The captain, along with Dixon and Winterburn, was one of three players in Arsenal's line-up that afternoon who'd also played the last time the Gunners beat United away from home, in October 1990.

'You know, the last time we won at Old Trafford,' he said, 'we won the league.'

# 19

# What it Meant

As the television cameras panned across the section of Old Trafford that housed away supporters in the immediate aftermath of Arsenal's seismic victory, the image of one fan leapt from the screen.

With a grey scarf swept casually around his neck, clenched fists protruded from his black leather jacket. His eyes bulged beneath his curly black locks as he roared the word 'Yes' three times before beating together his palms to applaud the Arsenal players celebrating below. Sky Sports' match director lingered on this fan's reaction of raw, untethered emotion for four seconds. Four seconds that changed Barry Ferst's life.

'It was the relief of getting the win on the day, but more the excitement at the fact that we could actually do it, win the title,' Ferst remembers of his famous eruption.

'It was literally the fact that we could win this. I'd have been happy with a draw, but actually winning it, you realized that if we go on to win our games in hand, we'll be in front.

'There was something in the air that felt like maybe things would go our way, but as the game wore on you started to wonder whether it was going to happen. United had been so good through the Nineties. When you looked at our players, you were talking to your mates, saying, "We can do this," but you're just being optimistic. Now, it was like, "Shit, we actually can. It's in our hands. If we win every game, that's it."'

Ferst had been an Arsenal supporter all his life. His first trip to Highbury came in 1969 when, just five years old, his dad took him to watch a North London derby. As a season-ticket holder and regular away traveller domestically and in Europe, he estimates that he'd missed no more than a handful of Arsenal's matches across an eight-year period prior to the Old Trafford victory.

'I don't want to say that Arsenal were the most important thing in my life at the time,' he says, 'but it probably was in reality. My partner at the time probably wouldn't like me saying that, but Arsenal were far more important to me than her. I was 34 – it was no way for a grown man to act.'

His post-match fist pumping was picked up by TV broadcasters because it was obvious in an instant how Ferst's passionate celebration would resonate with viewers. He might have been a diehard Arsenal supporter, but in that moment every football fan could understand the strength and specificity of what he was feeling. Yet despite his unexpected supporting role in the most anticipated football fixture of the season, the slower communication channels of the day – with no social media, no culture of text messaging and no widely accessible high-speed internet – news of his newfound notoriety was slow to reach Ferst.

'I had a couple of phone calls with people saying "You're famous",' he remembers. 'They didn't explain it particularly well. They just said, "They keep showing you on the TV." When it came to the evening, I settled down to watch *Match of the Day*. I was looking at shots of the crowd, thinking, "I must be in there somewhere." I assumed that people that knew me had spotted me in the crowd and recognized me as one of hundreds of people in a shot. But when it happened, it was like, "Oh, bloody hell!" I didn't think I was going to be on the whole screen. I was completely shocked.

'On the Monday morning, it started. I worked at a branch of Barclays bank at the time. I got to work early. One of my colleagues said, "Did you have a nice weekend?" I said, "Yeah, it was all right. Did you?" And he said, "Yeah, but I didn't make a fool of myself on the telly." It kind of rolled from there. It was quiet in the morning. I could get from the tube station to the bank quite easily. Come the journey back in the evening, there were a lot more people out. What was normally a five-minute walk took three-quarters of an hour, with people wanting to stop and chat.

'Working in a branch, a lot of people get to know you, but a lot more did after that, it seemed. I don't know if Barclays got any extra accounts after it, but it was always nice going to the pub after work.

'My friend who I went to games with was happy it wasn't him. It didn't bother me too much. I found it funny, really. The only thing I found a bit strange was that I was being treated a bit like a hero. It wasn't like I'd run on the pitch and nodded in the winner.'

Though he was amused by his overnight celebrity status, Ferst admits to being taken aback by how the resonance of his joyous Old Trafford outpouring has endured over time. When he went to watch Arsenal take on Sheffield Wednesday at Highbury two weeks later, he picked up a copy of the *Gooner* fanzine, as was his custom. When he turned over the latest issue, he saw a picture of his screaming celebration on the back cover accompanied by the words 'This is what it meant'. Sky Sports continued to use Ferst's image in advertisements for their football coverage for several years. His five minutes of football fame never fully faded.

'People still come up and ask for photographs when I'm at games,' he says. 'It's making their day, so I'm not going to knock them back. It's handy it was me and not my mate who was a bit more grumpy. I wasn't surprised it kept being used, but I was surprised at how long the notoriety went on. They kept using it, so I kept getting recognized. It still happens. I have long hair now, but people still recognize me.

'I get it. The passion shown was what many supporters would do. I know what it meant to other people.'

# 20

# The Outstanding Stand-in

By the time Arsenal travelled to Upton Park on 17 March 1998 to face off against West Ham in an FA Cup quarter-final replay, talk of a first Double since 1971 had reached full throttle. After beating Manchester United at Old Trafford three days earlier, they were in the driver's seat in the Premier League and, with no other top-four side left in the competition, they were favourites for the FA Cup, too.

But when the two sides could not be separated after 120 minutes in East London, Arsenal's Double dream rested on the relative randomness of a penalty shoot-out.

Ordinarily, Arsenal held an upper hand in such situations thanks to their goalkeeper. David Seaman was an outstanding penalty stopper. He once saved three spot kicks in a League Cup shoot-out against Millwall, a feat he repeated against Sampdoria in the Cup Winners' Cup semi-final in April 1994. His shoot-out success versus Sampdoria was made all the more remarkable for the fact he was nursing two cracked ribs at the time. At Euro 96, he'd saved a Gary McAllister penalty in England's group-stage win over Scotland before keeping out Miguel Ángel Nadal's effort to secure a quarter-final shoot-out triumph over Spain. When it came to repelling penalties, Seaman was as good as it got.

The same applied to goalkeeping in general. In 1990, when George Graham asked Bob Wilson, Arsenal's goalkeeping coach, whether the club should sign Seaman from Queens Park Rangers, where Wilson coached one day a week at the time, the legendary former keeper was unequivocal.

'He's the closest thing I've seen to Pat Jennings,' Wilson said. 'If you can get him, go for it.'

It was no coincidence that Arsenal not only won the league title in Seaman's first season at Highbury but did so while setting a record for the fewest goals conceded in a top-flight campaign. His performances at Euro 96 cemented his reputation as one of the best keepers in the world. He was ranked the seventh-best player in the Premier League by *The Independent* in 1997.

'You are there to be shot at,' Wilson begins in assessment of what made Seaman exceptional. 'It is a stupid position to have chosen, because you are always vulnerable to making a mistake. The first thing you need to show is that you are not scared of the position underneath the crossbar, and that is what we mean by the word "presence". As David went out on to the pitch, he'd look at me and nod or wink. He had extraordinary presence. He filled that goal mouth. He made the goal shrink. That's the greatest strength you can have as a goalkeeper.'

Seaman was gruff and imposing, a six-foot-four Yorkshireman with a thicket of sweeping brown hair and a moustache that belonged to a bygone era. He was also a gentle giant with a warm and ever-present chuckle. He was known simply and affectionately by teammates as 'The Goalie'.

But what happens when the goalie is not The Goalie?

'I grew up in Salzburg, close to the old stadium,' says Alex Manninger. 'I joined SV Salzburg at age seven and worked my way up. It was easy for me because I was close to the facilities of the club. Also, some people thought I should become a skier. Looking back now, I don't think they would have waited for me in the mountains. I think I made the right decision to stay in town and play some football.'

Born in the shadow of the Alps in 1977, Manninger describes his childhood as 'very pleasant'. He was the only child of separated parents, but there was no acrimony within his divided family. He split his days between his father, a banker in the city, and his mother, who worked in a local courthouse.

He started playing football at seven but as an outfield player at first. It was only when the coach of his youth team asked who was 'brave enough' to don the gloves in place of an absent goalkeeper that he stumbled into his future.

'No one lifted their hand,' Manninger remembers. 'All of a sudden, someone said, "Alex, you can do it." And I said, "All right, I'll do it." From then, I stayed more in goal. It took about another year, at about 12, when I got my first gloves and became a goalkeeper.'

He stood out quickly in his new position. He was an exceptional athlete and had a gymnast's agility. But as he progressed through the ranks at SV Salzburg – who'd later become Red Bull Salzburg – he came to realize his opportunities would be limited at first-team level.

'Salzburg, in these days, were very successful,' he says. 'They won the league and played in the UEFA Cup. They had a great run. There was always a couple of goalkeepers you couldn't go past at 18, so I looked for somewhere I could play. In '96, Grazer gave me a chance and I took it.'

He joined Grazer AK, the smaller of the two main clubs in Graz, after future two-time Manchester United Champions League opponents Sturm Graz. Smaller though Grazer might have been, Manninger's debut match for the club could hardly have been more big-time – against Inter at the San Siro in the UEFA Cup.

'When you've just turned 19 and are starting in the San Siro, you think, "Bloody hell, this isn't what I'm used to,"' he says. 'You get an idea of modern, top-class football. It was something I was looking forward to experiencing.'

Manninger soon began to appear on the radar of clubs across the Continent. There was interest from the German Bundesliga as well as from Udinese in Serie A. He learned early in the 1996–97 season that Arsenal had been watching them, with chief scout Steve Rowley dispatched to analyse the young goalkeeper's potential a handful of times. Manninger flew to London in April to meet with Wenger.

'The thing I remember is he spoke in German,' he says. 'I thought, "How is this possible? A French coach in England talking in German." Then I learned he came from Strasbourg, he speaks about six languages and he'd been in Japan before. He was one of those guys who changed football in the last 20 years. I didn't know that before. Many others didn't know his career before he came. He was a nice person. Human. A genius in football.'

Impressed with Wenger and the way Arsenal were integrating foreign players and ideas, he joined the club in the summer of 1997 in a £500,000 deal. While he didn't expect a great deal of first-team action initially, he saw the potential for a perfect apprenticeship on the training pitches at London Colney, where he'd work with Wilson and alongside Seaman and John Lukic, the veteran who'd kept goal for the '89 title side and had returned to the club as third-choice keeper.

'I was impressed by Seaman's quality in goal,' Manninger says, 'and I was happy that I got him back into fishing more again. I'd heard he was a fisherman. I said, "David, I was born a fisherman. Since I was able to walk, I went fishing with my dad." We went fishing together one afternoon, and from then on we went a few times. We worked out a few nice lakes around North London where he lived. We had some good days at lakes.

'At the age he was, he was so calm. He had his master's degree as a goalkeeper. He was one of the goalies you would watch as a boy. I was lucky to work with him for four years. Him and John Lukic were master goalkeepers. Lukic, with his experience – hundreds of games, titles – he gave me a great hand as well. John was there before a game, after a game. We became friends. He was probably one David Seaman looked at. It was probably the best mixture at this time at an English club. Bob Wilson was David's coach and knew David inside out, but I was lucky to get that coaching situation.'

As much as they might have bonded on those fishing trips, there was a healthy competitive tension between Seaman and his young understudy. Manninger lacked the England goalkeeper's experience, but he lacked for nothing in terms of confidence.

'Outwardly, they got on great,' Wilson says. 'But unless you believe "I'm going to be better than him", you ain't going to be better than him.'

Arsenal's post-Christmas surge towards title contention could have been halted at its outset. When making a save to deny Darren Huckerby in the 2-2 draw with Coventry City on 17 January, David Seaman broke a finger. The loss of their stalwart between the sticks had the potential to derail Arsenal's season.

'As far back as the autumn,' Manninger says, 'Arsène asked me, "Are you ready?" I said, "Look, boss, this is what I'm waiting for. This is why I moved over." It was Middlesbrough, my first game. I remember David called me to wish me luck. From that day on, it took off. We were hungry. The spirit was there from the first day. Every game, the belief got bigger. Different people scored. Different people kept clean sheets. I think it was a master's degree for a lot of players and for Arsène himself. It was something special.

'In those days, I had no reference. There were no Austrian players and no young goalkeepers playing in the Premier League. I could see how someone else reacted if they made a mistake – how do you perform? How do you recover? That made things a little bit difficult. I was fresh at this time. It was all new to me. I didn't have the experience.'

Manninger had played just two first-team games for Arsenal prior to Seaman's injury, both in the League Cup. With the number one out, he would play thirteen in a row.

Whether it was a case of nervousness or eagerness, he made an error that led to a goal in this first game of that run, away to Middlesbrough in the FA Cup. The 20-year-old keeper rushed from his penalty area in the second half and was beaten to the ball by Paul Merson, who fired into the unguarded net. Fortunately for Manninger, Arsenal were already two goals up at the time and his misjudgement did not prove costly.

Remarkably, considering his inexperience and the pressure of the situation into which he was thrust, that was the measure of Manninger's mistakes. From then on, he found his feet and showed what he was capable of with his hands. He produced acrobatic match-saving stops week upon week, highlighted by saves against West Ham and Wimbledon that helped Arsenal keep piling pressure on Manchester United at the top of the league. The members of the veteran back four in front of him were won over. 'Alex was a great goalkeeper,' says Nigel Winterburn. 'He was so agile. He was a little bit hyper at times, but he was such an agile goalkeeper. A terrific goalkeeper. I didn't feel that him coming in for David Seaman was an issue.'

Wenger was convinced, too. 'He has showed that, under pressure, he is very strong,' the manager said. 'And that's why I think he is an Arsenal player.'

By far the biggest test of Manninger's stint as Seaman's stand-in came at Old Trafford. With his father in attendance, the young Austrian was not overawed by the moment. In addition to the spectacular reflex saves for which he was becoming known, the youngster excelled in an art mastered by his opposite number, Peter Schmeichel, by racing quickly from his goal line to smother shots from Teddy Sheringham and Andy Cole.

'I remember my dad was there,' he says. 'He wasn't at a lot of games, but we had a UK trip organized for him. It made this game more special that my dad was there with a couple of friends. They drove all the way up to Manchester on the day of the match.

'Being in goal, winning this game and changing the attitude after this game, we believed more after that game. Manchester United were Manchester United in these days. You knew if you beat them, you could beat the rest as well.'

On to the FA Cup quarter-final replay against West Ham three days later, Manninger was once again in imperious form, producing several athletically impressive stops, in particular as he denied John Hartson and John Moncur from close range

It was the third meeting between Arsenal and West Ham in the space of two weeks and the fifth clash between the two sides that season. They were familiar foes and, it seemed, they had each other figured out.

Arsenal had won the two sides' first encounter of the season comfortably. Dennis Bergkamp, Ian Wright and a brace for Marc Overmars had wrapped up a 4-0 rout at Highbury in September. Their

League Cup face off in January had been much tighter, with Wright and Overmars again scorers as the Gunners squeaked out a 2-1 away win. The second Premier League meeting, on 2 March, ended scoreless and their first attempt at an FA Cup last-eight showdown finished 1-1, necessitating the return date at West Ham's home.

The Gunners faced an uphill battle at Upton Park after the thirty-second minute, when Bergkamp was sent off for crashing an elbow into the face of West Ham midfielder Steve Lomas. It was a moment of recklessness for which 'The Iceman' would feel remorse.

'The one with Steve Lomas, I wasn't happy with that,' he said. 'He pulled my shirt from behind as we were breaking out from the corner, and I smashed him with my elbow. But he was bleeding and I felt bad about it. He didn't deserve that, not at all. It was meant like "Get away from me!" but when you do it in such a way that you hurt someone, straightaway you think, "That's not nice." I also hurt the team – they had to play for an hour with ten men, so the whole thing was not good.'

Arsenal could have been further disadvantaged in the second half when, away from the ball, Martin Keown grabbed Samassi Abou by the throat. The West Ham striker reacted with a push before felling Keown with a headbutt. Referee Mike Reed consulted with his assistant and then allowed both players to escape with only a verbal warning.

A 20-yard bullet of a strike from Anelka put the travelling ten men ahead in the final minute of the first half. The teenage striker pulled his yellow away shirt over his head in celebration. But former Gunner Hartson's precise near-post finish with six minutes to play sent the match to extra time. It was the fourth of Arsenal's cup fixtures that season to require extra time and it would be the second to necessitate penalties, with no further scoring in the additional 30 minutes.

So as the shoot-out began, it was not the familiar, formidable figure of Seaman guarding the goal for Arsenal, but instead a 20-year-old Austrian, distinctive for his bright orange jersey and flushed cheeks.

Stephen Hughes stepped up first for Arsenal and converted a low shot into the left corner. David Unsworth then rolled a calm effort into the net for the home side as Manninger guessed wrong with his dive.

Second-half substitute Christopher Wreh was first to miss, striking the post with the third kick of the shoot-out, but Hartson erred right after, firing wide.

Luís Boa Morte and Frank Lampard scored to keep the score even, but then Rémi Garde smashed the ball well wide of his countryman Bernard Lama's goal. Israeli midfielder Eyal Berkovic stepped forward with the chance to give West Ham the lead in the shoot-out.

'I remember a couple of talks with David Seaman and John Lukic,' Manninger says of his pre-penalties preparation. 'When you're a young guy, you try to pick up as much as possible. They helped me then. I was close at a couple. I thought, "Bloody hell, there's five; I should at least get one." When it's the most important one, it makes the dive worth it.'

The dive was very much worth it. Manninger exploded to his right and beat away Berkovic's effort with a powerful left palm.

Patrick Vieira, Lomas and Tony Adams all scored their kicks. Abou took the twelfth strike, needing to score to keep West Ham in the cup. Manninger anticipated the striker's low shot to his right and stretched for the ball with a long dive, but it wasn't needed. Abou shot wide. Arsenal were through to the semi-finals. The Double dream was alive.

'One of my English best friends is a West Ham supporter and he still speaks about this game. It was something special,' Manninger says. 'I remember the penalties. During the game, it was already something special. We were right up in the league, and you don't know if it's because of the different players or whether there's a different attitude, but West Ham played a great game. They probably couldn't believe they didn't win in the end.'

If West Ham had wondered how they lost, they needed only to look across to the fresh-faced alpine athlete between the posts for Arsenal. Manninger had once again been outstanding. A hero in the cup, the six consecutive clean sheets he'd kept in the league was a club record and he was named the Premier League's Player of the Month for March. But he would not begin April as Arsenal's starting goalkeeper.

'Immediately David was back in,' Wilson says. 'If you're looking at the complete picture, the closest to perfection, there was never any question of who was the most consistent goalkeeper.'

Seaman's broken finger had healed sufficiently for the England goalkeeper to resume his regular role as Arsenal's customary custodian for Sheffield Wednesday's visit to Highbury on 28 March. It was back to the bench for Manninger, albeit with a sky-rocketed reputation and a belief that his time would come again.

'I've still got the little Player of the Month trophy,' Manninger says. 'Arsène got the Manager of the Month award at the same time.

'Sometimes I look back and see the little trophies and think about how it's probably been a different career from what I expected, but I know I did something right. Little trophies like that make you remember.'

Manninger played for Arsenal for another three seasons, although he was never able to unseat Seaman as the club's undisputed number one. He later had spells with Red Bull Salzburg, Siena, Juventus and Augsburg in an itinerant career that culminated with a short spell as a back-up at Liverpool during the 2016–17 season. Although, as he admits, his time at Highbury didn't pan out as he'd hoped and expected, his contribution to Arsenal's 1997–98 campaign would not be forgotten.

# 21

# No Question

Even when faced with the evidence of Arsenal's deserved victory over his side at Old Trafford, Alex Ferguson was not ready to concede the title to the Gunners, nor admit to the superiority of Arsène Wenger's men.

'They played well today,' scowled the fiery Scot, 'but I don't think they are as good a football team as us, though they looked strong and determined. If they win their games in hand they will go ahead of us, but they will find out they start dropping points towards the end of the season, there's no question about that.'

It was a bold, hubristic prediction from Manchester United's manager. Arsenal quickly got to work to prove him wrong.

**Arsenal 1-0 Sheffield Wednesday, 28 March 1998 – Highbury, London**

ARSENAL: Seaman, Adams, Dixon (Garde 52'), Keown, Winterburn, Hughes, Overmars, Parlour (Grimandi 74'), Vieira, Bergkamp, Wreh (Anelka 57')

SHEFFIELD WEDNESDAY: Pressman, Atherton, Barrett, Hinchcliffe, Sedloski, Stefanovic, Walker, Pembridge (Whittingham 83'), Booth, Carbone (Hyde 67'), Di Canio

GOAL: Bergkamp 35'

**Ron Atkinson:** 'I knew a little bit about Arsène Wenger before he came over because my fitness coach, Roger Spry, had worked with him in Japan and had been on one or two European coaching courses with him. He briefed me a little bit on him. He spoke very highly of Wenger. My first game after I went back to Sheffield Wednesday in November 1997 was against Arsenal and we beat them 2-0 at Hillsborough. But then they went on this incredible run. We'd played Manchester United in March and we beat them, which was when Arsenal were coming back into the title race. Wenger had them playing some nice attacking football and he didn't have to worry too much about the defence because the famous back five were already there. Some of the French signings he made were unbelievable – Anelka, Vieira, Petit. And there were some good, solid citizens alongside them, players like Ray Parlour. Then, of course, they had Dennis Bergkamp, who scored against us in this game, and Marc Overmars. Things fell into place nicely for him, but he'd changed the whole philosophy of how they played. People talk about how he changed the diet and stuff like that. I think it was more about how he changed the way they played after taking over that was impressive.'

|   |         | **Games Played** | **Points** |
|---|---------|------------------|------------|
| 1 | Man Utd | 32               | 63         |
| 2 | Arsenal | 29               | 57         |

**Bolton Wanderers 0-1 Arsenal, 31 March 1998 – Reebok Stadium, Bolton**

BOLTON: Branagan, Bergsson, Cox, Fish, Todd (Salako 52'), Phillips (Johansen 86'), Frandsen, Sheridan, Thompson, Blake, Holdsworth

ARSENAL: Seaman, Adams, Keown, Grimandi, Winterburn, Overmars (Hughes 45'), Parlour, Petit, Vieira, Anelka (Platt 84'), Wreh (Bould 64')

GOAL: Wreh 47'

**Mark Fish**: 'I remember we gave them a tough time. We made it very difficult for them. It was my first game against Arsenal after coming to the English Premier League. Having watched them when I was growing up in South Africa, Arsenal were one of the teams you always wanted to play against. They had formidable players, but that day we did as much as we possibly could do. It was always a good footballing experience playing against Arsenal. When you're playing against the best players who set a standard as high as they did, it brings you up a level. They bring the best out of you. It makes it easier when you go for the first tackle and you're successful; it gives you confidence. If you go for it and the striker goes past you or Overmars or Anelka skin you with their pace, it's going to be a long 90 minutes for you. Manchester United came with the pedigree of winning the Premier League. Arsenal at that time, with Arsène Wenger coming in, changing things and bringing in so many quality foreigners, it was harder and more exciting to play against them. The players they had and the style of football Wenger had them playing, I enjoyed it. In my nine years in England, I was part of a winning team at Highbury just once. It was pretty much the same with United. Those two teams stood out, but in this period Arsenal stood out most. Their attack was a lot more formidable and a lot more daunting in comparison to United. They played the best football and had some of the best players not only in the Premier League but in the world. They lifted up the league and they created something unique.'

|   |   | Games Played | Points |
|---|---|---|---|
| 1 | Man Utd | 32 | 63 |
| 2 | Arsenal | 30 | 60 |

**Arsenal 3-1 Newcastle United, 11 April 1998 – Highbury, London**

ARSENAL: Seaman, Adams, Bould, Winterburn, Garde, Overmars (Hughes 76'), Parlour, Petit, Vieira, Anelka (Boa Morte 85'), Wreh (Platt 62')

NEWCASTLE: Given, Barton, Albert, Dabizas, Griffin, Pearce, Batty, Hamilton (Ketsbaia 60'), Speed, Barnes (Andersson 66'), Shearer

GOALS: Anelka 41', 64', Vieira 72'; Barton 79'

**Andy Griffin:** 'I remember Vieira scoring a goal from quite a distance out. Highbury was the stadium I went to and conceded the most goals in my career. Partly because the pitch was reasonably small. And that team had immense pace, particularly in Anelka and Overmars. I played against some of the greatest wingers and forward players in modern history in my career. When I look back at my most difficult opponents, Marc Overmars was an exceptionally difficult player to play against. I would compare him to somebody like Eden Hazard, where he can drift inside on to his right foot. If you tried to show him down the line, he had the pace to go down the line on to his left foot and then cut across you. He was an exceptionally difficult player to play against. Playing against that team, it felt as if it was boys against men. They were extremely physical, they covered the grass exceptionally well, you didn't seem to get much time on the ball whatsoever and not only were they hungry for success and tough and rugged, they had some incredible ability on the ball as well. They were such a powerful, quick and aggressive team.'

|   |         | Games Played | Points |
|---|---------|--------------|--------|
| 1 | Man Utd | 34           | 67     |
| 2 | Arsenal | 31           | 63     |

## Blackburn Rovers 1-4 Arsenal, 13 April 1998 – Ewood Park, Blackburn

BLACKBURN: Fettis, Davidson (Valery 58'), Henchoz, Hendry, Kenna, Flitcroft, McKinlay (Ripley 79'), Sherwood, Wilcox, Dahlin (Beattie 79'), Gallacher

ARSENAL: Seaman, Adams, Bould, Winterburn, Garde, Overmars (Hughes 87'), Parlour, Petit, Vieira, Anelka (Platt 69'), Bergkamp

GOALS: Gallacher 51'; Bergkamp 2', Parlour 7', 14', Anelka 42'

**Chris Sutton**: 'I was out injured at the time and I remember watching this match from the stands. Arsenal were on a good run at that particular time. Their confidence was high. Everyone talks about Bergkamp and his influence, and Petit and Vieira, but Ray Parlour was a big part of that team as well. He was a tremendous athlete. And Nicolas Anelka was probably better in this phase, as a young player, than he was later in his career. He was a bit of a surprise package. Stéphane Henchoz was a really good defender and I remember Anelka giving him the runaround. He had tremendous pace and he was a skilful player as well. I actually think that was a better team than the Invincibles side that went unbeaten through a whole season a few years later.'

|   |         | Games Played | Points |
|---|---------|--------------|--------|
| 1 | Man Utd | 34           | 67     |
| 2 | Arsenal | 32           | 66     |

### Arsenal 5-0 Wimbledon, 18 April 1998 – Highbury, London

ARSENAL: Seaman, Adams, Upson, Winterburn, Garde
(Dixon 14'), Overmars, Parlour, Petit, Vieira (Platt 70'),
Anelka (Wreh 76'), Bergkamp

WIMBLEDON: Sullivan, Cunningham, Blackwell (McAllister
83'), Perry, Gayle, Thatcher, Ardley (Francis 75'), C. Hughes
(Cort 45'), M. Hughes, Roberts, Clarke

GOALS: Adams 12', Overmars 17', Bergkamp 19', Petit 54',
Wreh 88'

**Marcus Gayle**: 'When I look at that Arsenal squad and what was happening under Arsène Wenger, it was revolutionary, in terms of the training and the good habits he was bringing in. And that team reflected it. You got the sense this was something new. They were super-strong. They had a different type of mental strength. I always look back at that '98 team as a great period for Arsenal. We could play our best game, with nine-out-of-ten performances from everybody, but if Arsenal had clicked into gear there was no way we were beating them. Our game plan was to try and force any team with that kind of talent to drop their levels. We'd try and win the game before it's even started, with our antics and mind games. But Arsenal back then were a formidable team. They had a squad of dominant players.

'They were super-skilful, but they were super-physical as well. They could mix it. Dennis Bergkamp was no slouch or pushover – he was very physical and he was blessed with tremendous ability in his game. It set the tone for the quality of players they were getting in. Their balance was right. The foundation was English and the flair was from abroad. It worked perfectly.'

|   |         | Games Played | Points |
|---|---------|--------------|--------|
| 1 | Arsenal | 33           | 69     |
| 2 | Man Utd | 35           | 68     |

### Barnsley 0-2 Arsenal, 25 April 1998 – Oakwell, Barnsley

BARNSLEY: Watson, Eaden, Barnard, De Zeeuw, Moses, Jones, Bullock, Redfearn, Tinkler (Bosančić 65'), Fjørtoft (Hendrie 75'), Marcelle (Ward 51')

ARSENAL: Seaman, Adams, Dixon, Keown, Winterburn, Overmars, Petit, Platt, Vieira, Anelka (Wreh 75'), Bergkamp

GOALS: Bergkamp 23', Overmars 76'

**Neil Redfearn:** 'I was up against Patrick Vieira. He was an unbelievable player. He was so athletic and had so much quality in the simple things he did. They had the ability to pass one-twos and play the ball through the opposition. You had world-class players playing with confidence. It was the perfect storm. We'd been really naive earlier in the season. Arsenal were probably the first really top team we played, when we went to Highbury. They gave us a proper battering. We did well to keep it to 5-0. But then we grew into the season. We started getting results. At that point, we were getting close to getting out of the relegation zone. The game against Arsenal at Oakwell was a lot closer. But Dennis Bergkamp, when we were trying to close down and make it difficult for Arsenal, he'd just got this composure and this serenity about him.'

**Darren Barnard:** 'We enjoyed the Premier League season. We were on a hiding to nothing. We were a very small club and we were looking to stay in the league if we could, but we knew it was going to be an uphill task. When you're at home, you try to use the crowd to get you through. It's about trying to stay in the game as long as possible when you're up against the bigger teams. You want to keep their chances to a minimum and then try and nick a goal. David Seaman produced a wonder-save from me at one-nil, then they go up the other end and score. We were desperate for three points because we were fighting relegation, but they were desperate for three points as well. We gave a good account of ourselves, but their extra quality showed in the end.'

|   |          | Games Played | Points |
|---|----------|--------------|--------|
| 1 | Arsenal  | 34           | 72     |
| 2 | Man Utd  | 35           | 68     |

**Arsenal 1-0 Derby County, 29 April 1998 – Highbury, London**

ARSENAL: Seaman, Adams, Dixon, Keown, Winterburn, Overmars, Parlour, Petit, Vieira, Anelka (Platt 82'), Bergkamp (Wreh 30')

DERBY: Poom, Dailly, Laursen, Rowett, C. Powell, Bohinen
(Solis 82), Carsley, Delap, D. Powell (Burton 74'), Sturridge,
Wanchope
GOAL: Petit 34'

**Deon Burton**: 'The fact we'd beaten them three-nil at Pride Park earlier in the season gave us lots of confidence before we played them at Highbury. But Arsenal back then were very good, so we knew it was still going to be tough to get a result. We always used to play with three forwards against Arsenal and it worked well for us a lot of times. On this occasion it didn't because we lost, but it was a close game, just one-nil – boring, boring Arsenal! When I came on in the second half, we were a goal down and chasing an equalizer. Jim Smith, our manager, and Steve McClaren, his assistant, just told me to work hard and try to get us back into the game. But when you're playing against one of the best defences in the world at the time, it was obviously going to be so, so tough. Arsenal are one of the only teams I never scored against, so that says it all. They were a top, top side back then and it was a privilege to have the opportunity to play against them.'

| | | Games Played | Points |
|---|---|---|---|
| 1 | Arsenal | 35 | 75 |
| 2 | Man Utd | 36 | 71 |

So much for Ferguson's certainty. The narrow victory over Derby at Highbury was Arsenal's ninth win in a row. If they could add a tenth the following weekend, when they were to host Everton, they'd be Premier League champions with two matches to spare.

# 22

# Perfect Day

On Saturday 2 May 1998, Arsène Wenger was at his home in Totteridge, listening to the afternoon's Premier League results filter through on the radio alongside Boro Primorac and Damien Comolli. They heard of Liverpool handing a 5-0 thumping to West Ham, Bolton's 5-2 win over Crystal Palace and a 6-2 victory for Tottenham away at Wimbledon. Manchester United weren't in action until the following Monday, with Leeds their opponents. But if Arsenal could overcome Everton at Highbury on the Sunday, the result at Old Trafford would be immaterial – the Gunners would be champions.

As the full-time scores were reported from around the country, David Dein called in.

'Arsène, if you win tomorrow, it's done,' the vice-chairman said. 'But we're relaxed, there's no pressure.'

Everyone in the room agreed.

Dein's visit was only fleeting. After he'd left, Wenger turned to his two guests. 'We're under massive pressure,' he said. 'They want me to think there is no pressure – they *are* the pressure.

'But I'm OK. I know exactly what we're going to do to win tomorrow.'

After one training session in the final month of the season, one of the coaches suggested the players needed to be doing more work in order to be ready for the upcoming crunch period. Wenger, ever the diplomat, replied, 'Yes, that's a good point' – those who'd worked with him previously came to understand that this type of 'yes' from the manager typically meant 'no'.

He shared a ride home from training with Comolli who was visiting from France. 'What did you think of that idea?' Comolli asked. 'We're not going to do more,' Wenger said. 'We're going to do less. The players are purring right now. I don't want to do anything to upset their rhythm or tire them out.'

Wenger had been wary of putting his players through extra work at the end of a long season ever since he felt it cost him a European title in 1992. His Monaco side had reached the Cup Winners' Cup final that year. Two days before taking on Werder Bremen at the Estádio da Luz in Lisbon, he ran an intense, tactically demanding training session covering the high press. His most important midfield player sustained a dead leg in the drill in a collision with a teammate. He thinks Monaco lost the final because of this. 'I will never forgive myself for doing this extra, high-intensity drill forty-eight hours before the final,' he told Comolli. 'Now I know I should do less, not more.'

The Frenchman's caution proved prudent. Arsenal produced some scintillating attacking displays along the nine-game winning streak that brought them to within a victory of the title. They pulverized Blackburn at Ewood Park with four goals in the first half. They blasted Wimbledon 5-0 and put three past the Newcastle side they'd meet again in the FA Cup final on 16 May. But it hadn't all been plain sailing. There were a handful of hairy moments that could have derailed their quest for a Double if not for the defensive fortitude honed long before Wenger's arrival and the stamina the manager had cultivated through workload management, diet and fitness.

The FA Cup semi-final, a scrappy 1-0 victory over second-tier Wolverhampton Wanderers, was one such example. 'We played terrible,' Gary Lewin says. 'Martin Keown had his eye socket smashed. He had to come off at half time.' Sheffield Wednesday and Derby had been edged out narrowly, too. There is one grind of a game that sticks out most in the memory of the Arsenal contingent, however, which saw the Gunners clinging to a 1-0 victory after a second-half red card for Keown.

'I remember the game at Bolton, coming in at half time at nil-nil,' says David Platt. 'They'd absolutely thrown everything at us. The ball was raining in from every angle – long throws, free kicks in their own half. It was a midweek evening game under the lights in Bolton. I remember coming in at half time and thinking, "Christ, it's a bloody hard game." They knew that if they tried to play against us at football, they're going to get turned over. So it became an onslaught. I was number 7 and Tony Adams was number 6. At that time, the dressing room was set out by shirt numbers. I sat down next to him and Arsène started talking. At the end of him speaking, when it was like, "Right, get yourselves ready again," Tony just pulled me and said to me, "This is the game: you and Ray Parlour sit in front of me and Bouldy. We stay there, they don't score. I guarantee you, they don't score. If those three [the attacking players] don't do their job, it's their fault." We won the game one-nil. It was Tony, really, saying, "Let's not chase this game, because it's coming at us. Let's just make sure that they're not going to score." And the second half was a war. It wasn't me looking to be the match winner. It was me saying, "OK, I'm going to be part of this defensive block that says, "You don't score. Throw what you want at us, but we'll stand up to it." And Tony's point was, "We're not going to lose the game. If they [the attacking players] don't score a goal, it's their fucking fault."'

'Those sort of results build up confidence,' Lewin says. 'It definitely makes you feel that you can challenge, but it's about sustaining. I think the bigger games were ones like going to Bolton and winning one-nil. I think they're the ones that build up as much belief as the big games. Everyone can raise themselves when they play Manchester United or Liverpool. But when you're going to Bolton away, can you do the same? They're the games that really build belief.'

For a peripheral figure, Wreh's contribution to Arsenal's 1997–98 campaign should not be underestimated. He made 24 total appearances, scoring just 4 goals. But three of his strikes had earned 1-0 victories. The Liberian lasted only two more years as an Arsenal player, departing in 2000 after a string of loans. He left a small yet significant mark at Highbury, both for his crucial goals and his quirky character.

'He scored in the FA Cup semi-final and he scored a brilliant goal away at Bolton,' club photographer Stuart MacFarlane remembers. 'He wasn't that good a footballer, but I remember saying to him, "Is that the best goal you've ever scored?" He just looked at me and said, "I score goals like that all the time."

'Nowadays, every player or every players' agent is on my case all the time for pictures for social media and stuff like that. Christopher Wreh was the first player that ever asked me for pictures. Every time I saw him – "Print me some pictures, print me some pictures." Maybe he was a bit of a pioneer in his time. He was a good character.'

With Dennis Bergkamp injured, Wreh's vital goals earned him a starting berth alongside Nicolas Anelka against Everton as Arsenal prepared to leap over their last Premier League hurdle.

'It doesn't matter if we don't score early,' Adams bellowed to his teammates in Highbury's home dressing room before leading them out to face Everton and attempt to wrap up their first Premier League title.

'We will win this game. Be patient.'

The Arsenal players didn't need any convincing. The hard work of chasing down Manchester United had been done. Having earned a three-game margin for error, they felt little pressure, only a conviction that this would be the day they'd become champions.

'The thing that stands out to me from that game is that I never, ever thought before it or during it when I was playing that there was going to be anything except a substantial win,' says Platt. 'I felt like this is where we'd win the league. Going into the game, it never seemed in doubt.'

It was a confidence apparently shared by the majority of the Arsenal fans inside Highbury on that baking-hot May afternoon. The weather was glorious and the Gunners were in imperious form. As the sun beat down on North London, it was difficult to escape the feeling that fate was shining on Arsenal.

'We turned up knowing we were going to win the league from the minute we arrived off the tube,' says Arsenal.com writer Josh James. 'I was usually quite a nervous watcher, but I remember feeling like nothing could go wrong. I had so much faith in that team. There was no doubt. It was the perfect day.'

Arsenal radiated that belief from the second they took to the field. A quick fast break saw Wreh bring an excellent diving save from Everton goalkeeper Thomas Myhre. Then, in the sixth minute, Parlour won a free kick in the right corner. Petit swung over a high delivery towards the back post. Adams was nearest but it was the man marking the Arsenal captain, Slaven Bilić, who got the decisive touch, inadvertently heading into his own net. In front of the home dugout, Wenger shook his fists in celebration – albeit without quite the vigour Barry Ferst had mustered at Old Trafford in March. Arsenal were on their way. They were a bullet train that could not be stopped.

Much though Myhre tried. The Everton goalkeeper produced a second stunning stop, this time denying Ray Parlour's diving header. And Myhre almost thwarted Overmars after the Dutch attacker stole possession and raced clear in the twenty-eighth minute, but the winger managed to squeeze his left-footed strike underneath the Norwegian.

John O'Kane, Everton's young right back, had felt confident of his prospects ahead of the match. But he hadn't fully appreciated the magnitude of the task that chasing Overmars presented.

'I wasn't fazed,' the former Manchester United defender says. 'I was new on the Premier League scene. I'd just broken into the team and I was excited to be playing in one of the great stadiums against a top team. I wasn't really thinking about how I had to mark Overmars. I was like, "Yeah, bring it on." But then you get out there and it's a different story. They ripped us apart. My main focus that day was to enjoy myself and to try and stop Overmars. I can honestly say that in all my career I never played against anyone as quick as him. And his runs were just ridiculous. I tried to get tight, but then he spins you. If you drop off, he'll run at you. So what do you do? I wasn't the kind of player to smash him in his kneecaps.'

O'Kane was, however, the type of player to swing a malicious elbow once overcome with the frustration of chasing Overmars's shadow.

'I was a bit naughty in the game,' he admits. 'I was running back from one of our attacks and they were on the break. It was when they scored their second goal. 'I was on the right side, running back after we'd lost the ball. Emmanuel Petit was on the same side. He was just getting up after being injured in a challenge. I'm not this kind of player, but I elbowed him in the head. I was chasing back and I just smashed him in the back of the head. Nowadays it would be a red card. He went back down and then he chased me up the pitch.'

O'Kane lasted only until half time. Howard Kendall, the Everton manager, shuffled his deck during the interval. He switched 18-year-old left back Michael Ball over to the right side of the backline, throwing the teenager in the line of Overmars's fire. But while O'Kane remembers being roasted by the Dutch flyer, Ball reserves his highest praise for Arsenal's other wide man.

'It was a roasting hot day in London – not good for my pale skin,' he says. 'The first half was the longest 45 minutes. I ended up chasing Ray Parlour everywhere. I played against some world-class players, but I always say Ray Parlour was my hardest opponent. He wasn't a flashy type of winger, but he made you sweat. You had to work for anything you got against him. I was a young full back. I used to like to get forward. But any time I went forward, Ray was there, following me. I think that was why Arsène Wenger played Ray Parlour every game. He could take on that workload.

'All they were looking for was that first goal. They got it from an own goal after about five minutes, and after that they were just in second gear, cruising around. We couldn't get near them. We were getting pulled apart through their clever play. At the time, most teams played the same way. I wouldn't say it was kick and rush, but it was about who had the most desire to get their head on the ball, stop crosses and win the game. Arsenal seemed to have a way of dictating games by slowing it down and taking an extra touch. They had the quality, with Overmars, Petit, Anelka. They could just control games. They had composure on the ball. They knew where their players were. They trusted each other.

'We got run ragged in that first half. We went in two-nil down at half time, but it could have been three or four. Howard Kendall wasn't happy at half time. He made a few changes to switch things around. He moved me to right back. I'd never played right back in my life. I had no right foot. I had to mark Overmars. We went back out with the aim of trying to keep it tight and then maybe try to nick a goal from a set piece to get back in it. But I lost the ball in midfield. Overmars picked it up and just ran through from the halfway line and scored. It was the goal that killed the game for us.'

Overmars struck his second goal in the fifty-seventh minute, giving Arsenal an unassailable lead. The Everton defence's efforts in chasing down the Dutch winger had been futile. The Gunners could now not be caught, neither in this game nor the title race. With such breathing space, there was room to indulge in a little sentimentality.

Ian Wright rose from the substitutes' bench with 12 minutes to play. He came on for Anelka, replacing his long-term replacement. It was Wright's first appearance since 8 February. With his antics after December's defeat to Blackburn now a distant memory and the mood inside Highbury flipped completely since that dark winter afternoon, he received a standing ovation from the 38,269 supporters in attendance. All was forgiven.

'I remember going to Arsenal in 1991. Just a few months before I signed for Arsenal, I remember then going to a game and they were champions. I said, "I would love this to happen to me." If I'm going to be totally honest, I thought it was going to happen a lot sooner than it did at Arsenal. Wenger came and put that right. I remember going to that game and it was a party. From the time I got around to Upper Street and Liverpool Street, everybody's banging on the car. It was amazing.

'Every time I came out to warm up, the crowd went crazy. It was amazing. It was like being on drugs. It was like being on a high.'

Wright was desperate to score. The World Cup was approaching and he wanted to prove his fitness ahead of the tournament for which he'd been so crucial to England's qualification thanks to his display against Italy in Rome earlier in the season. Since he'd been out of action, Michael Owen had made his senior international debut. The 18-year-old Liverpool striker would finish as the Premier League's joint-highest scorer for 1997–98. His emergence had pushed Wright further down Glenn Hoddle's pecking order ahead of the England manager naming his squad for the competition that kicked off in France the following month.

Arsenal's fans were equally eager for him to find the net. The first title of the Wenger era was looking increasingly like being the first and last of the Ian Wright era. The occasion deserved to be marked with a goal from the man himself.

It wasn't to be. But if the supporters inside Highbury could have selected another ideal candidate for rounding off their rout of Everton with a goal, they would have chosen the man who slammed home Arsenal's fourth in the eighty-ninth minute.

No goal could have better encapsulated the stylistic changes Wenger had wrought. It was sparked by a piece of combination play between two players who produced uncharacteristically artful touches; two defenders for whom such creative play would have been utterly unthinkable during the George Graham years.

Steve Bould, the grizzled, 37-year-old centre half, had come on for Wreh in the eightieth minute – to play in *central midfield*. When he picked up the ball on the halfway line as the seconds wound towards full time, Adams bolted forward.

'Put me in! Put me in!' the captain hollered.

With a vision and deftness of technique that had apparently lain dormant for most of his 18-year career, Bould spun and dropped an inch-perfect ball in behind the Everton defence for Adams to chase.

Adams then chested down the bouncing ball as he raced towards goal. And with one stunning swing of his left foot, the player once labelled a 'donkey' for a perceived lack of technique crashed an unstoppable half volley into the top-right corner from the edge of the penalty area.

'And it's Adams, put through by Bould,' exclaimed Sky Sports commentator Martin Tyler as the Arsenal captain burst through on goal. 'Would you believe it?!'

That morning, the front-page headlines of the national newspapers had been dominated by the news that the actor Kevin Lloyd, who had played DC Tosh Lines on ITV's popular police drama *The Bill*, had died due to alcoholism. It provided Adams with a stark reminder of how different his life might have been by that stage had he not found sobriety less than two years earlier.

As he celebrated his wonder goal in front of Highbury's North Bank, he stretched his arms out wide, closed his eyes and breathed in the moment. It is a pose since immortalized as a statue outside the Emirates Stadium. The emotions Adams felt as the scene unfolded in real time needed no explanation. The catharsis that washed over him was palpable.

'It was a beautiful moment,' Adams said, 'and as I closed my eyes to savour it, I simply felt a great calm and peace.'

'You only read that in storybooks,' says David Dein. 'It was *Roy of the Rovers*. Tony has been such a wonderful player for Arsenal. Such a tower of strength as captain. The whole stadium erupted.'

'If you'd told me that one centre half would chip it through to the other . . .' Nigel Winterburn trails off mid-sentence, still disbelieving of the goal. 'And then Tony's bursting through and I'm thinking, "Where the heck is he going?" It just sat up beautifully and he connected so nicely. That picture of Tony with his arms aloft, that was a great accolade not only to him but finishing the season and winning the title in front of our own supporters in a game we completely dominated.'

'I was amazed really,' says Parlour, reflecting on a perfect climax to a perfect afternoon. 'I thought it would go down to the wire. We had two games to go after Everton: Liverpool and Aston Villa. It was a magnificent day. That will always stand out as one of the best days in my career because it was my first title and it was at Highbury. I thought the North Bank was going to fall down. It was rocking, absolutely rocking. The circumstances of the game as well, with Tony scoring the last goal, was amazing. Tony was probably one of my best mates in the team. I roomed with him for nine years. To see him score a goal like that . . . It could have gone anywhere. It probably should have ended up in the stand – it usually would have. Bouldy setting him up as well was really special. That was an amazing day.'

Some members of the opposition even found themselves caught up in the overwhelming joy of the occasion.

'They were phenomenal,' says O'Kane. 'In the end, I enjoyed the celebrations. I got brought off before Adams scored. I remember watching the celebrations and thinking it was a privilege to watch them. My mum was there. She never supported anybody at the time; she just supported me. But that day she saw Petit and just fell in love with him. Arsenal were her team from that day.'

A makeshift stage was erected in the middle of the Highbury pitch. Before Adams could step up to collect the Premier League trophy, he had to walk past a giant inflatable pint of beer advertising the Premier League's chief sponsor, Carling. The Gunners skipper was winning the battle with his own alcohol problem. Football still did not even recognize it had one.

The rest of the Arsenal squad filed on to the stage behind Adams to collect their winners' medals. Alex Manninger was among them. At the time, title-winning players were required to feature in at least ten league games to earn a medal. The young goalkeeper had only played seven Premier League matches, but special dispensation was given in light of his unquestionable contribution to Arsenal's success. He had not conceded a single goal in those appearances, after all.

'We requested it and I think they gave it without even thinking,' Manninger says. 'I keep it in a little safe. Every now and again I look at it. Not many Austrians have that little thing. It makes me proud.

'My dad was at the game against Everton. I wanted to show him and to give him something back, to say that, at 20, I had won a trophy. It made all the work I'd done in my youth, all the washing my mum did, the travelling my dad did to bring me to games, worth it. It gave a little payback, a little thanks. Something must have been right, because I was up there at 20. It was a nice moment to share with him.'

The celebrations continued back in the home dressing room. Adams circled the room, speaking individually with his teammates to thank and congratulate them on a spectacular season. Cans of lager were cracked open, Champagne bottles were uncorked, shaken and sprayed as the players jumped and sang. Stephen Hughes, lost in the revelry, sprayed beer on Adams, some of which landed on the captain's lips. Adams scolded the young midfielder and Hughes sat distraught among the party until the sober centre half calmed down and told him not to worry about it.

There was one old indulgence that Adams permitted himself amid the celebrations. He took himself away to Pat Rice's office and unwrapped a Mars bar.

## 23

# Don't Stop Me Now

When Arsène Wenger gathered his players at the Chelsea Conrad Hotel on the eve of the 1998 FA Cup final, he felt a need to shake them out of their post-title malaise.

Since confirming themselves as Premier League champions with their emphatic victory over Everton two weeks earlier, Arsenal had allowed their standards to slip. They lost both of their remaining league fixtures, hammered 4-0 at Liverpool three days after the Highbury title-clincher and then beaten 1-0 by ten-man Aston Villa thanks to a cheekily chipped Dwight Yorke penalty that embarrassed David Seaman.

Their opponents for the Wembley showpiece, Newcastle United, had endured a miserable campaign, finishing eleventh after having been runners-up the previous two seasons. They were in horrific form, with just two wins from their last twelve league games, but they were not without talent. They'd have Alan Shearer, English football's most expensive player, starting up front and backed up by internationals in nine of the other ten positions. Wenger knew his players could not afford to slacken off and sleepwalk into the final.

'I have been observing everyone since we won the title,' he said, 'and we have changed. We got here because we were a team and we looked to our own performance. Lately we have been looking at each other's performances.'

The manager delivered his message with customary calm, but there was a sternness behind his words that was intended to reawaken his players' focus. Arsenal's choice of suit for the season-closing occasion suggested a businesslike attitude towards their final remaining fixture, too – a black-shirted Hugo Boss ensemble, a polar opposite of Liverpool's gaudy cream selection from two seasons earlier, when they'd lost to Manchester United.

The one extravagance the Arsenal squad afforded themselves in the build-up to the final was to record and release an FA Cup single. A retrospectively bizarre custom that has since, mercifully, died out, it was common for cup finalists to take to the recording booth to butcher an adapted cover song or a clunkily written original tune. Arsenal opted for a reimagining of Donna Summer's 1979 song 'Hot Stuff', a song whose popularity had been rekindled the previous year by its inclusion in the film *The Full Monty*. The idea for the track had supposedly come to David Dein in a dream, but the tone-deaf tweaked rendition was closer to the stuff of nightmares. 'Gonna see the Arsenal playing some hot stuff / Let's see the Arsenal showing them how!' the players sang. 'Come on you Arsenal, yeah you're the hot stuff / Keep telling us we're boring, we'll just keep on scoring now!' Thankfully, they at least kept their clothes on. The single peaked at number nine in the chart, with all proceeds donated to the Arsenal Charitable Trust.

Unlike Dein, Dennis Bergkamp's dream would not be realized. He had been named the PFA Player of the Year in April, becoming just the third foreigner to be voted the country's top performer by his fellow professionals. 'It is great to have an FA Cup final to look forward to and I hope I can play in that,' the Dutchman said upon collecting the award. 'It's a dream come true to play at Wembley and I am looking forward to that.' But a hamstring strain that had kept him out of Arsenal's last three league games also threatened his place in the Gunners' FA Cup final line-up. Bergkamp had watched the cup final as a child in the Netherlands and longed to contest English football's oldest prize at Wembley. He endeavoured to regain fitness in time to be considered for selection, even missing his brother-in-law's wedding to focus on extra rehabilitation work with Rob Ouderland, a Dutch physio he'd enlisted.

'Leading up to the cup final, it looked like he was going to make it,' remembers Gary Lewin. 'He'd gone through all the different objective markers from the medical team. He joined in training on the Thursday and the Friday and it looked like he was going to make it. On the Friday, he finished training. He came in and said, "I'm not right. I don't want to let anyone down." So the decision was that he wasn't going to play.'

Though Bergkamp was disappointed to miss the final, he'd made his decision with one eye on the upcoming World Cup in France, for which Holland were among the favourites. When he felt his hamstring tighten while practising free kicks in training the day before the Wembley date with Newcastle, he determined he could take no risks.

The club's medical staff expected the news of Bergkamp's absence to be guarded closely, so as not to allow Newcastle manager Kenny Dalglish time to prepare a game plan for an understrength, Bergkampless Arsenal side. Wenger saw differently.

'We all thought everyone would keep dead quiet about it,' Lewin says. 'No one will say anything about it and it'll be a surprise on the day. Arsène walked in and said, "I've just announced at the press conference that Dennis isn't available tomorrow." We went, "Why did you do that?" He said, "Think about it. For Newcastle, Dennis is one of our biggest players. They find out today he isn't playing. They get a massive buzz from that. Tomorrow morning, they'll wake up and remember they're playing Arsenal in the cup final. If we leave it until tomorrow and tell them before the game that Dennis isn't playing, that big buzz they get, they're going to get in the dressing room before the game. I don't want that." That was a criticism that people threw at Arsène throughout his career, that sometimes he was a bit too honest. But his philosophy is: tell the truth, otherwise you'll get caught out.'

Plugging the Bergkamp-shaped hole in his side's attack was the only real selection conundrum Wenger faced before the final. He chose Christopher Wreh to partner Nicolas Anelka. Ian Wright, who'd been fit enough to start the final two league games, was named only among the substitutes.

On the morning of the match, Wenger's team talk before leaving the hotel was brief. He simply listed his choice of 11 starters. He felt no need to discuss Newcastle's strengths and weaknesses at all. The opponents were not even mentioned. He knew that if his team played to their capability, they'd win. The players felt sure of that, too.

'Newcastle weren't a bad side,' says Ray Parlour. 'To get to the final, they had some good players – the late Gary Speed, David Batty in midfield, Stuart Pearce on the left-hand side where I was playing, Shearer up front. We weren't in good form at the time. We'd lost to Liverpool and the last game of the season against Villa, so we weren't going into the cup final in great form, but we knew we could just switch a button and we're back in full flow again.'

'I remember feeling as certain that we were going to win that game as any other game I've played in,' Lee Dixon says. 'It was, "We're going to beat Newcastle and that's it." I never felt in any danger at all. I never thought they would ever score. I just thought probably Nicolas will get a goal and Marc will score, and we'll probably win two or three-nil. It was the culmination of the Double. It was very matter-of-fact, really.'

On the coach journey to the famous old stadium, Adams did the rounds, speaking to his colleagues individually, dishing out encouragement where he felt it might have been needed. He told David Platt that he was sure they'd win; he told Martin Keown he was certain his central-defensive partner could cope easily with the day's searing heat; and he reminded the whole team to enjoy the moment.

'The English players were saying this was more important than winning the league,' remembers Marc Overmars. 'I thought, "You're crazy! How can you say that?" For them, it was the best day ever. I knew the importance of this game, of course; I had watched it in Holland. When you play a final, you must win the final. But, for me, the league was ten times more important.'

Upon arriving at Wembley, the players inspected the immaculate turf, the mid-May heatwave causing them to sweat into their Hugo Boss suits. 'I remember going on the pitch and going, "My God, it's roasting!"' Parlour says. 'It was like a hundred degrees on the pitch. Proper roasting.' After changing into their playing kit and completing a scarcely needed warm-up, Adams rallied the troops one last time before leading them out for the 3pm kick-off.

'Come on, boys,' the captain roared. 'Let's make some memories.'

Arsenal should have been ahead early on, but Anelka headed over from 6 yards after a precise build-up move started by Adams led to Parlour finding the French striker with a cross from the right. The Gunners didn't have to wait long for a breakthrough, though. After 23 minutes, Emmanuel Petit located Overmars behind the Newcastle backline. The winger shrugged off Alessandro Pistone before firing between goalkeeper Shay Given's legs and into the net.

Newcastle twice almost mustered an equalizer in the second half – first when defender Nikos Dabizas headed against the bar from a set piece, then when Shearer pounced on a Keown stumble only to crash a left-footed shot off the post.

But then, in the sixty-ninth minute, Anelka atoned for his earlier wastefulness to put the result beyond doubt. Again it was Parlour who fed the teenager, looping a high ball over the Newcastle backline. In what was becoming his trademark fashion, Anelka raced clear of his closest defender, Steve Watson, before finishing hard and low across the goalkeeper. With that strike, he became the third-youngest player to score in a cup final.

'The big turning point, you could argue, was when Shearer hit the post when Martin fell over the ball,' Parlour says. 'He had that big chance to make it 1-1, and then suddenly you're in a different game. But as soon as he missed that and we got the second goal, it was all over, really.'

'They pushed right up on Anelka and he blew right through them,' says Pat Rice. 'It was like, "Bye-bye!" He could have given them a 10-mile head start.'

Parlour's indefatigability was undiminished by the heat. He covered every blade of the Wembley grass. He almost added a third for Arsenal, sweeping inside from the right before smacking the outside of the post from a tight angle. The curly-haired midfielder was deservedly named Man of the Match and, despite Bergkamp having won both the PFA and Football Writers' end-of-season awards, Parlour was voted Arsenal's Player of the Season in recognition of his efforts throughout the campaign. For all Arsenal's game-changing foreign imports, the 25-year-old Essex boy who'd come through the club's academy had proven vital to a triumphant season thanks to his endless endeavour, connectivity and consistency.

'It was a great day,' Parlour says. 'I had such a great season that year.

I really enjoyed my football and I got Man of the Match in the final, so that was even more special. And that season was topped off with me getting Player of the Season. That's a massive honour, because that plaque, with all the names on it, if you can get on that, there are some amazing names on it. I was really honoured to be given Player of the Season. I improved a lot that season. I really knuckled down and I was training hard. I think Wenger knew that, as well. I played 34 games out of 38 in the Premier League, so I more or less played every week. What a season. It was fantastic. You're buzzing.'

Wenger had brought Platt on in place of Wreh in the sixty-second minute. The Arsenal manager made no further substitutions. Referee Paul Durkin blew the final whistle to confirm Arsenal's victory with Wright still rooted to the Wembley bench. In the moment, the England striker was not especially disappointed to have missed out on the action. He would have been, though, had he realized he would never play for Arsenal again.

'The reason why I wasn't so fussed about the FA Cup final is because I didn't realize I was leaving,' Wright says. 'Otherwise I would have loved to have come on in the cup final, in the last ten minutes, said goodbye at Wembley. But it was fine.

'You look at those moments and you're pleased that you had them, but I knew of Nicolas's emergence. I wasn't afraid of that. The reason I wasn't afraid was because I knew Arsenal were going to benefit. I genuinely thought I was going to stay at Arsenal until I retired in 2000, which was my plan. I was going to go to the end of my contract, then I was going to retire. I had television beckoning. Everything was going well.

'The evening time is when I realized that things were happening with Arsène and me. That was the only time he ever said to me that he really regretted not putting me on in the cup final. I thought, "That's strange. He never normally says things like that." But the penny still never dropped. I thought he was just being nice to me because we were drinking wine, everybody's chilling and he was just maybe in a reflective moment, thinking, "Maybe I should have given him ten minutes." If I knew I was leaving, for instance if that was my retirement year, don't worry, I would have told him, "You better get me on here so I can at least say goodbye to the fans at Wembley."'

It wasn't until after the World Cup that Wright discovered his fate. Although his injury troubles meant he wasn't selected for Glenn Hoddle's England squad, he had been in France to cover the tournament as a television analyst. While there, he and his agent were called to a meeting with Dein and Wenger in a hotel room.

In a sequence he likens to a Mafia execution, Wright was invited into the room and Wenger began to speak. 'We have accepted an offer for you from West Ham,' the Frenchman told the shellshocked striker. 'I would love you to stay, as much as I know you would love to stay, and I know you've still got a lot to offer somebody. At the moment, however, we don't have the space for you.'

'It was like in the film *Goodfellas*,' Wright says, in reference to the scene from Martin Scorsese's 1990 Mob flick in which Joe Pesci's character is murdered. 'You go into the room thinking you're going to be a made man. In the end, you get whacked. I didn't know what was happening. When I went to meet them, it didn't click to me, because I never thought I was ever going to leave Arsenal once I got there. I never wanted to leave – apart from the time I was with Bruce Rioch and he was forcing me out almost. But when I went into that room, it was only when we started talking I realized, "This is it. I'm being whacked. I'm not being made."

'I actually thought they might have been saying they wanted to give me a year's extension. The last thing I thought was I was being let go. I was devastated. Once I left the room, I realized he actually doesn't want me here anymore, Arsène Wenger. That was one of my darkest days. I remember that day and that night. It was like I was walking around in a trance. I was walking around in this continuous night-time; it just felt dark. Obviously, I was going to West Ham. We sorted out the West Ham deal pretty quick. I had to, during that time, relieve myself of the Arsenal vibe so I could go and play for West Ham. In my football career, even with the injuries, getting that news at that moment was the lowest point of my life. I was devastated. Me and Mr Dein were very emotional, because he means the world to me. That's what happens in football. It's ruthless.'

After Adams had led the squad up the 39 steps to Wembley's Royal Box, where he'd received the FA Cup from the Duchess of Kent and lifted it high into the scorching London sky, the players completed a lap of honour with the trophy. Wright and Dixon then took the cup to the centre circle and sat and reflected on the season and the privilege of their position, a moment the striker described as 'priceless'.

The television cameras captured Wenger and Adams in a warm embrace after the manager had joined his players on the pitch. The centre back had become the first Arsenal captain to lead the club to three league titles and here, with the addition of the FA Cup, the first to inspire a Double since Frank McLintock in 1971.

'Now you've seen the best Tony Adams,' the captain said. Wenger told Adams how proud he was of him and how proud he should be of himself for all that he had overcome.

Wenger was the second foreign manager to lift the FA Cup, beaten to the distinction of being the first by Ruud Gullit, who'd won it the previous season with Chelsea. The Frenchman had already become the first non-British or Irish coach to win the top-flight title two weeks earlier, however, as he was thus the first to do the Double.

'Arsène Wenger may have dressed like an undertaker for Wembley, but he is a Prince of Light for the English game,' wrote Rob Hughes in *The Times*.

When the Arsenal staff and squad eventually headed back to the changing room, they left the pitch to a warm ovation from the Newcastle supporters positioned around the players' tunnel. The grace in defeat of the opposition's supporters struck a chord with the man who'd begun their team's downfall.

'I think it was the hottest day in England in my whole three years,' Overmars says. 'I can remember the game very well, and the way Newcastle fans respected us when we came off the pitch – that was unbelievable. One half of the stadium was black and white, the other half was red and white. When we came off the pitch and needed to go back to the dressing room, it was in the black-and-white stand, but they gave applause. That made a big impression on me.'

Once they reached the changing area, many of the players plunged straight into one of the old stadium's giant communal baths. They took their newest piece of silverware for a splash, too, as well as an unsuspecting colleague.

'After the cup final, I got into the dressing room,' says Stuart MacFarlane. 'There was a massive great big bath. All the boys were jumping in the bath and they had the FA Cup on the side of the bath. David Seaman jumped off this window ledge into the bath. Then the next minute, I was in the bath. They'd thrown me in the bath, fully clothed. They'd got my cameras off me. It was a bit of a giggle, but then I realized I had to get out of there and walk through the mixed zone, which had maybe 150 journalists, out the press exit, through the crowds, get in my car and drive back home afterwards.

'I managed to drag myself out the bath. They were all laughing at me. I walked out the tunnel. The mixed zone was completely silent, because I was literally out of a swimming pool with a trail of water behind me. I could just hear people laughing at me as I disappeared out of the press entrance. And it was a bit embarrassing, but that's the sort of thing that I will always remember.'

The merriment and memory-making continued on the journey up the M1 as Arsenal travelled from Wembley back to Sopwell House. The players bounced and sang, passing the cup between them, as Queen's 'Don't Stop Me Now' blasted from the coach's sound system.

Such a good time.

# 24

# Vive la Révolution

The day after finalizing the Double at Wembley, Arsenal paraded their two trophies from an open-top bus that weaved its way through North London before depositing the players and staff for a reception at Islington town hall.

It was a journey of just 2 miles, but it lasted 90 minutes. The red-and-white double-decker crawled slowly to allow all three hundred thousand fans that had gathered in the streets to get a glimpse of their conquering heroes.

Ian Wright led the joviality from the top deck, dancing and showing off the silverware. A white banner hung over the front declaring, in bold red letters, 'ARSENAL F.C. 1998 Double Winners'.

'The best thing about that season was going on the bus, going round and seeing all the fans,' says Ray Parlour. 'A quarter of a million people lined up around the streets. It was a really proud moment. You see all the fans; you see their faces, their happiness. That's an amazing feeling for a player, to go on that bus and think, "Look how many people you've made happy." It's brilliant.'

Marc Overmars, one of the smallest members of the group, stood at the front for a prime vantage point, his arms resting atop the banner and his compatriot and friend Dennis Bergkamp beside him. He'd finished the season with 16 goals in all competitions, the best tally of his career.

'When I look back, I am proud we played with that kind of English mentality,' he says, 'that we won the Double with six or seven English players, and with Tony, who came out of a not-easy period. That's special.

'After the games, we had a small area where we waited for our wives and kids. I saw his parents. They were proud to see Tony as a captain. Those small things are still in my head. That's just a lovely memory.'

Matthew Upson offers the perspective of a young player stepping into a top-flight environment for the first time and finding himself part of historic success. He remained an Arsenal player until 2003, although he was never able to consistently crack the first team. Still, the experiences of his first campaign at Highbury helped shape a career that saw him go on to represent England while starring for Birmingham, West Ham and Stoke in the Premier League.

'It was a whirlwind,' he says. 'I was a young kid coming from playing for Luton Town. Now I'm playing for Arsenal and on the bench while we're winning titles. I was soaking it all up, loving every minute of it. It was such a great group of players for me to be around, to see how they operate and to see their mentality. It was just a massive journey for me.'

There were few more experienced players among Arsenal's number than David Platt, but this was the former England captain's first time on an open-top bus parade. As he looked around at the hordes of fans celebrating with him and his colleagues, he felt a deep satisfaction about his decision to join the Gunners three years earlier.

'It was everything I'd come back from Italy for, because it was a wrench to leave Sampdoria,' he says. 'That's what I'd come back for. I hadn't come back to join Arsenal Football Club. I'd come back to join Arsenal because I wanted to win things. I still think that if I had gone to Italy as a league winner or as an FA Cup winner, there's every chance

I would have stayed in Italy. This was something I could look at and think, "It was worth it."'

Like Wright, lifting the FA Cup was to be Platt's last action as an Arsenal player. He decided to retire at the end of the season, a decision he would reverse a year later to join Nottingham Forest as player-manager.

The player whose arrival the previous summer had edged Platt out of the line-up was the coolest cat on the coach as the team made its way towards the town hall. With his hair pulled back into his trademark ponytail and sporting shades and striped T-shirt, Emmanuel Petit took in the scene from his spot at the front corner of the bus. When reflecting on the 1997–98 campaign, his thoughts turn to the harmony the manager cultivated.

'It was not only based on football,' he says. 'It was based on many, many things. This is what I love about Arsène. I have nothing against any managers who are only focused on football. For me, you need to put more humanity into your management. You need to be more developed with the food, with the sleeping – everything. He was always the first one trying to develop everything and trying to improve the team. For me, it was no surprise when he came to England, because sometimes destiny sends you signs. The fact that David Dein used to go to the south of France with his boat, used to know some friends that Arsène knew as well, and all of a sudden they were at a dinner and their relationship increased and developed. I think that was a desire of David Dein's. I think he fell in love with Arsène straight away. I think it was mutual. This is why, when trying to build something successful, you need to build something as human beings. That's really important.'

Lee Dixon echoes Petit's emphasis on the importance of the Wenger–Dein axis.

'The relationship that Arsène had with David Dein is something that sticks in my mind,' he says. 'David seemed to have a real special relationship with him. They trusted each other and he was a bit of a confidant. That relationship stands out for me to be a real turning point. At the height of our success and my success with Arsène, David was integral and at the forefront of everything. He was very visible at the club.'

Aside from the departures of Wright and Platt, the majority of Arsenal's Double-winning core remained in place as they sought to defend their dual crown the following season. They would fall agonizingly short. They were pipped to the Premier League title by Manchester United on the last day of the campaign and eliminated from the FA Cup at the semi-final stage by the same foes, as Alex Ferguson's men added a Champions League triumph to complete an unprecedented Treble.

It would have served as scant consolation in light of their unsuccessful title defence, but Wenger's men had earned the respect of their enemies.

'They just had a bit of everything really,' United winger Ryan Giggs said of Arsenal's 1998 side. 'Quality with Bergkamp, pace with Anelka and Overmars, the experience of the back four, and then the toughness of Vieira and Petit in midfield.'

'The side that I regard as their greatest ever is not the Invincibles of 2004 but the 1998 Double-winning team,' said Gary Neville. 'They were the strongest domestic team I have ever played against, by far.'

Wenger led Arsenal to another Double in 2002. By then, Petit and Overmars had been sold to Barcelona in a £30 million joint deal and Real Madrid had purchased Nicolas Anelka for £22.3 million. Rather than being derailed by such headline-grabbing exits, Wenger again proved his savvy eye for talent by upgrading on his outgoing stars, with Robert Pires and Thierry Henry signed for less than their predecessors had been sold.

That was the final title Adams, Dixon and Seaman would win with the club. The other original members of the old guard, Steve Bould and Nigel Winterburn, had left in 1999 and 2000, respectively. Parlour, Bergkamp, Martin Keown and Patrick Vieira remained for Arsenal's next championship, forming part of the triumphant Invincibles, who won the Premier League in 2003–04 without suffering a single defeat.

Wenger's reign extended to 22 years before, in 2018, he stepped down. A toxic rift had developed between sections of the fan base who fiercely disagreed on the Frenchman's continued suitability for the job. There were no more league titles after 2004. There was a Champions League final in 2006 and Wenger would take his tally of FA Cups to a record seven. In later years he was derided for how Arsenal had fallen from perennial title contention and instead began to settle for Champions League qualification as their primary aim, a knock-on effect, many assessed, of the costly construction of their new home, the Emirates Stadium, which opened in 2006.

Yet despite the sourness of how his Arsenal reign ended, the changes Wenger influenced not only at Arsenal but across the entire landscape of English football in his early years with the club cannot be overstated. Yes, the English game would likely have caught up with its Continental counterparts in respect of diet, nutrition and training methods at some stage, but the Frenchman's arrival and rapid success acted as an accelerant towards that enlightenment.

In a column for *The Times* headlined 'Wenger Leading English Towards Exit From Insularity', the writer Rob Hughes praised the Arsenal manager's approach to wedding Continental influences with old-fashioned ideals of British football in the wake of the 1998 Double. Wenger, Hughes wrote, showed 'what there is to learn from overseas'.

Wenger's success at Arsenal, and the style with which it was achieved, removed the stigma foreign coaches faced. At the start of his final season, 12 of the Premier League's 20 managers were from outside the British Isles.

It can be debated which of Wenger's great teams was the stronger, but there can be no disputing the fact that the 1998 Double winners were the most important and influential.

That serendipitous spark of a lighter that ignited Wenger's cigarette in 1989 ended up lighting a fire under the English game.

# Acknowledgements

I'm a fiend for Nineties nostalgia. I can't get enough of it. I was born in the late 1980s, so my formative years came in the final decade of the last century and I find myself constantly harking back to that period – just ask my Spotify account. It was at this time I fell deeply in love with football. I don't know exactly what did it, but it was probably some combination of the thrill of filling out the latest Merlin Premier League sticker album by trading swaps in the school playground – 'Got, got, need! I'll give you Gary Pallister and Robbie Earle for that Newcastle shiny!' – play-by-mail management simulations and trying (unsuccessfully) to copy Benito Carbone's bicycle kick technique in my best friend's back garden. So, I suppose, ever since I began to pursue writing as a career, it was inevitable that I'd eventually want to take on a project like this book, to relive the halcyon days of my youth by delving into the story of one of the decade's best and most influential teams.

But Tony Soprano once said that '"Remember when" is the lowest form of conversation.' Now, I wouldn't ordinarily seek career advice from a murderous Mob boss, but he's not wrong in this instance. In order for *Arsène Who?* to have any relevance a quarter of a century on from when the stories it covers took place, for it to be a worthwhile investment of your time and money, I knew it had to have more substance than simply 'remember when'. It had to contain anecdotes you – hopefully – haven't heard before and offer a fresh perspective on the ones you have. It had to paint a vivid picture of a bygone era while also providing a contemporary contextualization of the events within it. And it had to have the authority of those who were there – the players, coaches, backroom staff, opponents – sharing memories and insights in their own words. Without the hundreds of hours of interviews with Arsenal's 1998 Double winners and dozens of key figures in that team's orbit, this book could not exist. So to everyone quoted within these pages, I offer my deepest and most sincere thanks. I'd like to extend an extra-special thanks to Lee Dixon, too, for so kindly providing a foreword.

Another essential ingredient in this book's making was the hours and hours spent speaking with fans, journalists, coaches and players who helped me attain the deepest possible understanding of this era of English football, of Arsenal and of Arsène Wenger. Some were quoted, some were not, but all were vital in shaping *Arsène Who?* Crucial, also, were so many kind colleagues who graciously opened their contact books for me, helping me reach the two hundred-plus people I interviewed, as well as those who helped with the translation of interviews and correspondences with non-English speakers. All listed below fit into one of these categories, and to all I am eternally grateful:

John Cross, Graham Hunter, Per Mertesacker, Robert Pires, Henry Winter, Patrick Barclay, Oliver Holt, Philippe Auclair, Paul Hayward, Tim Stillman, Jon Spurling, Alf Galustian, Callum McFadden, Gavin Blackwell, Will Unwin, Stephen Tudor, Harry De Cosemo, Josh James, Roscoe Bowman, Ronny Johnsen, Henning Berg, Steve McManaman, Sue Campbell, Jill Armstrong, Andrew Allen, Tim De'Ath, Kevin Whitcher, Martin Tyler, Clive Tyldesley, Alan Smith (former Arsenal player), Alan Smith (former Crystal Palace coach), Alan Smith (former England physio), Lee Canoville, Alex Fynn, Leo Moynihan, Andy Gray, Andy Impey, Albert Morgan, Tony Attwood, Andy Roxburgh, Danny Sweetman, Alvise Cagnazzo, Valur Gíslason, Dave Jones, David Elliott, Michael Michael, David Winner, Frank McLintock, Harry Harris, Marvin Berglas, Ian Stone, Isaiah Rankin, Jasper Rees, Jason Crowe, Kevin Ball, David Elleray, Gary Newbon, John Curtis, Les Ferdinand, Markus Hörwick, Neil Banfield, Vic Akers, Peter Wood, Matt Dunn, Simon Yaffe, Gino De Blasio, Chris Evans, Andy Mitchell, Dan Williamson, Adam Digby, James Morgan, Marc Iles, Paul Fennessy, Sarah Ewing, Johnny Cochrane, Jeremy Smith, Sam Pilger, Alexandra Dubois, Paul Morrissey, João Malha, Stefan Wölfel, Doug O'Kane, Ian Stone.

Thank you, also, to Trevor Davies and everyone at Octopus Books for believing in this book and giving me the time, freedom and support to see it through. Thank you to Clare Hubbard for whipping the manuscript into shape with a meticulous and embarrassment-saving copyedit. And thanks to my agent, Kevin Pocklington, for his patience, advice and guidance throughout.

Being able to write books for a living is a privilege and a joy. At least for the most part, that is. As someone who types slowly and is easily distracted, the process of transcribing interviews is always my least favourite aspect of the job. I shouldn't complain, I know. This is not backbreaking work – I am not digging for coal nor performing brain surgery. But if there is anything approaching metaphorical heavy lifting in this profession, it's the transcribing. That being said, I often found myself amused during the process of typing up the interviews for this book due to how often they were soundtracked by babbling – sometimes tantruming – toddlers. In total, *Arsène Who?* was a project around three years in the making. That means for our first-born, Dylan, who turned five a week after the final manuscript was submitted to the publisher, Daddy has been speaking to boring, boring footballers about boring, boring Arsenal for most of his life. And for Finlay, who joined us in 2021, it's all he's ever known. They are a constant inspiration and my greatest motivation, whether that's when hearing their adorable gabbles trapped in time in my interview recordings, when they perk me up at my desk with a pause for a 'cuggle', or when they nap just long enough for me to squeeze out a paragraph or two. Thank you, my beautiful boys.

Finally, my greatest gratitude is reserved for my Sophie. This book has been a joint effort. Without your help carving out time in our life as exhausted parents of two gorgeous yet demanding little boys, I wouldn't have been able to do this. Your encouragement through the most testing moments means the world to me. And your constant, boundless and vitalizing support is my foundation. None of this is possible without you. Thank you.

# Bibliography

Adams, Tony and Ridley, Ian, *Addicted*, Collins Willow, 1998

Adams, Tony and Ridley, Ian, *Sober: Football. My Story. My Life.*, Simon & Schuster, 2017

Auclair, Philippe, *Thierry Henry: Lonely at the Top: A Biography*, Macmillan, 2012

Bergkamp, Dennis and Winner, David, *Stillness and Speed: My Story*, Simon & Schuster, 2013

Cox, Michael, *The Mixer: The Story of Premier League Tactics, from Route One to False Nines*, HarperCollins, 2019

Cross, John, *Arsène Wenger: The Inside Story of Arsenal Under Wenger*, Simon & Schuster, 2015

Ferguson, Alex, *Managing My Life: My Autobiography*, Hodder & Stoughton, 1999

Ferguson, Alex and Moritz, Michael, *Leading: Learning from Life and My Years at Manchester United*, Hachette, 2015

Fynn, Alex and Whitcher, Kevin, *Arsènal: The Making of a Modern Superclub*, Vision Sports Publishing, 2008

Fynn, Alex and Whitcher, Kevin, *Arsène & Arsenal: The Quest to Rediscover Past Glories*, Vision Sports Publishing, 2015

Fynn, Alex and Whitcher, Kevin, *The Glorious Game: Arsène Wenger, Arsenal and the Quest for Success*, Orion, 2003

Graham, George, *The Glory and the Grief: The Inside Story*, Andre Deutsch, 1995

Hartson, John, *The Autobiography*, Orion, 2006

James, Josh, Kelly, Andy and Andrews, Mark, *Arsenal: The Complete Record*, deCoubertin Books, 2018

Kuper, Simon, *The Football Men: Up Close with the Giants of the Modern Game*, Simon & Schuster, 2011

Lawrence, Amy, *89: Arsenal's Greatest Moments, Told in Our Own Words*, Century, 2019

Lawrence, Amy, *Invincible: Inside Arsenal's Unbeaten 2003–2004 Season*, Viking, 2014

Lawrence, Amy and MacFarlane, Stuart, *The Wenger Revolution: The Club of My Life*, Bloomsbury Sport, 2018

Merson, Paul, *How Not to Be a Professional Footballer*, Harper Sport, 2011

Palmer, Myles, *The Professor: Arsène Wenger*, Virgin Books, 2005

Parlour, Ray, *The Romford Pelé: It's Only Ray Parlour's Autobiography*, Century, 2016

Petit, Emmanuel, *Franc-Tireur*, Editions Solar, 2015

Rees, Jasper, *Wenger: The Making of a Legend*, Short Books, 2003

Rivoire, Xavier, *Arsène Wenger: The Authorised Biography*, Aurum Press, 2007

Seaman, David, *Safe Hands: My Autobiography*, Orion, 2000

Spurling, Jon, *Highbury: The Story of Arsenal in N5*, Orion, 2006

Spurling, Jon, *Top Guns: Arsenal in the 1990s*, Aureus Publishing, 2001

Storey, Daniel, *Portrait of an Icon*, Ockley Books, 2017

Vieira, Patrick, *My Autobiography*, Orion, 2005

Wenger, Arsène, *My Life in Red and White: My Autobiography*, Weidenfeld & Nicolson, 2020

Whitcher, Kevin, *Gunning for the Double: The Story of Arsenal's 1997–98 Season*, Sporting Editions, 1998

Wright, Ian, *A Life in Football: My Autobiography*, Constable, 2016

Yousif, Layth, *Arsène Wenger Fifty Defining Fixtures*, Amberley Publishing, 2014

# Index

# Photo credits